Situating Poetry

SITUATING POETRY

Covenant and Genre in American Modernism

Joshua Logan Wall

Johns Hopkins University Press
Baltimore

© 2022 Johns Hopkins University Press
All rights reserved. Published 2022
Printed in the United States of America on acid-free paper
2 4 6 8 9 7 5 3 1

Johns Hopkins University Press
2715 North Charles Street
Baltimore, Maryland 21218
www.press.jhu.edu

Library of Congress Cataloging-in-Publication Data

Names: Wall, Joshua Logan, author.
Title: Situating poetry : covenant and genre in American modernism / Joshua Logan Wall.
Description: Baltimore : Johns Hopkins University Press, 2022. | Includes bibliographical references and index.
Identifiers: LCCN 2021063007 | ISBN 9781421443782 (hardcover ; acid-free paper) | ISBN 9781421443799 (paperback ; acid-free paper) | ISBN 9781421443805 (ebook)
Subjects: LCSH: American poetry—20th century—History and criticism—Theory, etc. | Modernism (Literature)—United States. | New York (N.Y.)—Intellectual life—20th century.
Classification: LCC PS310.M57 W35 2022 | DDC 811/.5209112—dc23
/eng/20220223
LC record available at https://lccn.loc.gov/2021063007

A catalog record for this book is available from the British Library.

Special discounts are available for bulk purchases of this book. For more information, please contact Special Sales at specialsales@jh.edu.

CONTENTS

Acknowledgments vii

Introduction 1

PART 1 COVENANTAL SPACES

CHAPTER 1
A Congregation of Readers: James Weldon Johnson's
God's Trombones 23

CHAPTER 2
Renewing the Covenant: Charles Reznikoff's Recitative 60

PART 2 CIRCULATING MODERNISM

CHAPTER 3
Immigrant Publics: Lola Ridge On and Off the Page 93

CHAPTER 4
Louis Zukofsky and the Poetics of Exodus 127

PART 3 LIMIT CASES

CHAPTER 5
A Covenantal Limit Case: Robert Hayden Beyond the Lyric 165

CODA
The House We Build Together 191

Notes 201
Index 229

ACKNOWLEDGMENTS

The ideas and readings in this book have developed over more than a decade, across seminars, essays, café tables, conference talks, illegibly scrawled notes, and classrooms of my own. At the University of Michigan, the earliest versions of many chapters began in conversation, written and spoken, with my dissertation committee: Larry Goldstein introduced me to the poetry of Lola Ridge and happily talked about Robert Hayden. Conversations with Josh Miller helped me think about the purpose and promise of archival research. Gillian White challenged me to define and hone my understanding of poetic genre and theory. The earliest pieces of this project began in a seminar paper for Deborah Dash Moore (though only a sentence or two remain), who later taught me a tremendous amount about writing. Julian Levinson indulged my intellectual whims and tangents, contributed a few of his own, but always knew how to guide me back toward what I was truly interested in. (He also deserves credit for the book's title.)

I benefited from the generosity and advice of others within and beyond the University of Michigan: Jonathan Freedman, Sasha Hoffman (who taught me Yiddish, even on the days I didn't want to learn it), Misha Krutikov, Doug Mao, Anita Norich, Ranen Omer-Sherman, Shachar Pinsker, Maeera Shreiber, John Whittier-Ferguson, the members of the U-M American Jewish Studies Reading Group and the Poetry & Poetics Workshop. Lisa Curtis and Denise Looker make the English Department Writing Program a wonderful place to work and teach each day. I'm grateful for the interest that Elaine Sproat and Jeffrey Twitchell-Waas showed when I approached them about quoting, not insubstantially, from Lola Ridge's and Louis Zukofsky's work—Elaine, in particular, deserves credit for several factual corrections on a draft of chapter 3 and providing me with correspondence between Ridge and Johnson.

Although this book has been tied to the University of Michigan from its inception, I've been blessed throughout my life by the teachers I've encountered. In a nonexhaustive list: Carol Brown, Dick Aylor, Kathryn Balbach, and Pat Mulloy. Andrew Campbell, Michael Goldberg, and Anne Glosky first introduced me to modernist literature. All of them encouraged me to read and write and teach. At Northwestern University, Christine Froula and Robert Wallace did as well. My undergraduate thesis advisor, the late Kathryn Bosher, taught me how to conduct academic research—but, more importantly, how to mentor students. I miss very deeply the conversations about this project that we were never able to share.

Beyond individuals, a handful of institutions deserve credit for providing me with opportunities to work on this project, in all its iterations. *Situating Poetry* became a book, rather than a dissertation, while I was a Frederick Donald Sober Post-Doctoral Fellow in English Language and Literature at the University of Michigan. Through the Rackham Graduate School at U-M, I was supported by a Pre-Doctoral Research Fellowship, a Humanities Research Fellowship, a One-Term Dissertation Fellowship, funding for summer research, and a variety of conference travel grants that allowed me to present early versions of this research. The Department of English Language and Literature and the Frankel Center for Judaic Studies also provided funding for conference travel; the Frankel Center, moreover, provided funding for research and language study. Any project drawing on archival research owes a debt to librarians; mine goes to those at the special collections libraries of the University of Texas, Yale University, the University of Chicago, and the University of Michigan.

My family's support has also left its mark on this book, and I owe thanks to Zach and Katy, Janis, and Uncle Marvin. Large swaths of *Situating Poetry* were written while sitting at the desk that once belonged to my maternal grandfather, Stuart Yussman (z"l). The stories that my father's parents, Kenneth (z"l) and Pauline Wall, told me as a child have left their clear imprint on this work; I certainly wouldn't have realized why Reznikoff's "Israel" and "King David" were so interesting without them. My father, Ken Wall (z"l), may have set me on the path to talking about poems for a living: my first memories of extended literary analysis involve sitting in his car as he held forth on the lyrics of Bruce Springsteen, Johnny Cash, and (of course) Commander Cody and His Lost Planet Airmen. My mother, Lisa, and stepfather, John, have given so much and without request: I love you.

By the time you're holding this book in your hands, my wife, Rachel, will have undoubtedly celebrated the much-anticipated departure of the two hundred or so library books in boxes under my desk that have followed us through, I believe, three residences now. For the entirety of our marriage, she's had to share time and literal, physical space with this project—and, in the strange spring and summer of 2020, when so much about our own circumstances was uncertain and unsettled, she gave me the freedom to write (more freedom, honestly, than I deserved or should have accepted). It's a cliché of the acknowledgments genre, but it's true: without her, this book wouldn't exist.

And then, of course, there's Abigail, whose arrival early that year gave me something to write for (and who is sitting on my lap as I write this paragraph). Jotting down lines of verse in the delivery room gave me a different understanding of what it might mean to situate poetry—and her early references to rhyming children's books as "songs" speaks, probably, to an underlying truth at which all these pages just gesture vaguely. I'm tempted to dedicate this book, following Zukofsky, "For my daughter—when she can read." But I'm legitimately worried that condition will already be fulfilled by the end of 2022—and she will (God willing) be a sister by then. So I'll just say: *for my children*.

For use of portions of chapter 2: Copyright © 2020 Johns Hopkins University Press. This article first appeared in *Modernism/modernity*, Volume 27, Issue 1, January 2020, pages 27–49. Published with permission by Johns Hopkins University Press.

For use of excerpts of poetry by Robert Hayden: "El Hajj Malik El-Shabazz." Copyright © 1970 by Robert Hayden, "John Brown," "[American Journal]." Copyright © 1978, 1982 by Robert Hayden, from COLLECTED POEMS OF ROBERT HAYDEN by Robert Hayden, edited by Frederick Glaysher. Copyright © 1985 by Erma Hayden. Used by permission of Liveright Publishing Corporation.

For use of excerpts of poetry by James Weldon Johnson: "The Crucifixion," and "The Judgment Day" from GOD'S TROMBONES by James Weldon Johnson, copyright 1927 by Penguin Random House LLC, renewed 1955 by Grace Nail Johnson. Used by permission of Viking Books, an imprint of Penguin Publishing Group, a division of Penguin Random House LLC. All rights reserved.

For use of excerpts from "Stone Face" (*Dance of Fire*) and "Morning Ride" (*Red Flag*): Elaine Sprout.

For use of excerpts from works by Louis Zukofsky: All Louis Zukofsky materials copyright © Musical Observations, Inc. Used by permission.

Situating Poetry

Introduction

An American Tale

The scene shouldn't be too hard to imagine. It's sometime between 1909 and 1912; the dates on the newspapers stacked outside storefronts and fluttering, discarded, on the sidewalks are hazy. On the streets of lower Manhattan, south of Houston, where the grid starts to break down and the roads curve gently, sometimes colliding at angles, a small Jewish boy between the ages of five and eight runs as if he's compelled by something other than sheer terror of the group pursuing him. Fleeing toward the East River on Grand or Canal, he hears cries of "Christ-killer!" and "Kike!" growing closer behind him. The older boys' faces are steeled in determination to exact retribution for the murder, by his ancestors, of their Lord and Savior some 1,888 years before. These are, the boy would recollect a half century later, his "Italian neighbors." Only when they corner the boy does something remarkable happen, the words spilling from his memory in an odd, Yiddish trochaic tetrameter:

> dort hot er dem lid gezungen,
> dos gesang fun Hayavata'n,
> dort bazungen zayn geburtshaft
> un zayn leben ful mit vunder,
> zayne tfiles un zayn fasten,
> zayne tkhaten un zayn layden,
> um di menshen tsu bagliken,
> um zayn shvot tsu derhoyken.[1]

The Italian boys pause and watch him. He continues. They don't know what to make of this child, of this scene, of these odd verses, their beat perhaps strangely familiar to one or two of them who pay more attention in school than they might like to let on. Recovering their menace, they fish in their pockets for spare pennies, and toss them, laughing, at the Jewish boy. Through it all, the child keeps chanting, his foreign words echoing off the walls around them. Finally, bored, the Italians leave our young poet in peace.

The poem the young Louis Zukofsky recited that day—and, by his telling, on many others as well—is more recognizable in its English original:

> There he sang of Hiawatha,
> Sang the Song of Hiawatha,
> Sang his wondrous birth and being,
> How he prayed and how he fasted,
> How he lived, and toiled, and suffered,
> That the tribes of men might prosper,
> That he might advance his people!

By his account, Zukofsky had memorized the popular Yiddish translation of Henry Wadsworth Longfellow's *Song of Hiawatha*—all of it—by the time he was five.[2] *Dos lid fun Hayavata* was the work of the American Yiddish poet Yehoash, né Solomon Bloomgarden, part of an oeuvre that, through its globe-spanning cosmopolitanism, laid claim to America. Yehoash's poetry was the first influence, a truly formative one, on Zukofsky's poetry—but that's a story for a little later. Like all legends, this narrative rubs uncomfortably against the facts we know to be true: Zukofsky was five in 1909; Yehoash's translation wasn't completed until 1910.

Nevertheless, surrounded by a violent mob in a New York alley, Zukofsky managed to communicate something beyond the words themselves—maybe even despite them: after all, they would have been unintelligible to his Italian neighbors. The poem that caused them to pause also made them, as another poet, James Weldon Johnson, would write in his memoirs about an even more fraught encounter with a violent mob, "look at each other"—at their victim-to-be, that is—a moment in which "a quivering message from intelligence to intelligence has been interchanged."[3] This exchange is imperfect and fails to achieve permanence: these bullies do not become Zukofsky's friends; they do not come to love him. But this shouldn't distract us from what *does* occur: they do not beat him. They acknowledge him, somehow, even if just in this moment, as part of a shared public.[4] To put it in terms perhaps excessively Levinasian, in the pause created by the poem, they see the face of the other and decide against committing violence against him. In the middle, mediating this interaction, stands a poem—a translation into Yiddish of an English-

American Fireside poet's attempt to write an American epic in a new, American epic meter, about a Native American tribal leader.

From our perch in the twenty-first century, this vignette cries out for an overdetermined reading: that Zukofsky's recitation claims or embodies or enacts a pluralist, open-ended Americanness out of a melting pot of ethnic, religious, and linguistic experiences. It's an effective illustration of the ways that American community comes into being less through blood, soil, or generational descent than through textual mediation, the imagined ties between us strengthened by literature. But Zukofsky was only a child—and while this pluralism sets the stage for many of the themes that follow in his poetry and those that this book reads alongside him, we can't rightly say that he did more than hit on them unintentionally.

Yet the poem's situation remains for us to consider: the spaces in which a poem is encountered, the circulatory routes it has followed to get there, and the often time- and place-bound natures of these qualities. This means more than simply thinking about poetry alongside terms like "audience" or "readers"—not poetry as a means of creating community but as an action that creates publics. "A public," writes Michael Warner, "is constituted through mere attention"—a deceptively simple statement.[5] What he means is this: publics are not communities. They exist only so long as we pay attention—as we join our attention toward a shared object. Or, in Warner's words, "Publics commence with the moment of attention, must continuously predicate renewed attention, and cease to exist when attention is no longer predicated."[6] Just because Zukofsky's recitation of the Yiddish *Hiawatha* fails to create a permanent *community* doesn't mean a *public* never came into being—and this is important. A time- or place-bound, impermanent public, constituted through mere attention, shows the possibility of community, something broader and more abstract, made up, we might say, of a series of overlapping publics.

"*Everything* begins with attention," Alan Jacobs echoes.[7] Whether attention is voluntary or coerced, how the giving of it is chosen or withheld—these are fundamental questions of human experience, in his telling. Jacobs writes this at the beginning of a critique of the discourse genres produced by twenty-first-century technology, particularly social media. But in doing so, he points to something more fundamental. Genre emerges from the way we choose to *give* our attention: when we identify the category of thing to which we give it and follow, reflexively, a set of norms about the mode of attention it requires or deserves. Poetry and its subsidiary genres are not just ways of writing, thinking, or speaking but ways of paying attention. To situate poetry is to return to specific moments of attention, to consider how and why they are given, to consider (in all their particularity) what kinds of public they produce.

The extent to which this way of reading poetry—of *attending to it*—has been overlooked emerges nowhere more clearly than in Warner's casting poetry in contrast to public and public-creating speech:

> Poetry is not actually overheard; it is read as overheard. And similarly, public speech is not just heard; it is heard (or read) as heard, not just by oneself but by others. The contrast may be carried through point by point. Public speech is no more addressed to a particular person than is lyric. Both require a very special apprehension of apostrophe. In the case of lyric, we regard the event not as communication but as our silent insertion in the self-communion of the speaker, constructing both an ideal self-presence for the speaking voice and an ideal intimacy between that voice and ourselves. In public speech, we incorporate an awareness of the distribution of the speech or text itself as essential to its addressee, which we nevertheless take to be in some measure ourselves.[8]

Note the elision in the fourth sentence: poetry becomes lyric; the norms of poetry are reduced to those of a particular subset. Warner points toward a readerly and critical reality in which poetry, as a broad mode of giving and demanding attention, has grown largely synonymous with a single genre of poetic attention: the lyric (to be even more precise, and as we'll discuss shortly, with a single *century's* idea of what lyric means). I point to Warner not to criticize—this idea of poetry provides a useful, illustrative counterexample that allows his observations about public speech more generally to show through—but because he gives eloquent voice to a series of assumptions about poetry's nature shared across much scholarship. He assumes that poetry is situated in a relatively stable format: on the page, the individual encounter, the private reading. "Lyric speech has no time: we read the scene of speech as identical with the moment of reading," he writes. "Public speech, by contrast, requires the temporality of its own circulation."[9] In reality, this contrast isn't quite so definitive. "Lyric speech," as one mode of giving attention, may well be timeless, but our individual encounters with poems are not.

In *Situating Poetry*, my aim is to explain what took place on that unknown day on an unknown street somewhere on the Lower East Side and harness its lessons in application to modern and modernist poetry more broadly. Doing so requires asking questions about spaces (*Where is a poem situated?*) as well as circulation (*How did it come to be situated there?*). This book's first part focuses on spaces and its second part on modes of circulation—but the two remain intertwined. The circulation of James Weldon Johnson's *God's Trombones* across decades plays a central role in chapter 1's study of its church-bound spaces, while situating Lola Ridge's "Stone-Face" within the spaces of labor activism helps to explain, in chapter 3, the challenges her works face in print circulation. More fundamentally, this book explores what happens when we read seemingly lyric (or anti-lyric) poems through or in dialogue with forms of attention conventionally associated with other genres. These genres include both poetry's (commemorative verse, ekphrasis, epic, elegy) and those of other, nonpoetic modes of speech: song, news, the law, a labor rally, a church on Sunday, a museum exhibition. The quintet of poets examined here constitute no formal movement and are joined less by their biographies or poetic methods (though there are links, to be certain) than by their shared answer to a final question, one that we can't lose sight of when situating poetry: *When this poem calls forth a mode of attention, what kind of public does this attention produce?*

Modernism, broadly construed, might be defined as the joint exploration of attention given to and demanded by then-new technologies—mass print, recorded sound, radio broadcast, photography, film, the car, the skyscraper—with attempts to deploy and manipulate these new technologies in order to produce (new) modes of attending to poetry. Our reflexive, delimited assumptions about the modes of attention that constitute poetry have impoverished our understanding of the publics that poetry—especially modernist poetry—can produce. In the linked stories I'll tell in the chapters that follow, poetry calls forth modes of attention in order to produce accessible, democratic publics. This doesn't mean that their poetry is easy to understand. Much of it runs toward and embraces difficulty rather than eschewing it. Rather, poetry teaches its readers how to pay attention to others and to their community in ways that embrace the emerging pluralism of twentieth-century citizenship in the United States. This process runs through their engagement with the tropes of American civil religion.

But first, we need to talk a little more about genre.

Beyond the Lyric

That *any* poem mediated the young Zukofsky's street-corner encounter is remarkable. The fault, Shakespeare's Cassius might have put it had he become a poet rather than a politician, lies not in our verse but in ourselves: in the assumptions and frameworks of reading that we bring, even (especially) when we do not know that we bring them, to the poems that we read. Virginia Jackson, Yopie Prins, Mark Jeffreys, and other scholars working under the heading of historical poetics have turned inquisitive eyes on these assumptions.[10] They contend, rightly, that our idea of what a poem is (like the idea of a poem in any era) is not a transhistorical constant but the product of history. Since the late nineteenth century, they aver, we have come to think of "poetry" and "lyric" as synonymous. Lyric, Jeffreys writes, "did not conquer poetry; poetry was reduced to lyric"—a process Jackson describes as the "idealization of poetry" and then the lyricization of that ideal.[11] As people were trained to read not only for a specific idea of poetry but for a specific idea of *lyric* poetry, the result has been that "the history of various genres of poetry was read as simply lyric, and lyrics were read as poems one could understand without reference to that history or those genres."[12] In other words, the idealized lyric that emerged from the late nineteenth century through the mid-twentieth century continues to shape the twenty-first century's definition of "poetry."

Gillian White attributes this "view of lyric poems as expressive objects that 'speak' to the reader without, paradoxically, the reader's need to understand anything of the history of the work's production, reception, or circulation" to the New Critics and their continuing legacy.[13] Yet the New Criticism was able to coronate this view of (lyric) poetry because it described what many readers of poetry *already* believed. A century before the New Critics, in 1833, John Stuart Mill declared, "We should say that eloquence is *heard*; poetry is *over*heard."[14] Eighty-five years later, W. B. Yeats announced, "We make out of the quarrel with others, rhetoric, but of the quarrel with ourselves, poetry."[15] I turn to them not to declare them engines of change but because they give voice to the history of our shared assumptions about what a poem is and does.

Mill and Yeats disagree with each other, to be certain: Mill's poetry (like his eloquence) is "the expression or utterance of feeling," while Yeats frames both in the language of agon: rhetoric and poetry alike emerge from, and participate in, struggle. Yet each theorizes poetry as fundamentally asocial. In direct contrast to eloquence's "feeling pouring itself out to other minds, courting their sympathy, or endeavoring to influence their belief, or move them to passion or action," Mill's poetry is disinterested, mere "feeling confessing itself to itself in moments of solitude, and embodying itself in symbols which are the nearest possible representations of the feeling in the exact shape in which it exists in the poet's mind."[16] It is fundamentally self-contained, an object that needs only itself to exist, a poem that could still be a poem without a single reader: a singularity of versification, the ideal Poem toward which all Poets strive as an unmoved mover, capable of both reading and writing itself.

Even the contemporary and late-twentieth-century avant-garde, which often cast themselves as explicitly anti-lyric, bear the imprint of this distinction between poetry and eloquence. Poet-critics including Charles Bernstein, Lynn Hejinian, Ron Silliman, and Bob Perelman, write Jackson and Prins, "no longer needed the lyric as a generic placeholder, but . . . continue[d] to need the lyric as the definition of the kind of poetry it [their avant-garde] is not."[17] Insofar as the Language poets reinforce the view that a poem is a thing to be looked upon, perhaps better suited to a museum than the world, even their deliberate artifice is not so different from the formats in which much poetry is first encountered as art in the United States: the textbooks and Norton anthologies of high school and college classrooms.[18] The world engagement of Claudia Rankine's recent "American Lyrics," *Don't Let Me Be Lonely* (2004) and *Citizen* (2014), pushes beyond the norms of lyric reading—but in claiming the genre, she continues to participate in the idealization of poetry as lyric precisely by attempting to expand its bounds.

"Eloquence," writes Mill, "supposes an audience. The peculiarity of poetry appears to us to lie in the poet's utter unconsciousness of a listener."[19] This, Jackson observes, is only a consequence of the idealization of poetry as "lyric." "When the stipulative functions of particular genres are collapsed into one big idea of poems as lyrics," she writes, "then the only function poems can perform in our culture is to become individual or communal ideals. Such ideals might bind particular groups or subcultures (in slams, for example, or avant-garde blogs, or poetry cafes, or salons, or university, library, and museum reading series), but the more ideally lyric poems and poetry culture have become, the fewer actual poetic genres address readers in specific ways."[20] In other words, the idealization of poetry as lyric—even by poets who attempt to resist or expand that genre—results in the attenuation of the specificity of address that, for Warner, gives life to *publics*.

Another way of putting this—one that draws on a contemporary of both Yeats and the poets considered here—is that the idealization of poetry as "lyric" depends in large part on the removal of the poem from what T. S. Eliot refers to as its "social function." Writing in 1945, he rejects pat distinctions between the functions of poetry and prose: they exist in a tense dance, perhaps even a competition; in modernity, prose has the upper hand: "The poem, the ostensible aim of which is to convey information, has been superseded by prose." So, "Didactic poetry has gradually become limited to poetry of moral exhortation, or poetry which aims to *persuade* the reader to the author's point of view about something. It therefore includes a great deal of what can be called *satire*, though satire overlaps with burlesque and parody, the purpose of which is primarily to cause mirth."[21] This insight is not particularly unique or profound. However, it points us toward an important element of Eliot's understanding of poetry. Genre, in essence, exists downstream from (and depends on) poetry's historically dependent social function.

Social function is necessarily *situated*. For Eliot, it is situated in the history, habits, and language of a nation; for a contemporary critic like Barry McCrea, it is situated more locally, in the voice of the vernacular poem against the national ideal.[22] My purposes are smaller; unlike Eliot, I'm not concerned with pinning down the essence of capital-*P* Poetry. Yet the approach he illustrates need not be quite so totalizing as he ultimately settles on. The social function of poetry can emerge from settings smaller than the formation of national character—or even the dynamic of the local in tension with the nation. Social function and the genre(s) that follows from it can inhere in a diversity of settings: a protest, a mailing, a magazine, unveiling a painting, mourning—even, as we'll see, in settings the poem itself imagines. Situated in anthologies and perfect-bound collections, these social functions fall away. Even archival research risks excising poetry from its situation: a situation is not simply context but social function as well.

The variety of poetic forms, verse schemes, and genres has always been more diverse than the assumptions of lyric and anti-lyric reading allow us to see. These forms, often, are precisely the kind of public, exhortative verse that both modernism and lyric reading eschew. To read "beyond the lyric" is not to critique or diminish lyric poetry—but, by acknowledging its others, to offer it the respect born of difference, as one genre of poetry among many, as one set of reading practices best suited for particular poems. But not for all poems. As Meredith Martin's work on the varieties, development, and social roles of verse forms in late-nineteenth- and early-twentieth-century Britain draws to a close, she reflects on her own practices as a reader of poetry: "I am learning to ask, when poets were inventing or experimenting with prosodic systems, with what else, in addition to the measure of the line, were they wrestling?"[23] This question is not simply one that a historically aware approach to poetics and lyric theory demands of scholars; it is a question that many poems require their readers—any readers—to ask.

Yet, as Dorothy Wang observes, even when this question is asked, it is not asked equally of all poets. There is a "double-standard in poetry studies" that forms the field's most pervasive, if often unconscious, flaw: "Form, whether that of traditional lyric or avant-garde poems, is assumed to be the provenance of a literary acumen and culture that is unmarked but assumed to be white."[24] As a result, "critics are more likely to think about formal questions—say, poetic tone and syntax—when speaking about [John] Ashbery's poems but almost certain to focus on political or black 'content' when examining the works of Amiri Baraka."[25] "All writing," she insists, "is situated in both the aesthetic and social realms."[26] I'd refine (or perhaps complicate) this further: because both the aesthetic and social realms emerge from and depend on acts of recognition and modes of attention, they're not so easily separable. If social function is a river and genre the ocean downstream, then poetry emerges at the ecotone: the point of contact and transition.

The poets most affected by our shared assumptions about how a poem ought to be read are those who differ from the poets and critics whose works helped to codify those assumptions. In the early 1990s, Cary Nelson began his important labor of literary recovery with the lament that "we no longer know the history of the poetry of the first half of this [the twentieth] century."[27] In the three decades that have followed, scholars have done much to fill out and restore our knowledge of various forgotten and repressed authors: racial and linguistic others; political radicals and outsiders; women; immigrants; "difficult" personalities; those who simply fell victim to time's passage. Our sense of literary history expanded and fuller, we now face another difficulty: we no longer know how to *read* the poetry of the first half of the twentieth century, trained as we are in poetic reading by that limited range of works that initially remained.

To return to our opening vignette: the young Zukofsky was, of course, neither author nor translator of the poem he recited at the bullies circling around him. Yet, a nascent poet, he still recognized that situation matters; his recitation was hardly "unconscious of a listener." With what else, we might ask, beyond the measure of the memorized line, was he wrestling in that moment? With the threat posed by his audience, with the need to communicate his humanity to them, with the need to enact some—*any*—kind of change within them. "But," I hear you protest, *"Hiawatha* isn't *lyric* poetry at all!" This is precisely the point. Both the poem and the context Zukofsky offers as the Ur-moment of his poetic consciousness cannot be reconciled with the idealized poem or the reading practices assumed, in various forms, by Mill, Yeats, the New Critics, the Language poets and their successors (among others). The poem is not lyric; the form in which he encountered it—a translation—is precisely one that must be aware of its audience. By not sharing the language of the original, it calls this audience into being. Its genre emerges at the same moment as its public—and, in many respects, is coterminous with it.

Civil Religious Discourse, Modernist Covenants

Zukofsky's unintentional childhood experiment in public-creation took place against the backdrop of a broader crisis of the American public. I mean this in a precise sense: as a central, textually mediated way of calling that public forth, American civil religious discourse strained under growing instability in the first decades of the twentieth century. Philip Gorski frames the crisis well in his 2017 study of the evolution of American civil religion:

> Was it possible to be a "light unto the nations" as well as a "defender of democracy"—to lead by example but also to rule by force? What would become of the "city on a hill" if it could no longer remain free of "entangling alliances"? Did the closing of the frontier and the growth of the corporation spell the end of "republican virtue"? Indeed, could propertyless "wage slaves" actually become good citizens? How could the "mixed" and "balanced" constitution of classical republicanism be maintained in an era of plutocracy and corporate power? Could the power of "the many" still function as a counterweight to the power of "the few"? Could the *res publica* coexist peacefully with the *res privita*? For that matter, could a self-consciously Protestant culture integrate an increasingly Catholic and Jewish population? Finally, could the civil religion be reformulated in nontheistic terms to accommodate the growing ranks of nonbelievers? In sum, could the civil theology of a geopolitically isolated society of small property-holders of WASP heritage be reformulated for a powerful and pluralistic nation of wage-earners?[28]

Modernist poets were well positioned to address this period less as a catastrophe than an opportunity. The strategies that modernists used to understand themselves as moderns bear remarkable similarity to those deployed within the discourse of American civil religion, even from its origins in the early seventeenth century. The mere acts of settlement and colonization entailed an abandonment of roots; the creation of a public through the quest for an authentic, autochthonous past would fail as inevitably in Salem as in Joyce's Dublin. So both discourses draw on a textual past. For American civil religion, this has meant not Greco-Roman myth or local folklore but revisions of the biblical typology that emerged from the Protestant Reformation. The short version is that Colonial, Revolutionary, and antebellum Americans often came to think of themselves as *Americans* by imagining themselves as Israelites fulfilling the biblical imperative to settle a (new) Promised Land. Whereas earlier biblical typology read the Old Testament into the New, American biblical typology read the Old Testament (and, to some extent, the New) into the encounter with the "New World."[29] In the waning years of the seventeenth century, we come to find no less a figure of colonial puritanism and New England government than Cotton Mather "wearing a skullcap in his study and . . . calling himself a rabbi."[30] To "make it new" was, from the beginning, a central act of creating what it meant to be "American."

Civil religious discourse offered James Weldon Johnson, Charles Reznikoff, Lola Ridge, Louis Zukofsky, and Robert Hayden a means of resolving modernist alienation and disinheritance that was not available to their European brethren. Their poetry asks the same questions that Gorski poses earlier but as outsiders twice over. This dynamic sets them apart. In Sacvan Bercovitch's seminal works of the 1970s, he observes that American biblical typology created a public designed to absorb outsiders—even (especially) those who wish to stand askance from normative public practices. The foundational role of the jeremiad (think Jonathan Edwards's "Sinners in the Hands of an Angry God") enables the absorption of critics and criticism into the American community itself. There is room for the liminal space of the angry prophet, the fire-breathing critic of things as they are who is also the idealistic believer in the national project. Condemning the public's failings seems like it should be a mode of discourse that establishes what Warner terms *counterpublics*, "defined by their tension with a larger public, . . . structured by alternative dispositions or protocols, making different assumptions about what can be said or what goes without saying."[31] But American civil religion recognizes these critiques, when formulated in certain ways, as part of its own discourse. A method of absorbing criticism is built into the system. Indeed, the role of critical, alienated outsider can, in this way, become a means of entering the American public.[32]

At the same moment as literary modernism's rise, Gorski observes what we might think of as a covenantal renaissance in American letters and public discourse: a flourishing of attempts to reimagine and repurpose the covenantal community created by American civil religious discourse. John Dewey (teaching at Columbia while Zukofsky, Reznikoff, and Johnson studied there) and W. E. B. Du Bois (to whom Johnson turned for advice on *God's Trombones*) were its Progressive-era exemplars, but Frederick Douglass was the first great exponent of this view. His writings transformed covenantal and civil religious discourse so that "the point was not to return to the eternal social order of a bygone golden age, nor even to recover the original meaning of the founding principles," but "to more fully realize the moral meaning of those principles, even when that meant abandoning established interpretations."[33] So, in James Darsey's reading, American radicals of both the Right and the Left draw on the rhetorical tradition of Hebrew prophetic writings to produce their critiques of a larger American center—to speak as critical outsiders, that is, while remaining within the bounds of the public they address. For Michael Walzer, the biblical Exodus in particular offers a historical paradigm for revolutionary thought in the twentieth century, something looser than either medieval or puritan typology but resembling the use that modernists made of, for example, the *Odyssey*: a "narrative frame" or "story [that] made it possible to tell other stories."[34] Like Walzer, Melanie J. Wright observes the use of an Exodus framework within novels of the American modernist Left during the first decades of the twentieth century, a trope deployed by both Lincoln Steffens and Zora Neale Hurston.[35]

The quintet of poets at the core of this study are figures of this moment. They are critics of the American present that they see around them—but, sometimes despite themselves, they remain believers in the moral meaning of foundational American ideals. Their writing, I've said, teaches ways of paying attention to others and to community. These modes of attention allow for the at least *momentary* enacting of a more democratic, pluralist American public—of engaging in the covenantal renewal at the core of twentieth-century American civil religious discourse. Their works do more than speak to readers, call out to them, or even challenge or condemn them—they act, that is, on more than the individual alone. By creating conditions that allow for and call on readers to understand themselves not as isolated individuals but as members of a situated, communal public, their poetry serves as the mechanism through which covenant is enacted, revised, and renewed. These publics are called on to reimagine themselves within covenantal and typological Americanness: as members of a church congregation, a jury, a labor rally, or refugees in flight, shaping a larger public through the collective experience of covenantal spaces and poetic circulation.

This is not to say that they set out to recover the religiosity of the past or to participate in a quest for authentic religion. They are too much the product of their secular age, in which one can't help but be aware that both religion and its absence are available options and that either must be actively *chosen*.[36] Religious history and pluralism enter their works as the turn not to a personal past but to a textual past: a chosen, constructed one. The religious backgrounds and choices of the poets in this study are varied. Three of the five—Johnson, Reznikoff, and Zukofsky—were openly and clearly secular; Johnson, Reznikoff, and Hayden expressed nostalgia for the simpler, presecular faith of their childhood and ancestors. Johnson, openly agnostic, had been raised, like Robert Hayden, in a religious household and accustomed to the worship and theology of the Black church tradition. Hayden, too, left the church—but for an adult conversion to the Baha'i faith, in which he and his wife were active members. Lola Ridge was educated by nuns in New Zealand—and though she seems not to have remained in communion with the Catholic Church, her works display a deep (indeed, passionate) Christian mysticism. Zukofsky and Reznikoff were both the children of Jewish immigrants—but grew up at different stages of secularization. The former was raised in an Orthodox household; by contrast, Reznikoff's parents had made the initial break from traditional observance. Their relationships to Jewish texts differ: for Reznikoff, translation becomes a mode of recovery; for Zukofsky, an imaginative modernizing.

As a study of works by African American poets and Jewish and Irish immigrants, the present volume could be placed into the category of ethnic—or *multi*ethnic—modernism. At the same time, it's something else—a study of modernism and religious pluralism. Framed in this way, rather than as a study of modernism and *religion*, the book pays attention to religion in order to develop alternative, complementary ways of thinking about ethnicity—in particular, as a form of Warner's idea of the counterpublic: discourse spaces "defined by their tension with a larger public [whose] participants are marked off from persons or citizens in general."[37] Dorothy Wang and Anthony Reed have each offered compelling, formally attuned studies of ethnic poetry that have helped to guide my approach.[38] But they focus on single groups: Asian and African American poetry, respectively. The reason for such isolated studies of American ethnic poetry, Steven S. Lee suggests in his innovative 2013 study, *The Ethnic Avant-Garde: Minority Cultures and World Revolution*, is that the production of truly multiethnic readings of American literary experiments requires looking outside the United States, to other ethnically plural nations, for alternative formulations of ethnic pluralism, group formation, and interethnic relations.[39] Lee thus finds an overlooked paradigm for reading the interwar ethnic avant-garde in the early Soviet Union.

Situating Poetry keeps its gaze at home. In the American ideal and reality of religious pluralism and the ways this shaped twentieth-century revisions of American civil religion, I find another paradigm. Poetry's frequently non-narrative forms of meaning-making can work together with attention to religious pluralism to explore the ways in which categories of ethnic classification are formed in literary studies, to identify where and how their boundaries grow porous, and to draw the lessons gleaned from studies of individual groups into dynamic conversation. Reading poets alongside each other as, on the one hand, members of ethnic groups and, on the other, members of religious groups uncovers networks of solidarity that cross borders of ethnicity—and sometimes tensions that divide them.

Multi- and postethnic approaches developed within the field of Jewish Studies offer, here, useful conceptual models for both ethnic studies and modernist studies.[40] During the wave of immigration that brought millions of Jews to the United States between 1880 and 1920, Jews (or "Israelites" or "Hebrews") were viewed outside the bounds of American whiteness, a race apart, darker in hair and complexion. Their religion, too, marked difference from a predominantly Protestant United States, and Jews became a central touchstone in the period's debates over immigration and national character. By the mid-twentieth century, however, religious pluralism had proved simpler to accommodate than ethnic pluralism: in the 1950s, Judaism entered into Will Herberg's influential formulation of a three-part, religious paradigm for American identity as (in his book's title) *Protestant, Catholic, Jew*.[41] Yet this acceptance of religious difference depended at least in part on the ethnic homogenization of Jews of European descent entering into American whiteness (as did other, often Catholic, ethnic whites whose families immigrated from southern, central, and eastern Europe at the turn of the twentieth century). The history of American Jewishness, this is to say, highlights the contingent, slippery, and necessarily incomplete nature of identity-based categories and readings. Turning to the works of poets—Jewish and otherwise—who lived and wrote during these decades, *Situating Poetry* reads beyond narratives of identity and identification in a way that resembles the incomplete, porous, and overlapping grammars of form and syntax that produce poetic meaning.

Dramatis Personae

The chapters that follow explore the works of five poets: James Weldon Johnson, Charles Reznikoff, Lola Ridge, Louis Zukofsky, and Robert Hayden. They are not offered as representatives of their backgrounds—African American, Jewish, and Irish immigrants; religious minorities; multilingual writers; politically marginalized. Rather, they highlight the shared and divergent paths toward poetic innovation taken by those who wrestled with their status as

American outsiders. They show that discussions of form and ethnic poetry need not and should not be limited to the application of formal innovation to address ethnic experience. Even when this avoids the language of belatedness, it does not avoid its premises. Rather, such discussions show that even a central formal practice might be independently or originally developed through the poetic negotiation of ethnic subjectivity.

The examples of Zukofsky and Reznikoff reveal how we've been limited. I often explain their relevance to nonspecialists in twentieth-century poetics through the role of "poet's poet": their works continue to shape the contemporary avant-garde as they did postwar experimental poetry. Yet, even in this role, they are often read as "Poundian"—as vectors of his poetics not tainted by his sins, evidence that the *poetry* might remain worthwhile, if the anti-Semite's practices can be used to examine Jewish life. Even when their contemporary advocates resist this adjective, their arguments are shaped by reading practices that can't capture the full breadth of Reznikoff's and Zukofsky's innovations and—indeed—their continuity with earlier formal and generic conventions.[42] Their works, like Longfellow's *Hiawatha* or Yehoash's Yiddish translation, are neither lyric nor anti-lyric.

Ridge and Johnson offer a different kind of counterpoint. Widely read and well-known poets during the 1920s and 1930s, their reputations fell into markedly different forms of posthumous decline. Johnson's poetry not only survived but thrived in nonscholarly settings: churches, performance, popular LPs—even science fiction thrillers and *The Ed Sullivan Show*. At the same time, he was the straw man against whom a first wave of scholarship on African American modernism pushed during the 1980s and 1990s, garnering him a reputation for antivernacular elitism from which he is only beginning to recover.[43] Ridge, by contrast, has retained vocal academic champions since her death in 1941—but remains largely unread except by them and their students.[44] Johnson's poetry, in essence, didn't need academia to survive: it has thrived when situated *off* the printed page, finding new life in modes of circulation that repeat and reimagine its original contexts. The printed page, however, too often fails to transmit anything of the situatedness of Ridge's poetry. Works that may have been vivid and vibrant in radical magazines and labor rallies fall flat in the classroom anthology. This contrast helps set the stage for the limit case offered by Robert Hayden's work in chapter 5: seemingly lyric poetry that thrives on the printed page but, when situated in public-creating contexts, reveals its entanglement within a network of sometimes-unexpected genres.

Though by no means a formal group, these poets and their verse crossed paths and circulated in the same literary and physical spaces of New York City in the 1910s, '20s, and '30s. Johnson arrived on the scene of the Harlem Renaissance fully formed as an elder statesman, dressed in three-piece suits with carefully knotted ties; he was deliberately mannered, holding his tongue through meetings with President Woodrow Wilson, toward whom he felt nothing short of physical revulsion. Political efficacy flowed through moderation: organize; threaten to withhold votes; make the case for legal reform on shared principles of good governance; write at set hours of the day. Ridge, on the other hand, was a bohemian through and through. Born in Ireland and raised in New Zealand, she abandoned a husband and then a son, devoting herself full-time to poetry and radical activism.

Whatever the two poets' surface differences, they were also well acquainted with one another, moving in overlapping literary circles. By 1925, Ridge was sending Johnson drafts of her poetry and expressed her excitement about the March issue of *Survey Graphic* edited by Alain Locke, the foundation for his *New Negro Anthology*—and in which Johnson's poem "The Creation" appeared (more on that in chapter 1). Johnson, in turn, introduced Ridge to Countee Cullen, whose first collection of poems, *Color*, would be published later that year.[45] They also shared a publisher—Viking Press—that viewed them as companions. A pamphlet advertising its "Spring Books of 1927" gave Ridge's *Red Flag* prominence on the center page. Above it sat a blurb for the elaborately produced, elegantly bound work on which Johnson staked his reputation as a poet: *God's Trombones: Seven Negro Sermons in Verse* (figure 1).[46] And both poets sold books. Johnson's volume became what it was intended to be: a staple of parlors and churches, the performance of his poems crossing racial divides.[47] Ridge's poems, best-sellers in their day, came to life at labor rallies. A thousand miles away, they also met in the reading habits of a young Robert Hayden, who encountered Ridge's verse in the same Detroit public library reading room he came across Johnson's "The Creation" in a copy of *The New Negro*.[48]

Charles Reznikoff's address in New York changed frequently, but at least for a time, he lived at 5 West Fourth Street, near Washington Park and not far from the Fifth Avenue, Greenwich Village headquarters of the NAACP, where Johnson worked.[49] Like Johnson, Reznikoff was an attorney, having graduated from nearby New York University in 1915. Reznikoff, self-publishing his works from a printing press in his parents' basement during the 1920s, sold them (so the title pages indicate) at The Sunwise Turn, "A Modern Bookshop"

POETRY

GOD'S TROMBONES
Seven Negro Sermons in Verse
by JAMES WELDON JOHNSON
Editor of "The Book of American Negro Spirituals," etc.
With illustrations by AARON DOUGLAS

AMONGST Negroes, particularly, the old-time preacher was spiritual leader and prophet; in his sermons he epitomized the yearnings of the race. His exhortations were of an ecstatic quality, akin to the famed spirituals. These sermons—landmarks in the story of a people—seemed doomed to extinction by neglect, when their essence was caught and sublimated by a real poet, and now they cannot die!

"A good deal has been written on the folk creations of the American Negro: his music, his plantation tales and his dances; but that there are folk sermons, as well, is a fact that has passed unnoticed," says the author in a richly informative preface. For years Mr. Johnson has made an intensive study of these sermons. His first experiment in transmuting a Negro sermon into his own poetry was *The Creation*, now recognized as one of the finest recent poems. This volume includes, in addition to *The Creation*, an opening prayer and six other Negro sermons in verse, among them *Go Down Death*, *The Judgment Day* and *The Prodigal Son*.

Aaron Douglas, Negro artist, enhances the beauty and power of this volume with eight full-page illustrations, and head and tail-pieces to each of the poems.

To be published in March. $2.50

RED FLAG
by LOLA RIDGE
Author of "Sun-Up" and "The Ghetto"

LOLA RIDGE has long been known to a group of discriminating readers of the best in American poetry as a poetess without compromise—one who dares to write as she feels and overleaps staid barriers of poetical conventions with verse that sings. This latest volume fulfills the high expectations of her admirers. The book is divided into series of poems called *Back Yards, Red Flag, Bermuda Sonnets, Under the Sun, Contacts, April, Sevens*, etc.

To be published in February. $1.50

Figure 1. "The Spring Books of Viking Press, 1927" (Box 61, Folder 222, James Weldon and Grace Nail Johnson Collection, Beinecke Rare Book and Manuscript Library, Yale University, New Haven, CT)

located in Midtown, not far from Fifth Avenue and the flagship Forty-Second Street branch of the New York Public Library, at 51 East Forty-Fourth Street. Ridge, too, gave readings here during the early 1920s, and we can imagine Reznikoff's terse, highly redacted lines making an odd partnership with either Ridge's effusive, Whitmanian free verse or her hermetic, mystically inclined sonnets.

Although the two poets wouldn't meet until the end of the decade, Louis Zukofsky spent the 1920s admiring Reznikoff's verse from afar, reading (like Johnson, Ridge, and Reznikoff) *Poetry* and *The Masses* along with the Yiddish papers read by his father, Pinchos.[50] It's even possible that he came across Ridge's poetry in one of these: the December 22, 1918, issue of *Der Forverts* included a lengthy review of *The Ghetto and Other Poems*.[51] In 1920, Zukofsky was a sixteen-year-old Columbia freshman, commuting from his parents' Lower East Side tenement to Morningside Heights, translating the works of Yehoash, and offering them to *Poetry* as representative examples of one of the great American poets of the age—albeit one whose writing, because in Yiddish, was not accessible to most American readers.[52] Like Johnson and Hayden, he was also impeccably dressed—as his wife would later recall, joking, he never went to weed their garden without first shaving and putting on a tie. Yet he, too, was active in radical politics—not in the anarchist circles of Lola Ridge but, befriending a young Whittaker Chambers, nearly joining the same Communist cell. (The explanation of his failure to do so varies: either Zukofsky, never a "joiner," declined to formally sign up or, laden with too many professional and literary aspirations, his application was rejected by the cell for being too "bourgeois.") William Carlos Williams, whom Zukofsky would befriend and whose early collections he would help edit and (with Reznikoff) help publish, had by 1925 already met Lola Ridge at one of her regular literary soirees.[53]

Each, in their own way, was already a prominent figure of New York's interwar literary avant-garde: Johnson, the elegant, well-connected, elder statesman so consumed by both literary and political work that he would nearly suffer a nervous collapse by the end of the 1920s; Ridge, the indefatigable networker, literary host, and pragmatic editor determined to see her visions through; Zukofsky, the single-minded and self-confident striver who would soon catch the eye of Ezra Pound; and the quietly successful Reznikoff, all the more striking for his silent indifference to the usual literary accolades. In Detroit, as Johnson and Ridge passed from the scene, a young Robert Hayden was beginning to publish his first poems—the labor-oriented work that, after studying with W. H. Auden, he would come to dismiss as his "'Prentice Pieces."

Yet all five fit at best uncomfortably within the genres and modes of circulating poetry that create canonicity. Scholarship, anthologies, high school or college curricula, even the retrospective "Collected Poems" all grant new and renewed life to some. But these formats, shaped by and bearing assumptions about how to read poetry, represent only a handful of poetry's situations. Each member of this study's modernist quintet grew acutely aware of this reality. They reacted differently. Johnson, like Eliot, would produce a theory of poetry's social role and seek to enact it in his own work. Lola Ridge attempted to create new spaces and routes for American modernism through her activism and editorial work. Reznikoff doubled down on his own patience, assuming total control of printing and distributing his work. For Zukofsky and Hayden, on the other hand, this reality was a temptation toward bitterness: they published in highly regarded venues, were praised and championed as young men by established poets, but found themselves ground down in middle age by day jobs teaching college composition and overlooked by a new generation of editors and readers. Only in 1966, at ages sixty-two and fifty-three, respectively, would they finally print collections with a commercial publishing house. Why was this the case in their lifetimes? And why has this been, in different forms, the case for all five since their deaths?

These questions drive the chapters that follow. To answer them, I'll turn to an approach drawing together archival research, textual and composition history, attention to multilingual intertexts, translation theory, postsecular studies, historical and formalist approaches to poetics, and reception history. But four fundamental questions about spaces, circulation, and the social function of poetry lurk beneath this approach and run through every reading: *Where is this poem situated? How did it come to be situated there? What mode of attention does this poem, thus situated, call forth?* and *What kind of public does this attention produce?* These are the questions, ultimately, that give birth to genre—and that can guide our receptivity to the performance of covenant in American poetry.

PART I

COVENANTAL SPACES

CHAPTER ONE

A Congregation of Readers

James Weldon Johnson's *God's Trombones*

James Weldon Johnson was among the most read, recited, and memorized American writers of the twentieth century. This would have been the case even if he had written nothing after the year 1900. A single work earns him this distinction, yet it has only rarely been read alongside his career as a novelist, poet, and songwriter. This, of course, is "Lift Every Voice and Sing," sometimes called the "Negro National Anthem" or "Hymn." (During the 1960s, the unofficial moniker would change again: the "Black National Anthem.") Sung in schools, in churches, at meetings of community organizations and the NAACP, the song's spread and growth was, by all accounts, organic and grassroots.[1]

The song's origins, in Johnson's telling, resemble religious revelation. In 1900, he was still the principal of the Stanton School, the African American elementary and middle school in the writer's hometown, a segregated Jacksonville, Florida. With a population of over twenty-eight thousand, Jacksonville was Florida's largest city at the turn of the century, and more than half the population was Black. Johnson was the first African American admitted to the Florida state bar, and his ambitions—and those of his brother, the composer J. Rosamond Johnson—already extended beyond the confines of the Jim Crow South. The brothers had collaborated on a comic opera, *Tolosa, or the Royal Document*, and spent the summer of 1899 in New York trying (and failing) to find a producer. So James Johnson wanted to do more for the city's celebration of Lincoln's birthday, on February 12, than deliver a simple address. "My thoughts began buzzing round a central idea of writing a poem on Lincoln," he wrote in his 1933 autobiography, *Along This Way*, "but I couldn't net them. So I gave up the project as beyond me; at any rate, beyond me to carry out in so short a time."[2] Instead, he and Rosamond continued their collaborative efforts, composing a song for the exercises, enlisting five hundred of Johnson's students as a chorus. The first line (the poem's title) came to him almost immediately, Johnson recalls, though the remainder of the stanza was a grind. Then inspiration took hold. The brothers worked simultaneously, Rosamond at a table, composing the music, and Johnson "pac[ing] back and forth on the front porch, repeating the lines over and over to myself, going through all the agony and ecstasy of creating." The "spirit of the poem had taken hold of me"; "I did not use pen and paper"; "I could not keep back the tears."[3]

By 1902, the brothers were in New York, working together with the musician Bob Cole as Cole and Johnson. Rosamond and Cole would perform in tuxedos on a stage bare of all but a grand piano, eschewing the blackface and vaudeville comedy still the norm for even African American singers. Johnson was the silent partner, focusing on lyrics and managing the trio's business affairs while inserting himself into New York's intellectual and cultural elite: taking writing courses at Columbia University, developing connections with Booker T. Washington and his supporters, and taking his first steps into politics with the Republican Party. They'd left Jacksonville in the wake of a 1901 fire that, through the deliberate choices of the fire marshal and city government, had devastated its African American community. The Stanton School burned. Johnson himself was nearly lynched.

The Jacksonville of the Johnsons' upbringing had been more cosmopolitan than this account indicates. The effect was largely created by their parents: an enterprising, multilingual, free-born Virginian and a mother who had immigrated from the Bahamas. They had met and married in New York City, and Johnson, despite being born in Jacksonville in 1871, would always consider himself "born for a New Yorker."[4] His father spoke fluent Spanish, and under his tutelage within the city's multilingual, multinational African American and Afro-Caribbean community, Johnson also learned the language.[5] Later, he would study Latin and Greek with a private tutor in Jacksonville and at Atlanta University; he knew French well enough to correspond with his wife in it. In 1906, this cosmopolitan rearing joined his political connections to set him on a new course: to US consulates in Puerto Caballo, Venezuela, and Corinto, Nicaragua. He stayed in the diplomatic corps until 1913, when the election of Woodrow Wilson upended his near transfer to a posting in the Azores and ultimately dashed any chances for career advancement. (As a Black Republican serving under an openly racist Democrat, he was doubly damned.) From 1920 to 1930, he was the NAACP's first African American secretary, a role in which he lobbied federal and state officials on behalf of antilynching legislation. Johnson traveled widely from the city of his birth, making his home variously in Latin America, Maine, Atlanta, Nashville, and (again and again) New York City, while also touring Europe and the Pacific. All the while, he wrote. There was a novel (*The Autobiography of an Ex-Colored Man* [1912]), three volumes of poetry (*Fifty Years and Other Poems* [1917], *God's Trombones* [1927], *Saint Peter Relates an Incident of the Judgment Day* [1935]), a history (*Black Manhattan* [1930]), three anthologies (*The Book of American Negro Poetry* [1922] and, with Rosamond, the first and second *Book of American Negro Spirituals* [1925, 1926]), memoirs, and more essays, speeches, and editorials than can be counted.

Perhaps in part because of the novelistic breadth of Johnson's own life's narrative, "Lift Every Voice and Sing" can, at times, feel almost like a footnote in his story. But nothing in his careers as a songwriter, newspaper editor, historian, novelist, or poet would ever reach—or unite—such a wide audience. This song, one of Johnson's earliest compositions, suggests new ways to read and understand the works that came later—in particular, the poetry that would, after 1906, replace songwriting as his primary literary outlet. Although the words to "Lift Every Voice" are lyrics in the most basic sense, because they are *song* lyrics rather than lyric poetry, they don't produce what Michael Warner refers to as an act of lyric speech, in distinction from public speech. "Lyric speech," Warner writes, "has no time: we read the scene of speech as identical with the moment of reading. Public speech, by contrast, requires the temporality of its own circulation."[6] That is, we encounter "Lift Every Voice," even on the page, less like Johnson's "Fifty Years" than like the words to "The Star-Spangled Banner": its performative contexts, in which the performance itself transforms the audience into a communal public, are inseparable from the text itself. My solitary, office-bound encounter with the words to "Lift Every Voice," printed in the Library of America edition of Johnson's works, links me, across place and time, with the public that first performed it and all those that have performed it since. I don't need to hear the melody for this to happen: it's an anthem, a "national hymn." Yet, as Warner also observes, the distinctions between public and lyric speech that create these genres are no more than conventions: "Poetry is not actually overheard; it is read as overheard. And similarly, public speech is not just heard; it is heard (or read) as heard, not just by oneself but by others."[7] Or, as Bonnie Costello puts it, "An I/You address often brings a 'we' into being," a way in which "poetry as an act not only refers and reflects but also imagines and formulates *potential* community."[8]

This chapter poses a series of questions foundational to the readings and arguments that follow throughout this book: What happens when we read seemingly lyric texts through or in dialogue with the conventions of reading typically applied to public speech? This, in turn, begs more fundamental questions about the project of studying poetry: How, in fact, *should* we study it? Exclusively on the page? Through the performed voice of the author? Through the sound of others, its audience, reading it aloud? Through receptions, adaptations, and public contexts? The legacy of "Lift Every Voice" suggests the necessity of an expansive response, one that doesn't rule out any one approach. It's difficult, after all, to draw clear lines that demarcate the writing practices, generic conventions, and textual histories of "Lift Every Voice," the songs composed by Cole and Johnson, and Johnson's later poetry, such as *God's Trombones. Fifty Years and Other Poems* (1917), Johnson's first book of poetry, includes pieces originally written as songs. Some (but not all) were then republished in 1935's *Saint Peter Relates an Incident*. While Brander Matthews's introduction to *Fifty Years* implicitly casts Johnson as an heir to Paul Laurence Dunbar, equally adept in lyrics "common to all mankind" and "the dialect verses," Johnson wrote in both veins for musical performance: "My Lady's Lips Am Like de Honey" and "Nobody's Lookin' but de Owl and de Moon" are in dialect, while "The Glory of the Day Was in Her Face" and "O Southland!" conform to the norms of diction and meter found in turn-of-the-century genteel verse (figures 2 and 3).[9] This suggests another way to classify the poems in *Fifty Years*: between those first published as musical (performed) texts and those first published as poetic (written) texts. These categories cut across those Matthews suggested the volume's first readers use, each containing both dialect and "universal" verse, allowing us to read both sets of distinctions in dialogue rather than in contrast. I've used the word "published" rather than "written" earlier because the collection itself and Johnson's archives indicate that the musical/poetic distinction was frequently blurred at the moment of composition. Looking back a century later, able to historicize and contextualize with the aid of archival materials, we can impose this new classification (poetic/musical) to aid our readings. But in doing so, we can't ignore the fact that Johnson himself did not make this distinction. So if we bear in mind Johnson's own understanding of poetics, we see that approaching his poetry without accounting for the ways in which it engages with and, indeed, *depends on* the conventions we deploy to read public speech acts (such as musical performance) is to do so incompletely.

Figure 2. Sheet music for "My Lady's Lips Am Like De Honey" (lyrics by James Weldon Johnson, music by Will Marion Cook), 1915. (Beinecke Rare Book and Manuscript Library, Yale University, New Haven, CT)

The public created by the performed, communal speech act of "Lift Every Voice" doesn't simply gather to passively appreciate music. Rather, its act of public-creation depends on the audience's active participation in the act of public speech. Just as Johnson's composition practices blur the distinction between the poetic and the musical text, "Lift Every Voice" blurs the distinction between audience and performer. Sung in schools, in pageants, in celebration of Juneteenth and Lincoln's birthday, at chapter meetings of organizations like the National Association of Colored Women's Clubs, and as the official song of the NAACP, "Lift Every Voice" became a central, foundational element of the early-twentieth-century fashioning of African American civic—and civil

Figure 3. Sheet music for "The Glory of the Day Was in Her Face" (lyrics by James Weldon Johnson, music by H. T. Burleigh), 1915. (Beinecke Rare Book and Manuscript Library, Yale University, New Haven, CT)

religious—life.¹⁰ This African American civil religious discourse establishes both overlapping and conflicting narrative and ethical norms with the dominant discourse of American civil religion, broadly construed.¹¹ So Johnson's words unite communities both in the pursuit of a capital-*L* "Liberty" (aligned with, for example, the Declaration of Independence) *and* critical revisions of earlier hymns of American civil religion. "Have not our weary feet," the song asks, "Come to the place for which our fathers sighed?"¹² What "My Country 'Tis of Thee" frames as the "land of the pilgrims' pride / Land where my fathers died" becomes, in this telling, "days when hope unborn had died." "Lift Every Voice" does not reject the ideals of American civil religion. Rather, it operates as a cultural iteration of what the legal theorist Robert Cover terms "redemptive constitutionalism," in which "associations whose sharply different visions of the social order require a transformational politics that cannot be contained within the autonomous insularity of the association itself."¹³ Not revolution but reinterpretation: an American civil religion—and therefore society—expansive enough to recognize its history for what it is and to grant full citizenship to African Americans. "May we forever stand," the song concludes, "True to our God, / True to our native land."¹⁴

In method and in outcome, this idea aligns neatly with the ways Johnson would describe the civic and social nature of art during the 1920s. For Johnson, art exists in society and therefore can and inevitably will affect it. It is itself a kind of actor, obligated along with the artist who created it. These obligations, in his telling, are at once cosmopolitan and local. Indeed, the way to frame the true measure of artistic value is the ability to fulfill both sets of commitments without sacrificing one for the other. In a 1928 essay, "Race Prejudice and the Negro Artist," Johnson describes the development and consequences of what he terms "the individual Negro artist"—in effect, the modernist (re)iteration of the capital-*A* Romantic Artist, as against the "folk" artist of earlier periods. This development produces two important consequences. On the one hand, such artists "are bringing something fresh and vital into American art," which "will be richer because of it."¹⁵ This is the global or cosmopolitan claim: Claude McKay and Bessie Smith are significant because they enrich the lives of all Americans. (So, too, he might have written in another context, because they can enrich the life of an "Aframerican" reader in Corinto—or a Yiddish speaker in Poland.) This is the aesthetic obligation of art and artist, in which art becomes a universal heritage.¹⁶

The second contribution, Johnson continues, which "is of deeper significance to the Negro himself is the effect that this artistic creativity is producing upon his condition and status as a man and citizen." The very fact of African Americans' contribution of cultural value counteracts "the stereotype . . . that the Negro is nothing more than a beggar at the gate of the nation, waiting to be thrown the crumbs of civilization. Through his artistic efforts the Negro is smashing this immemorial stereotype faster than he has ever done through any other method he has been able to use." "Through artistic achievement," he continues, "the Negro has found a means of getting at the very core of the prejudice against him, by challenging the Nordic superiority complex."[17] Johnson's belief in the ability of art—and poetry especially—to reshape American race relations is, to be certain, more than a little idealistic. But he repeated similar claims with such frequency throughout his writings and lectures that we can say either that his belief in it was genuine or that he genuinely believed it was necessary for the general public to *believe* that art had such power.[18] As it pertains to the destruction of stereotypes, the truth in this claim is apparent. If works playing off stereotypes, whether Dunbar's indulgence of chicken-theft motifs or Woodrow Wilson's White House screening of *Birth of a Nation*, could do harm, then their rejection and replacement—even by merely moving the depictions to neutral—could only do good. So, writing elsewhere, in "The Dilemma of the Negro Author" (1928), he insists that "there is not a single Negro writer who is not, at least secondarily, impelled by the desire to make his work have some effect on the white world for the good of his race."[19] Even if Johnson could not truly speak for *all* African American artists, it stands to reason that he *did* speak for himself.

God's Trombones, like "Lift Every Voice," engages in this pursuit through the construction of a civil religious public. Such texts ask to be recognized as a distinct genre. When we account for it when reading Johnson's poetry, we enrich and reshape our understanding of the history of modernist poetics. The formal technique through which "Lift Every Voice" engages in acts of redemptive constitutionalism, using both words and prosody to allude to earlier texts, serves as a central compositional practice in *God's Trombones*, one of several that combine to produce a modernist documentary poetics distinct from both the high modernist strain and Depression-era leftist variant familiar from scholarship. Johnson's modernism develops from sustained engagement with literary genres that were rejected by the New Poetry but that were central to his early literary production: public, commemorative verse and dialect poetry. In *God's Trombones*, Johnson draws on these conventions to engage with the biblical and prophetic typologies of American civil religion, ultimately writing the African American preacher into this discourse, expanding and opening it by framing the United States as a congregation: that is, within the specific space and moment of the African American church on a Sunday morning. *God's Trombones* operates within the same reimagined civil religious discourse as "Lift Every Voice." Johnson's later poetry follows the guidance of this song, which deploys musical performance to allow an assembly of (for instance) segregated schoolchildren to assert and radically reinterpret the seemingly exclusive claim in "My Country 'Tis of Thee" that the United States is "my native country."

Doing so requires a distinctive poetic form: a public poetry capable of marrying political and aesthetic, global and local, without sacrificing one to the other. Johnson's documentary poetics record the voice of the African American preacher by using the techniques of verse to transcribe its score, developing modernist practices in continuity with the genteel, public poetry that had defined his earlier efforts. At the same time, the panracial congregation that Johnson's poetry imagines draws on and reimagines the tropes, imagery, and rhetoric of American biblical and prophetic typology. The political community imagined by American civil religious discourse is thereby transformed and reset within the confines of the African American church. The African American preacher, long a formally determinative figure in African American writing (in the genre of the "preacherly text"), assumes a prophetic role once held by white (or WASP) figures, calling on the civic congregation to repent—to turn back, that is, to the secular, civic covenant that binds them and that Johnson's poems model among readers.

Though historically attuned, the readings that follow eschew simple chronology and begin with a study of the performance history of *God's Trombones* and, especially, the first poem Johnson wrote for the collection, "The Creation." In performance, these poems have been understood explicitly as public speech acts, a history this chapter places in conversation with more conventionally historicist and formalist contexts such as publication history, archival records, and prosody. When public reception guides our approach to "The Creation," we come to see an alternative history for modernist poetic form—particularly, the documentary poem—through the ways this poem embeds its nature as a public speech act in its textual, rhythmic, and prosodic qualities. That is, readings of performance history teach us to recognize qualities already present, though overlooked, within the poetic texts themselves. The second half of this chapter uses the approach developed through readings of "The Creation" and public performances to reread the collection as a whole. Johnson proposes that Americans stand in a covenantal relationship not only with each other but with the law itself. When equal access to that law is not granted, the public that this covenantal relationship creates takes the form of the crowd or mob. The alternative offered by *God's Trombones* is to reimagine the United States as a congregational space. The importance of these readings extends beyond *God's Trombones* and Johnson himself. Reading poetry *simultaneously* as a public and a lyric speech act offers an opportunity to place ethnic and immigrant poets at the center, rather than periphery, of American modernism. In doing so, we come to see how alternative, convergent genealogies of modernist form emerge from the experiences of American racial, religious, political, and linguistic outsiders, a thread that each chapter of this book develops further.

Performing *God's Trombones*, 1918 to 2019

"The Creation," written over the course of 1918 to 1920, marks Johnson's poetic turning point. A reader of *Poetry: A Magazine of Verse* since he was introduced to it by William Stanley Braithwaite in March 1913, barely six months after its 1912 debut, Johnson was aware of and deeply familiar with the stylistic innovations of the so-called New Verse it championed.[20] Nonetheless, he continued to write in the conventional forms with which he was most comfortable. He published in *The Century* and *Ladies' Home Journal*, not the little magazines he followed. With "The Creation," Johnson turns toward formal techniques now associated with modernism: free verse, rhythms designed to mimic spoken language, the use of "folk" material to address contemporary issues. This pivot by an established, middle-aged poet should be less surprising than decades of a "breakthrough" model of modernism suggests. John Timberman Newcomb's scholarship has shown that the New Verse emerged from an interplay between a genteel, a popular, and a nascent modernist sensibility in the years preceding 1910. Johnson, whose career bridges modernism, the late-nineteenth-century genteel forms it eschewed, and the popular songwriting it ambivalently embraced, can be viewed as a case study of those "lost predecessors" of modernism, who "first broke the ground, struggling to use verse to articulate the ambiguous meanings of their own modernity."[21]

Johnson's modernity, in its signal issues, its ambiguities, and its crises, contained much to mark it as distinct from the modernity with which the traditionally and institutionally central figures of modernism struggled. The Great War, urban atomization, cultural malaise, and expatriate alienation are, at best, tertiary issues for Johnson. Centering Johnson or the likewise peripheral poetry of Charles Reznikoff, Lola Ridge, or Louis Zukofsky does more than highlight underrepresented voices and the issues they emphasize. The argument of this chapter and the remainder of this book is that by hearing and recentering these voices, we can recognize the convergent ways in which central modernist techniques (e.g., documentary poetics) emerge from a variety of experiences of modernity, engage in civil religious (rather than purely alienated) acts of public-creation, and require contemporary readers to expand our notions of what "counts" as both text and context when we study poetry.

The origins of "The Creation," were, in Johnson's account, quite like those he attributed to "Lift Every Voice": sudden, epiphanic, with religious overtones, and in the context of public performance. In 1918, Johnson was traveling the country on behalf of the NAACP, lobbying politicians and rallying community support for antilynching legislation. One Sunday in Kansas City, he sat in a church as one dull, unremarkable preacher after another droned on and on. Suddenly, a new speaker broke through Johnson's torpor (and, presumably, the congregation's). He sounded like the preachers Johnson had heard in his childhood, and as he electrified the community, Johnson "took a slip of paper and somewhat surreptitiously jotted down some ideas for the first poem, 'The Creation.'"[22] After a lengthy period of writing, revising, and strategizing, "The Creation" appeared in the December 1, 1920, issue of *The Freeman*. A successor journal to that pivotal, early little magazine *The Seven Arts* that had absorbed its political-aesthetic worldview and much of its editorial staff, *The Freeman* marked a new category of publication venue for Johnson, a modernism announced not merely through what but where.[23] This was also the case for the poem's next two publications (each better known to literary history than its first appearance): in Johnson's anthology *The Book of American Negro Poetry* (1922) and, in 1925, as a central, transformative work in Alain Locke's movement-consolidating anthology *The New Negro*. It's the longest individual poem in the latter, arranged so that it is the first free-verse work to appear, marking a break with the old that makes way for the poetry of Langston Hughes, which immediately follows it.

While Johnson was publishing and republishing "The Creation," he was also at work developing a thematically unified collection of what he called "Negro Sermons in Verse" from it. This would become *God's Trombones*, released to acclaim by Viking in 1927. These poems link the rhythms of ragtime and popular song to the prosody of genteel poetry and the King James Bible to the voice of "the old time Negro preacher."[24] In doing so, he draws on the underexplored tradition of what Marcellus Blount, writing in 1992, identifies as the "preacherly text." The key figure in this tradition for Blount (as for Johnson) is Paul Laurence Dunbar—or, more precisely, the speaker in his poem "An Ante-Bellum Sermon." By necessity double voiced and subversive, the speaker "pretends to consign his sermon to the task of biblical exegesis to dupe those listeners who might be threatened by his real text"—that is, the coming of freedom to the South's enslaved people. Blount insists that this is not signification of the sort described by Henry Louis Gates Jr. but that these "double and antagonistic voices allow [the preacher] the freedom to console his black listeners and discerning whites."[25] In the literary representations of these so-called traditional sermons, they become both allusive and metalinguistic, relying on the listener's/reader's knowledge of external texts and meditating on the inadequacy of their own language.

Johnson adapts these conventions to offer more than consolation and deception. Like Dunbar's, his preacher has a sense of humor—but the community this preacher asserts is even more expansive, including even those whites who, in Dunbar's poem, don't get the joke or subtext. The images, references, and narratives his preacher references are largely those of the typological discourse of American sermons, rhetoric, and literature. By the time Johnson wrote, to employ a preacherly voice was to engage in a project of recovery. The preacher who is expected to deploy these typological referents, whose presence looms over the works of Hawthorne and Melville and within the scholarship of Sacvan Bercovitch, James Darsey, and Tracy Fessenden, is white, male, a New Englander, a puritan presiding over the foundations of American citizenship. The African American plantation preacher, on the other hand, was by popular association in the early twentieth century a comic figure (the expectation that Dunbar's "An Ante-Bellum Sermon" manipulates). Indeed, in a 1931 address at Fisk University, Johnson noted that the negative associations with this figure were so strong that he received letters from editors of African American newspapers asking him not to publish *God's Trombones*, for fear that it would only reinforce stereotypes.[26]

Johnson's track record, were it better known at the time, would not have assuaged these worries. Although his preface to *God's Trombones* describes the plantation preacher as "generally a man far above the average in intelligence, . . . not infrequently, a man of positive genius" and singles out as the most famous of these folk geniuses John Jasper (1812–1901), to whose Richmond, Virginia, church "thousands of people, white and black, flocked," in Johnson's early career, Jasper was not always such a genius.[27] In *Aunt Mandy's*

Chicken Dinner, a film scenario Johnson sold to Lubin Productions in the summer of 1914, the title character has invited a Reverend Jasper Jones for supper, precipitating the chicken-theft plotline that earns the film the full weight of its subtitle: "A Darkey Comedy."[28] Reverend Jones himself is composed entirely of "comic" stereotypes: dressed in an old, shabby suit, he thinks himself a dandy but merely looks ridiculous; he fantasizes gluttonously about the meal to come; he drinks whiskey from a hidden bottle; and in the concluding scene, he attempts to fight Mandy's husband, Mose, with his umbrella, only to be chased away as the title character swats at him with a broom.[29]

Johnson returned specifically to this figure from the nadir of his career as he worked on *God's Trombones*. A discarded "Introductory Poem" titled "The Reverend Jasper Jones" sets out, quite literally, to transform Jones from the figure Johnson had presented in *Aunt Mandy's Kitchen Dinner* into the dignified man of genius he would describe in the volume's preface. (In a note to W. E. B. Du Bois, Johnson acknowledged, "I originally intended to use [the poem] as a sort of preface to the sermons.")[30] In its final version, this poem enacts the metamorphosis that the collection itself seeks to effect. As it begins, Jones is still the comic grotesque: "A man of medium height but massive bones. / A ponderous head, a brow both wide and full," to which "Add on short arms, bow legs and ample feet."[31] But as the poem describes the cadences of his sermon (the details resemble those given in the final preface but in pentameter couplets), it transforms the reader's opinion of him: "in spite of self, you fell / Under the primal magic of his spell" as "He roused in you emotions at his will," building toward the conclusion that no one could "dare belittle Jasper's place" and an invitation that the reader, in the following poems, "Hear for yourself the Reverend Jasper preach." The effect, in sum, is that "You thought him more the seer and less the clown."[32] In doing so, Johnson deploys Jasper Jones to enact a very different type of public speech from that he engaged in as a writer of film scenarios. Cast explicitly into the role of congregants, readers undergo a kind of race awakening: from the experience of shame or bemusement to that of pride; for white readers, perhaps, the moment of recognition of literary genius. With the preacher directly addressing his audience, his challenge can't be mistaken for entertainment. He calls on readers, no matter their religion or race, to imagine themselves a member of this church congregation. The poems that follow speak as this preacher does. Unlike Dunbar's double-voiced minister, they call out to the readers as members of a shared community, like the mixed congregation of John Jasper's church that Johnson describes in the published preface.

Although this introductory poem was ultimately discarded and remains unpublished, it enables us to see the ways in which Johnson's verse imagines itself as a public speech act as well as read, textual, or "lyric" speech. Its legacy is on display in the century-long performance history of *God's Trombones*. Viking's first editions of the book were expensively produced and elegantly designed. They look and feel like prestigious mantelpiece items. With heavy, durable paper, stylized fonts, and woodcut illustrations designed by Aaron Douglas, emerging as one of the premier visual artists of the Harlem Renaissance, the book design alone won the publisher critical acclaim and awards.[33] Such volumes appear perfectly designed for lyric or "poetic" speech. But those who bought them didn't consign them to the armchair and bookshelf. Instead, they served as a guide for public readings and performances from the moment of publication. The marginalia displayed in figure 4 offers an example of this. Here, "The Prodigal Son" is orchestrated for performance; the director's notations make clarifying emendations and decisions about where distinct voices in the poem begin and end. Whether in the late 1920s or today, performances of *God's Trombones* place us within the public assumed and created by the preacher's words, that of the congregation. Performed in a church—as the majority of present-day versions of *God's Trombones* available on YouTube have been—or even by theater ensembles *as if* in a church, they create a congregational public, even if only momentarily imagined as we sit in the theater, in pews, or (today) at home in a desk chair, watching a preacher recite these poems as actual sermons.

Yet, from the beginning, many of these performances have also been decidedly secular, as Johnson himself was. In one very early instance, on February 17, 1929, the New World Dancers included a recitation of "Go Down, Death," a poem from *God's Trombones*, as one of the settings for its performance. For that evening's audience at the Fifty-Fourth Street Gallo Theater, Johnson's words were juxtaposed with works by the French composers Maurice Ravel and Claude Debussy, to which the dancers also performed.[34] In this case, a public performance of the poem insists on locating it within a high-cultural, modernist tradition. So, in its own way, does the performance of trombonist Chris Crenshaw's *God's Trombones*, an album-length composition based on Johnson's poems, by Wynton Marsalis's Jazz at Lincoln Center Orchestra in 2012. Even listening to a recording of the words of *God's Trombones* set as liturgical music—as with Gordon Myers's 1964 setting for the Gloriae Dei Cantores ensemble (not recorded until 1995)—no more creates a neces-

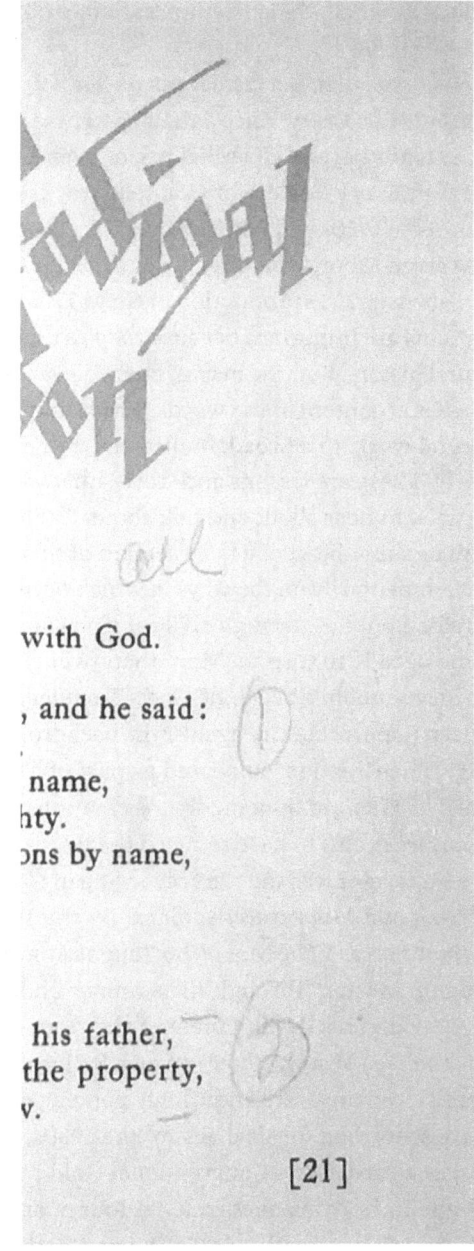

Figure 4. Marginalia for performance of "The Prodigal Son"

sarily Christian public, after all, than listening at home to Bach's *St. Matthew Passion* does.

Whether religious or secular, performances of *God's Trombones* function much like renditions of "Lift Every Voice": their discourse modifies a civil religious public that extends beyond the religious, or even specifically African American, frame. ("Lift Every Voice," for example, was taken up by Popular Front organizations of the 1920s and 1930s as a way of announcing labor's solidarity.) As Jackie Warren Moore, the director of the Paul Robeson Performing Arts Theater's February 2015 production of *God's Trombones*, explains in an interview, the poems are important because they're a central part of African American cultural history. But, she insists, their relevance extends beyond the Christian context and content of the words. They should be able to speak, like Johnson's original work, to a broad, multiracial, religiously plural audience: "It's also timely. These are lessons and stories that we need to hear and principles that we need to hear about and talk about."[35] These timely principles and stories will be the subject of a later section of this chapter. For now, it's worth lingering momentarily on the ways in which performances of *God's Trombones* have created publics through civil religious discourse.

The 1960s are the decade to turn to. More than twenty years after Johnson's 1939 death in an automobile accident, *God's Trombones* had entered the discourse of American popular culture against the backdrop of the civil rights movement. In 1951, "The Creation" appeared as part of a monologue in the postapocalyptic thriller *Five*, announcing the re-creation of human community after atomic warfare seems to have reduced the world population to five survivors. Far more important was the 1962 recording of *God's Trombones* released by Fred Waring and His Pennsylvanians. By the 1960s, Waring had already earned a reputation as "The Man Who Taught America How to Sing" and "America's Singing Master" through the summer choral workshops he had established in 1947 and his development of the "tone syllable" mode of musical education. *The Fred Waring Show* ran on CBS from 1948 to 1954, and Waring and His Pennsylvanians were enduringly popular, ranking among the best-selling and widest-touring musical acts of the 1930s, 1940s, 1950s, and 1960s; in 1984, he was awarded the Congressional Gold Medal. Released by Decca, the 1962 album *God's Trombones* includes four poems from Johnson's volume—"Listen, Lord," "The Creation," "Go Down, Death," and "The Judgment Day"—and, on its B side, five traditional spirituals: "Countin' My Blessings," "Sometimes I Feel like a Motherless Child," "Standin' in de Need of Prayer," "Were You There When They Crucified My Lord?," and "Jesus

Walked This Lonesome Valley." Side A opens with the sound of bells calling congregants into a church, followed by a chorus singing "Old Time Religion" in the style popularized by Waring, a white bandleader. The voices that follow, reciting Johnson's poetry, are those of Gertrude Jeanette, a pioneering African American Broadway actress, playwright, and producer, and Frank Davis, an African American baritone for the Pennsylvanians. Among both the performers and the target audience, Waring's *God's Trombones* enacts a mixed-race public. Indeed, through its aural establishment of a congregational public, called to prayer with church bells, the recording proclaims that Johnson's preacher is part of an "old-time religion" shared nationally, across racial lines. Most strikingly, in the same year that essays that would become James Baldwin's *The Fire Next Time* appeared in the *New Yorker*, Waring's album locates the possibility of an African American man demanding of a *white* public, "Sinner, oh, sinner, / Where will you stand / In that great day when God's a-going to rain down fire?" as unobjectionable and part of mainstream American religious, civic, and cultural discourse.

Within five years, *God's Trombones* had moved even closer to the heart of the United States' civil religious discourse, lodging itself at the intersection of an ecumenical, nondenominational Christianity and American popular culture: *The Ed Sullivan Show*'s 1967 Easter special. On March 26, Jim Henson's Muppets, the Dave Clark Five, and actors from *Green Acres* took to the stage of the church of television and popular song to bring Americans together to celebrate the holiday as a nation.[36] As part of this ceremony, Eddie Albert, the once-blacklisted (white) star of *Green Acres*, recited "The Creation": a poem on a religious theme, yes, and perhaps the evening's most religiously inclined moment, but also a poem that contains no reference to the birth, death, resurrection, or divinity of Jesus—a poem, that is, capable of pointing toward the God shared by Protestants, Catholics, and Jews, welcoming Americans to the celebration of a holiday framed less as Christian than *American* and requiring no creedal belief or confession, and leading white Americans to worship in the rhythm and diction of African American vernacular speech.

The poems of *God's Trombones*, situated in their postpublication performances, speak beyond the norms (and constraints) of twentieth-century lyric: they engage in the discourses of American civil religion and establish public-creating encounters. But to demonstrate the ways in which these publics are, indeed, *covenantal* requires attention to the content as well as the contexts of the poetry. These are not separate entities. Reception history and close textual readings should be no more thought of as incompatible than the literary-historical approaches of the new modernist studies and formalist scholarship are (or should be). Attending, first, to performance history rather than textual history can help to shift our readerly expectations. After all, public speech and lyric speech are distinguished as much (if not more) by what we expect and believe them to be than what they actually are. Viewed from this perspective, we can see the ways in which acts of public-creation are encoded in the most basic textual elements of *God's Trombones*, the formal, prosodic, and rhythmic qualities that often reside at the core of readings that idealize poetry as lyric.

Typological Documents: Scoring "The Creation"

The ways later publics have recognized themselves in performances of *God's Trombones* depend on textual practices embedded in Johnson's words, qualities as fundamental as spelling, rhyme, and prosody. They guide reader and poem into dialogue with a trio of genres: dialect verse, commemorative verse, and documentary poetry. A quick comparison with Paul Laurence Dunbar's "An Ante-Bellum Sermon" throws this into relief. The two poets create strikingly different "preacherly" texts in the service of changing generic expectations of preacherly performances. Dunbar undermines the expectations of a comic preacher to create a second, subversive community: what Warner would term a counterpublic. This preacher and congregation, for all their potential, remain outside the citizenship community established and enforced by American civil religion. Johnson rejects the comic preacher completely. In place of the preacher who "hides his real message under the guise of what is acceptable"—comic dialect, biblical exegesis—in order "to dupe those listeners who might be threatened by his real text," Johnson turns to a historical model in the Reverend John Jasper, whose eloquence drew together a multiracial congregation.[37] His preacher speaks in a voice unmarked by eye dialect, a "high," literary register that nonetheless retains a vernacular cadence. As Johnson explains in the preface,

> The old-time Negro preachers, though they actually used dialect in their ordinary intercourse, stepped out from its narrow confines when they preached. They were all saturated with the sublime phraseology of the Hebrew prophets and steeped in the idioms of King James English, so when they preached and warmed to their work they spoke another language, a language far removed from traditional Negro dialect. It was really a fusion of Negro idioms with Bible English; and in this there may have been, after all,

some kinship with the innate grandiloquence of their old African tongues. To place in the mouths of the talented old-time Negro preachers a language that is a literary imitation of Mississippi cotton-field dialect is sheer burlesque.[38]

This register, importantly, is not identical with "standard" or "literary" American English, indistinguishable from that of educated white Americans—though it is, by implication, *equal* to them. Johnson describes a literary register that draws on both English literary heritage—the King James Bible—and that of another people and language, the "old African tongues." His claim of a connection to Africa may well be groundless, but the intent still matters: Johnson frames the preacher's speech as an *alternative* register of literary American English, one with roots extending to Africa, well before the ancestors of Black Americans had met (and been enslaved by) the ancestors of their white fellow citizens, and which therefore cannot be dismissed as mere mimicry of the cultural referents of white Americans.

Johnson fuses the patrimonies of this alternate register through practices now associated with modernist documentary poetics. Just as Ezra Pound's documentary methods function by producing form from fragments (or reestablishing the possibility of form in a fragmented culture), Johnson's poetry recombines "the sublime phraseology of the Hebrew prophets," "the idioms of King James English," "Negro idioms," and "the innate grandiloquence of their old African tongues" to create the formal structure of the preacher's sermon. Modern technologies of documentation also inform Johnson's verse. But in place of mimetic recordings, as with John Dos Passos's newsreel, Muriel Rukeyser's newspaper and Senate hearing transcripts, or Zora Neale Hurston's tape recorder, he turns to the methods with which he was most familiar and follows the practices of the sheet-music industry. Rhythm, therefore, is as central to his documentary mode as to Pound's. But Johnson's documentary poetics work to subvert the "ideologically constructed expectations for black folk rhythms" that, Ben Glaser observes, were established in the minds of white audiences and reinforced by many modernists.[39]

The rhythms of the King James Bible serve as the prosodic score to which the preacher's words are set. The score of the KJV bears much in common with the ragtime compositions of Scott Joplin, Jelly Roll Morton, or the Original Dixieland Jass Band. He highlights the repetition and syncopation that characterize ragtime as vernacular qualities in the preface, but these are, in fact, the formal qualities through which the influence of the KJV on *God's Trombones* most clearly emerges. In the King James Version of Genesis 1, for instance, every verse except the first begins with the word "And"—in particular, the formulation "And God [+ verb]." In "The Creation," the "vernacular" repetition of Johnson's preacher follows the same syntactic patterns as the KJV's parataxis: of the first thirty-three lines (five stanzas), seventeen begin with "And," while four more begin with the syntactically and aurally comparable "Then"; eight of these instances are "And/Then God [+ verb]."

Syncopation proves even more central. Johnson orients his discussion of prosody around this concept: "The tempos of the preacher I have endeavored to indicate by the line arrangement of the poems, and a certain sort of pause that is marked by a quick in taking and an audible expulsion of the breath I have indicated by dashes. There is a decided syncopation of speech—the crowding in of many syllables or the lengthening out of a few to fill one metrical foot.... The rhythmical stress of this syncopation is partly obtained by a marked silent fraction of a beat; frequently this silent fraction is filled in by a hand clap."[40] Syncopation involves not only the variation of long and short lines but the variation of stressed syllables and play on traditional meter within and across those lines. For example, the first two lines, "And God stepped out on space, / And he looked around and said:" can be read as iambic trimeter, though it doesn't have to be. In a December 1935 recording, Johnson reads "stepped out" as a spondee; in a 1938 reading, it's an iamb. In each, Johnson reads "And he looked" as an anapest, a metrical unit that serves a central role in his syncopated prosody.[41] The next two lines, God's speech, "I'm lonely— / I'll make me a world," break completely with iambs and traditional verse length, establishing the heavily stressed quality of God's speech in "The Creation." The beginning of the next stanza, however, appears to return to conventional prosody: "And as far as the eye of God could see / Darkness covered everything." These lines can (but, again, don't *have* to be) read as iambic and trochaic pentameter, respectively; the slant rhyme of "God could see" / "everything" marks them as a couplet. And again, lines 3 and 4 break wildly from this meter: "Blacker than a hundred midnights / Down in a cypress swamp." It's not simply the frequency of stresses in a line—there's actually a slight *decrease*, from 5/10 and 4/7 to 4/8 and 3/6—but their arrangement. Johnson runs long strings of unstressed syllables together before hitting a series of stressed words and, in the process, throwing an ear that has been prepared—both by training and by the poem itself—to read or listen for meter measured in conventional, iambic feet off into the variations of jazz trombones.

These are the very prosodic qualities that characterize the King James's creation narrative. Take its first sentence: "In the beginning God created the heaven and the earth." Though prose, this sentence and those that follow scan remarkably well, even with the first required stress not falling until the fourth syllable ("be*gin*ning"). If these four syllables are marked off as a single foot—a fourth paeon (three unstressed syllables followed by a stress)—then the rest fall neatly into place: two iambs, then an anapest, and, to close the verse, another fourth paeon. If the reader listens for iambs, the result is something quite like the variations of Johnson's preacher. And if we further think of anapests and fourth paeons as variations on the iamb—as contemporary poetics sometimes asks us to think of trochees, spondees, and pyrrhics—then we find such variations embedded in the very parataxis that defines both the King James account and Johnson's: Genesis 1:2 begins, "And the earth," an anapestic sentence opening that recurs midverse throughout Genesis 1 and frequently at the beginning of verses in "The Creation."[42] The opening phrase "And God [+ verb]" can likewise be read trisyllabically, as a bacchius (an unstressed syllable followed by two stressed): the point being that while "And God," as a phrase, is an iamb, "And God [+ verb]," as a *formula*, can be read or heard as a variation on the iambic "standard."[43] As Johnson's manuscripts reveal, he wrote with precisely these prosodic qualities in mind, planning a score of iambs, anapests, and fourth paeons in the margins of his working drafts throughout the 1920s (figures 5 and 6).

Reading with historical prosody (the belief "that we cannot separate the practice of reading a poem from the histories and theories of reading that mediate our ideas about poetry")[44] as well as public performance in mind uncovers the ways in which the public speech act has been embedded within the written text. It also alerts us to an alternative, convergent genealogy of the modernist practices known as documentary poetics.[45] For Johnson, scansion offers a way to transcribe and record the poem's voicing: a practice of documenting and reproducing sound without recourse to emerging technologies of recording that shaped the documentary practices of both Anglo-American high modernists and Depression-era Left modernists. *God's Trombones*, by contrast, appears quite at home within Johnson's long-standing engagement with sheet music, from which he derived steady income throughout his life.[46] This influence permeated Johnson's literary output of the 1920s, including the first and second *Book of American Negro Spirituals* (1925, 1931), at which he labored while writing *God's Trombones*. Working again with

> Then God said to Noah, Bar the door!
> And Noah barred the door.
>
> And a little black spot began to spread,
> Like a bottle of ink spilling on the sky.

Figure 5. Johnson's margin notes calling for lines of varying anapests and iambs on a draft of "Noah Built That Ark" (Box 60, Folder 212, James Weldon and Grace Nail Johnson Collection, Beinecke Rare Book and Manuscript Library, Yale University, New Haven, CT)

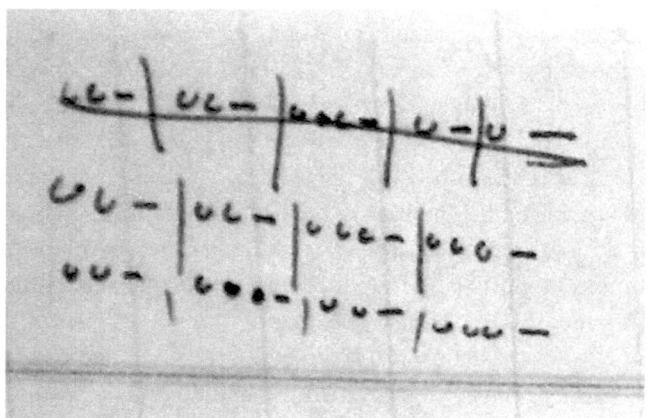

Figure 6. Johnson's margin notes delineating meter on a draft of "Let My People Go" (Box 60, Folder 215, James Weldon and Grace Nail Johnson Collection, Beinecke Rare Book and Manuscript Library, Yale University, New Haven, CT)

Rosamond, Johnson documented African American folk tradition and its cultural productions by quite literally editing, arranging, and scoring the texts in volumes that anthologized spirituals as sheet music with a scholarly introduction and notes.[47] This editorial role, in which Johnson prioritizes the voices and rhythms of his source material, prefigures the later documentary style of Pound's Adams Cantos or Reznikoff's *Testimony*.[48]

Johnson's documentary poetics depend as heavily on the generic conventions of nineteenth-century and fin de siècle verse as they do the recording technologies. *God's Trombones* is not meant to be fully mimetic.[49] Instead, language first used to describe Pound's later documentary experiments applies with accuracy: his poetry seeks less to record than to "memorialise past occurrences in such a way as to give them a material form and, in so doing ... reveal the ideas or concepts that cling to the form and that remain meaningful and useful in the present."[50] What David Ten Eyck and Lawrence Rainey see as a poetics of memorialization in Pound is, for Johnson, a poetics of commemoration, developed in continuity with the commemorative verse of earlier poems such as "Fifty Years." While, by the 1910s and 1920s, commemorative verse would be seen as an ossified, outmoded form by modernism and the New Verse, in the middle of the nineteenth century, as Edward Keyes Whitley observes, commemorative verse offered an alternative form to poets dissatisfied with the limited possibilities of lyric address—particularly to racial and religious outsiders. Instead of a lyric "posture of solitary isolation, ... commemorative poetry is instead characterized by direct address to an audience whose presence looms large in the poet's mind."[51] Characteristically, this audience is one assembled for an event of communal importance—the dedication of a church, a parade of foreign delegates, the passing of Lincoln's funeral train.

Through this commemorative function, Johnson's documentary poetry becomes a public-creating speech act with a civic purpose: precisely the role we have seen it take in performances over the past nine decades. The occasion of "The Creation" and the other poems in *God's Trombones*, rather than the historically concrete commemoration of specific events or figures, is the nonetheless real, recurrent, and temporally bound speech act of the Sunday sermon. Yet these poems function to commemorate, memorialize, and document not only sermons but also—and more importantly—the congregational public that these speech acts created and re-created each week. Both the published prefatory poem, "Listen, Lord," and the unpublished "The Reverend Jasper Jones" cast the reader into the role of congregant through second-person address and description of inward transformation. *God's Trombones* directly addresses its readers not in isolation but as members of a shared public. Drawing white readers into an African American church as congregants, Johnson binds them all under the terms of a mutual covenant, at once expanding the breadth and sharpening the implicit threat that recurs within the typological language and rhetoric of American civil religious discourse—of, for instance, the puritan jeremiad. "A nation under covenant," writes Gorski, "is not a nation under contract, but a nation *under judgment*. And the role of the prophet is to remind the nation of this, to preach an ethos of contrition and humility on the one hand, and to inspire acts of charity and justice on the other."[52] This reminder lies at the heart of Johnson's poems. So, his preacher reminds the members of his congregation, creating it out of the volume's readers as he does so, Americans should not imagine themselves as the Chosen People, their nation as a Promised Land, but as "proud and dying sinners / Sinners hanging over the mouth of hell."[53]

Covenantal Poetics and Modernist Practice

By commemorating the space and language of the African American church on a Sunday, *God's Trombones* engages in poetic genres of public speech. By addressing readers as members of the congregation, it asks them to imagine themselves as such. Its performative contexts and reception—crucial to the poem's legacy from the moment of its publication—along with its formal, prosodic elements, embed these qualities within the text itself. But the publics created through encounters with *God's Trombones* are more than commemorative. They are covenantal. That is, the poem mediates publics defined by promised behavior—here, to behave in ways that enable and encourage the recognition of African Americans within the community of citizenship and to refrain from behavior that interferes with this goal. The legal concept of covenant is defined by promised behavior alone. But religious, and particularly biblical, concepts of covenant treat these promises as the conditions that determine whether blessings or curses will be bestowed by a governing partner to the covenant (i.e., God). The sermons of *God's Trombones* tell the stories of those who either uphold the covenant (and meet with blessing) or fail to do so (and are punished). The public created by these poems, Johnson's preacher asserts, has been bound to the terms of covenant. He presents them with a choice between two kinds of civic communities, a choice no less stark than that presented to the Israelites in Deuteronomy 28. On the one hand, there is the congregation, a public committed to and governed by a shared, covenantal law. On the other hand, there is the mob, the dangerous, impulsive, and violent public governed by the collective force of individual passions.

In Johnson's imagining, the law itself serves in place of God as the covenant's governing partner. This covenant is civil religious, rather than merely religious. Johnson's lack of religious belief had been deeply held from an early age: he courted censure as a college student for openly professing his agnosticism. But as a trained attorney and civil rights activist, he does express a faith in the law, despite the many failings of the U.S. legal system. The United States is a nation of laws, ruled by laws; its founding promise, in this view, is equality before the law regardless of race, class, sex, or religion. By excluding individuals and groups from being subject to, protected by, and bound to uphold the law, the nation violates its founding covenant. Rather than an angry God ordaining punishment unto the third and fourth generations, the law itself enacts this punishment by breaking down into mob rule when subject to the covenantal violations of (for instance) the Jim Crow South. The message of Johnson's preacher, summarized while standing on one foot, is that of the covenantal ethics declared in Charles Reznikoff's "Israel" (to be discussed in chapter 2): "You are not to do each what is right in his own eyes."[54]

God's Trombones' emergent documentary practices bring the breadth of this covenantal vision for American civic life into full view. Beyond the blending of "literary" and "vernacular" voices, Johnson's poems engage in dialogue with his wider oeuvre. More than a historicist claim, this is a formal one. *God's Trombones* regularly interpolates the images, themes, and phrases of Johnson's earlier writings and of individual poems within the volume; these, in turn, are later interpolated into future texts (such as *Along This Way*). This practice establishes a field of referents that allows the work to directly address its readers, both white and Black, about contemporary racial politics and violence in the covenantal discourse of American civil religion. (In many ways, it also casts the preacher as a deft modernist skilled in the source-based poetics of an increasingly allusive modernist scene.) Noelle Morrissette, examining the interrelation of the many prefaces Johnson wrote to his own works and those of others, observes a practice of prose interpolation that crests between 1917 and 1927, the period in which he was at work on the first and second *Book of American Negro Spirituals*, *The Book of American Negro Poetry*, and a reissued *Autobiography of an Ex-Colored Man*, his 1912 novel. Within this "simultaneity of composition," she concludes, "Johnson's repetitions create a field of referentiality that significantly alters any understanding of these works as discrete entities." Rather, "each work presents a reverberating continuum between author and artist, art and audience, enhancing Johnson's simultaneous composition practice."[55]

What Morrissette terms a "theory of vernacular transcription" could also describe Johnson's orchestration of the voice of the preacher to the rhythmic score of the King James Bible. Such interpolation is an act of transcribing or orchestrating a new text to an earlier document, whether we're discussing his prefaces or his poetry. It developed naturally from the verse genres of Johnson's earlier career. The preacherly text deploys a kind of documentary interpolation, relying on the reader's knowledge of external sources, deploying citation, quotation, and allusion to allow a biblical narrative to speak about the present. Likewise, interpolation was characteristic of African American musical forms, including both ragtime and the popular songwriting Johnson engaged in with Cole and Johnson. As a lyricist, he demonstrated a marked predilection for it: for example, in his use of "Nobody Knows the Trouble I've Seen" in the song "Under the Bamboo Tree" (1902). Two decades later, T. S. Eliot interpolated "Under the Bamboo Tree" into "Sweeney Agonistes." If we readily call Eliot's practice modernist, we have no justification for not applying it to Johnson's.

This interpolation forms the backbone of the covenantal discourse in *God's Trombones*. For instance, in "The Prodigal Son," Johnson's preacher transforms the New Testament parable about divine love into a tale of an individual who falls away from covenant and the ways in which he is able to return to it and rebuild a community. The field of referents on which this depends treats *The Autobiography of an Ex-Colored Man* as a documentary source text on par with the Bible. This Prodigal Son, following the biblical narrative, takes his inheritance early, leaves his father's house, and squanders it in a far-off city. Although a passerby insists he's come to "That great city of Babylon," Johnson's language and the Aaron Douglas woodcut that accompanies the poem make it clear that this is really New York's nightclub scene.[56] Douglas, who would later be Johnson's (and then Robert Hayden's) colleague at Fisk University, produced a woodcut illustration for each poem. Reproduced in contemporaneous reviews and subsequent editions, the woodcuts also operate as part of the collection's documentary composite. In the center of this image, the silhouettes of a man flanked by two women in modern dress dance together beneath a ceiling lamp. Around the edges, a bottle of gin, trombones, a dollar bill, playing cards, and dice frame the scene.

This Babylon—New York, the city Johnson proclaimed his spiritual hometown—is not the quintessential land of exile but the paradigm of community that has failed to uphold its civic covenant. This iteration of the Prodigal Son leaves his family home and comes to the nightclubs of New York's Tenderloin district. There, he falls into sin—drinking, whoring, "Throwing dice with the devil for his soul." More notably, the people around him not only make no effort to help him but, as a nameless mass—a mob—take advantage of him:

> And he wasted his substance in riotous living,
> . . . .
> And they stripped him of his money,

And they stripped him of his clothes,
And they left him broke and ragged[57]

This is a scene drawn from Johnson's novel, not the Bible. The Ex-Colored Man, too, departs his family home and, in the nightclubs of the Tenderloin district, spends time among the same "Brass bands and string bands a-playing" as he becomes a talented ragtime pianist.[58] The poem follows the same progression as the novel's gambling-den scene. Shortly after the Ex-Colored Man's arrival in New York, a new acquaintance guides him to a gambling hall's upstairs high-roller room, where, playing craps for the first time, he wins two hundred dollars. On his way out, however, he notices a set of men begging for money to reenter the game and wearing nothing but "linen dusters":

> And as I looked about I noticed that there were perhaps a dozen men in the room similarly clad. . . . [My companion] told me that men who had lost all the money and jewelry they possessed, frequently, in an effort to recoup their losses, would gamble away all their outer clothing and even their shoes; and that the proprietor kept on hand a supply of linen dusters for all who were so unfortunate. . . . Sometimes a fellow would become almost completely dressed and then, by a turn of the dice, would be thrown back into a state of semi-nakedness. Some of them were virtually prisoners and unable to get into the streets for days at a time.[59]

In the weeks that follow, the Ex-Colored Man attempts to make a living at gambling and concedes, "I passed through all the states and conditions that a gambler is heir to. Some days found me able to peel ten and twenty dollar bills from a roll, and others found me clad in a linen duster and carpet slippers."[60] The primary difference is a difference of emphasis: in the novel's gambling scene, the gamblers themselves are responsible for the loss of their clothes and money. In the preacher's sermon, the Prodigal Son loses money in gambling halls—but "*they* stripped him of his money, / And *they* stripped him of his clothes, / And *they* left him broke and ragged."[61] Here, the failure occurs on the level of civic community, not the individual.

Nonetheless, falling away from covenant plays a crucial role in *The Autobiography of an Ex-Colored Man*. The novel's final line points directly to rejection of the covenantal community for the satisfaction of individual desire. The narrator, having made the choice to abandon his people, says, "I cannot repress the thought that, after all, I have chosen the lesser part, that I have sold my birthright for a mess of pottage."[62] He suspects that he is an Esau—Jacob's twin who, famished from a day of hunting, is desperate enough for Jacob's pot of lentil stew that he agrees to sell his birthright, the inheritance of the covenant of Abraham, for it. Esau's story, the interpolation of the *Autobiography* into "The Prodigal Son" implies, is another version of the Prodigal Son's. The Ex-Colored Man is a Prodigal Son who does not return home: having identified African American folk art as his truest inheritance, he forsakes the projects of collecting spirituals and of transforming them into an opera after witnessing a lynching in the South. Instead, for the sake of his children's safety and prosperity, the new widower chooses to live as a white man, a role in which he has always been able to pass. Yet Johnson's documentary practices frame "The Prodigal Son" as a parable about not only how communities are established and then broken but also how they are potentially repaired. Once again, it's the presence of the *Autobiography* within the poem that brings this into focus. There's another level on which the Ex-Colored Man is a son who *does* return. His father is a white man; by entering white society, he has, in a way, come back to his father's house. He does not, on this reading, sell his birthright but announces, like Johnson's Prodigal Son, "I will arise and go to my father."[63] This return fails. In a Paris theater, he realizes that he is sitting beside his father and a woman who must be his half sister. "I knew I could not speak," he narrates, "but I would have given a part of my life to touch her hand with mine and call her sister."[64] But he does not even try: his father does not, like the Prodigal Son's, plead "with tears in his eyes" for his return.[65] He doesn't even recognize his son. So, in silence, the Ex-Colored Man realizes that any reunification with his father and his father's family is impossible: "What should I say to him? What would he say to me?"[66]

On this reading, covenantal community is broken not by the Ex-Colored Man but, repeatedly, by his white father, who cannot (or will not) recognize the small birthright he has given his son: a gold coin the Ex-Colored Man wears on a chain around his neck. Even this, the physical symbol and reminder of their connection, has been damaged from the start: as a child, the Ex-Colored Man says, "I sat upon his knee, and watched him laboriously drill a hole through a ten-dollar gold piece, and then tie the coin around my neck with a string. I have worn that gold piece around my neck the greater part of my life, and still possess it, but more than once I have wished that some other way had been found of attaching it to me besides putting a hole through it."[67] In the New Testament parable, the son wastes an inheritance he does not value; here, the (white) father first damages and devalues and then does not acknowledge an inheritance that the (Black) son nonetheless attempts to prize. This is Johnson's "Dilemma of the Negro Artist" recast in the language and imagery of biblical typology, a parable of the United States, concluding with a permanently broken covenant and a country in which the contributions of African Americans to American culture will never be acknowledged. Unrecognized, he abandons his duties to African American folk arts and, passing, renders both himself and whatever contributions he might someday make unrecognizable. The ending of Johnson's poem offers a stark contrast with this scenario. This father welcomes his son home by placing "a golden chain around his neck."[68] The necklace that for the Ex-Colored Man signifies permanent separation, a physical reminder of his own devaluation, rejection, and isolation, comes to symbolize reconciliation between father and son. Returning home, he is welcomed *as himself*—not having permanently rejected his birthright for a mess of pottage, he can now draw on his experiences with dance and ragtime to add to the cultural store of his father's house. No longer, as Johnson puts it in "Race Prejudice and the Negro Artist," "a beggar at the gate of the nation, waiting to be thrown the crumbs of civilization" (as he might have been described, while in rags outside a gambling hall), "he is the possessor of a wealth of natural endowments and . . . has long been a generous giver to America."[69]

It's fair to ask precisely how Johnson's poem enacts this vision of the covenant restored even while avoiding starry-eyed idealism. (*God's Trombones*, it's worth remembering, was written while Johnson led the NAACP's lobbying efforts to pass antilynching legislation on the federal and state levels and as he supervised legal aid to those who were arrested for trying to defend themselves from racial violence—work so tireless that doctors eventually forced him to step away, convinced that he was on the verge of a nervous breakdown and physical collapse. The poet was no Pollyanna.) Significantly, the poem does not end like the parable, in which the Prodigal Son's older brother objects to their father's lavish welcome, appealing to a sterner justice. Indeed, Johnson elides this figure, mentioning him only once, as the poem begins:

A certain man had two sons.
. . . .
And Jesus didn't call these sons by name,
But ev'ry young man,
Ev'rywhere,
Is one of these two sons.[70]

The distinction between the sons is introduced only to universalize their experiences and allow them to blur into each other. While there are two sons, each is a potential prodigal, embedding a version of the parable in which the protagonist is *white* alongside the Black son of the *Autobiography*. This is at once a call from the preacher to his mixed congregation of readers, to imagine themselves, both white and Black, as siblings. Yet it also channels Johnson's earlier lynching poem, "Brothers—American Drama" (1917), which posits "The Victim" and "The Mob" as siblings. Another of the poems in *God's Trombones* takes up this model of broken sibling relations and a fallen-away covenant.

The Congregation and the Mob

In "The Crucifixion," Johnson turns to the phenomenology of racial violence. Both citing and cited by "The Prodigal Son," this poem reveals the intratextual interpolation and documentary practices of *God's Trombones*. Johnson's emphasis stands out within this widespread turn to the crucifixion in African American and leftist literary and visual culture from this period.[71] Johnson does not posit the strongest connection between the violence of the crucifixion and the violence of American lynching as the innocence, purity, or martyrdom of its victims, unlike Langston Hughes or Countee Cullen, who craft a "Black Christ." Nor is his point that of W. E. B. Du Bois's dozen crucifixion tales of the same period, that white Americans are unable to recognize both contemporary Black Christs and the biblical Jesus, a dark-complexioned Palestinian Jew. Johnson's Jesus remains white. Rather, with an interest fixed on the phenomenology of lynching rather than its iconography, Johnson insists that white Americans are unable to recognize their own participation in either the contemporary mob or the acquiescence of a Pontius Pilate. The crucifixion and American lynchings are analogous because they are both stories of the mob's triumph over the rule of law.

Johnson depicts lynching throughout his career in works that focus on the psychology of the lynch mob itself. These scenes invariably feature an amorphous white mob as their antagonist. For instance, "Brothers—American Drama," one of his earliest political poems, is structured as a dialogue between "The Victim" and "The Mob."[72] The man to be lynched, in these works, retains his subjectivity until the end, while the consciousnesses of those who have come to kill him are depersonalized and combined into a collective entity: dissolving their selves, they all act and think as one. This is even the case in "A Texas Carnival," an unpublished work in free-verse dialect written from the perspective of a member of a lynch mob. Its speaker can only recall the previous night's deeds through the plural pronoun "we"—never "I."[73] This "Texas Carnival" cannot be confused for a true community: it does not allow room for individual subjectivity. In the lynching scene in *The Autobiography of an Ex-Colored Man*, the narrator observes that, in the singular "crowd," "everything was being done in quite an orderly manner."[74] This orderliness is more grammatical than emotional. As the victim is brought forward, a burst of rebel yells indicates "the transformation of human beings into savage beasts"—yet the passive-voice description of their proceedings continues to depict the mob as a single self that knows exactly what it is doing: "A railroad tie was sunk into the ground, the rope was removed and a chain brought and securely coiled around the victim and the stake. . . . Fuel was brought from everywhere, oil, the torch."[75] Johnson's account of his own near lynching during the Jacksonville fire of 1900 again presents "the group" as a unified actor: "They surge round me. They seize me. They tear my clothes and bruise my body."[76] Johnson is saved only when an individual resurfaces within the mob, regaining his subjectivity not through the act of individual motion but through the recognition of Johnson's subjectivity: the provost marshal, a fellow member of the Florida bar, "breaks through the men" of "the rushing crowd." "We look at each other," Johnson writes, prefiguring, almost image for image, Emmanuel Levinas's discussion of the recognition of the face of the Other as the decision not to murder, "and I feel that a quivering message from intelligence to intelligence has been interchanged." Upon the provost marshal's recognition of his fellow attorney, he reimposes the rule of law, transforming "the howling mob of men" back into "soldiers under discipline" who take Johnson into official custody (from which he will be released without charge) rather than murdering him on the spot.[77]

"The Crucifixion" likewise depicts Judas at the head of a "crucifying mob." As in Johnson's depictions of lynch mobs and in a grammatical echo of the actions of the crowd in "The Prodigal Son," they act in a plural unity:

> And they beat my loving Jesus,
> They spit on my precious Jesus;
> They dressed him up in a purple robe,
> They put a crown of thorns upon his head[78]

Johnson's surprisingly neutral depiction of Pontius Pilate emphasizes this mob's explicit rejection of the rule of law. He is "the mighty Roman Governor. / . . . / Great Pilate on his judgment seat." His authority as a representative of the

Roman government goes unquestioned, while his perch on a "judgment seat" equates him with both the God of "The Judgment Day" and the courthouse authorities of the twentieth-century United States. His verdict, announced without apparent irony, is, "In this man I find no fault."[79] In contrast to the accounts of the Gospels, the execution that follows is not state sanctioned: Pilate does not grant his proxy to the crowd, and no Roman soldiers oversee it. As he watches the mob steal Jesus from his jurisdiction after a verdict of not guilty, Pilate resembles nothing so much as American legal authorities, self-convinced of their own inability to control or combat lynching. Seizing Jesus, the mob nails him not to a cross but to a *tree*, transforming the standard Roman punishment for sedition and rebellion into the actions of a mob working, like those in Johnson's lifetime, from the instruments conveniently at hand.

Johnson's "Crucifixion" is an account of mob justice, of the moment when the rule of law has broken down, overwhelmed by the mass passion that represents the antithesis of the legal basis for shared community. This is the same measured attorney's case he relied on as he campaigned for antilynching legislation during the 1920s, pointing out, again and again, that if the rule of law is dissolved anywhere, for anyone, it undermines the law's ability to establish civic order for everyone, everywhere. In this way, lynching was distinct from simple murder—only one represented a fundamental threat to the civic order. This is precisely the case Johnson made in his testimony before the Senate Judiciary Committee during the summer of 1922:

> In lynching, a mob sets itself up in place of the state and acts in place of due processes of law to mete out death as a punishment to a person accused of a crime. It is not only against the act of killing that the federal government seeks to exercise its power through the proposed law, but against the act of the mob in arrogating to itself the functions of the state and substituting its actions for the due processes of law guaranteed by the Constitution to every person accused of crime. In murder, the murderer merely violates the law of the state. In lynching, the mob arrogates to itself the powers of the state and the functions of government.[80]

Lynching, he goes on to say, deploying one of the period's most charged political labels, is not simply murder but "anarchy."[81] Throughout the 1920s, in newspaper accounts, in speeches about and against lynching, and in the case he presented while lobbying elected officials, Johnson repeatedly and consistently framed the issue as a question of upholding the rule of law against the rule of passion, which threatens to totally overwhelm it.

Lynching, in this account, is not only a matter of racial justice. Its most direct and palpable threat is directed, with violence, toward African Americans. But the disregard for the rule of law it represents damages and will ultimately destroy the rule of law as a civic covenant—as a set of obligations, responsibilities, rights, prohibitions, and procedures that bind individuals together into a community. Asking readers to reevaluate the crucifixion through this framework, "The Crucifixion" does not call on them to recognize (as in Langston Hughes's powerful poem) Christ in Alabama but the *mob* in Alabama. As the mob marches Jesus to the top of Calvary, they seize "Black Simon, yes, black Simon."[82] Unsated, at large, "they" turn toward new victims, actively transferring the cross to Simon's back. Beyond a symbolic transfer of victimhood, this moment helps to clarify the *typological* transfer that "The Crucifixion" enacts: within the frameworks of the prophetic, typological associations foundational to the idea of America since the early colonies (Promised Land, Chosen People, New Jerusalem, City upon a Hill, Light unto the Nations), Johnson asserts the place of racial violence in the recurrence of the crucifying mob.

The white reader-congregants of *God's Trombones* hold an unseemly position in this revised typology. Among the sins of the Prodigal Son—and the primary offense of his white iteration—is participating in or (at best) acquiescing to the mob. The idea of the crowd or mob draws a disproportionate share of the preacher's ire in "The Prodigal Son"—especially when one recalls that the New Testament parable contains no analogue. Although the "crowd in Babylon" is not *as* violent (guilty of theft but not murder), its actions lead no less certainly to the collapse of community, the absence of congregation. When the Prodigal Son first reaches Babylon, a passerby entreats him, "Come on, my friend, and go along with me. / And the young man joined the crowd." The preacher takes this narrative event as an opportunity to turn directly to his audience with a warning:

> You can never be alone in Babylon,
> Alone with your Jesus in Babylon.
> You can never find a place, a lonesome place,
> A lonesome place to go down on your knees,
> And talk with your God, in Babylon.
> You're always in a crowd in Babylon.[83]

The sin of Babylon, in this telling, is not gambling, corruption, or prostitution: these are merely symptomatic. It is, rather, to relinquish the subjectivity on which covenant depends for the mindless passion that prevents it, the sin of subsuming the individual within the mass and joining the mob. The lonesomeness of which the preacher speaks is not the atomization of the modern city—*that* is precisely the experience of the members of the crowd—but the knowledge of one's own lonely, unique subjectivity: that which precedes true covenantal connection. In "a lonesome place," praying on his knees, is where Jesus is first encountered in "The Crucifixion," as he pleads with God in Gethsemane while his companions sleep. Meanwhile, Judas and the mob come "Sneaking through the dark of the Garden," where they seize him, interrupting the encounter—here, with God, prophecy, and conscience—that is necessary to civic and self-transformation, to the recognition and reception of the "quivering message from intelligence to intelligence" within the crowd.

As "The Prodigal Son" draws to a close, the preacher turns to directly address his audience with a warning:

Oh-o-oh, sinner,
When you're mingling with the crowd in Babylon—
....
You forget about God, and you laugh at Death.
....
But some o' these days, some o' these days,
You'll have a hand-to-hand struggle with bony Death,
And Death is bound to win.[84]

As "sinner[s]," those who join the crowd fall away from covenantal community. The crowd dissolves individual conscience and places them under the sway of dangerous passions that directly threaten the rule of law. This is merely an assessment; covenantal violations carry consequences. So the preacher pivots to the reminder that what they dance with will eventually turn to consume them. The threatened punishment comes not from the divine but from the very actions of violating covenant: gutting the foundations of civil society will leave nothing in place to offer protection when these passions turn against even white citizens. Throughout *God's Trombones*, the preacher turns to such direct challenges to his reader-congregants, reminding them of the consequences of violating the civic covenant.[85] The purpose, however, is not to exclude the rebuked from the congregation but to offer them the means to return. As "The Prodigal Son" makes clear, there is always the possibility of repentance: to "come away from Babylon" and "Fall down on your knees, / And say in your heart: / I will arise and go to my Father."[86] The possibility of internal change—especially as figured among white readers—draws not only on the tradition of the sermon but on the genre of commemorative verse in which these poems participate. Edward Keyes Whitley observes the way in which racial, religious, and economic others found the potential to contest exclusive definitions of Americanness in commemorative verse during the mid- to late nineteenth century, deploying the genre to create a public that experiences "a sense of discord as they are forced to admit that the poet who is addressing them does not represent them."[87] Johnson's preacher claims a privileged access to the terms of an American covenant. He addresses congregants, even sinners, but does not represent them—though, if they return, he *might*.

The willingness to include white readers within the audience of *God's Trombones*, to directly address and unsettle them, enables the preacher's voice to come to a prophetic crescendo in the volume's final poem, "The Judgment Day." Standing before his congregation, speaking with the vocal technique that the preface to the collection has already described in terms of jazz music and prosody has scored to the King James Bible, the preacher describes how the angel Gabriel will follow God's command to "Blow your silver trumpet, / And wake the living nations." These blasts take on the variety of a virtuoso brass player (Gabriel) in a call-and-response with his bandleader (God):

> And Gabriel's going to ask him: Lord,
> How loud must I blow it?
> And God's a-going to tell him: Gabriel,
> Blow it calm and easy.[88]

Later, the answer changes: "Like seven peals of thunder." After his instrument has announced the end of days, the poet-preacher-prophet turns to address his congregation of readers directly:

> Oh-o-oh, sinner,
> Where will you stand,
> In that great day when God's a-going to rain down fire?
> Oh, you gambling man—where will you stand?
> You whore-mongering-man—where will you stand?[89]

As "liars and backsliders," they have fallen away from upholding the covenant in precisely the manner that the crowd-joining sinners of Babylon do in "The Prodigal Son." Indeed, the preacher interpolates fragments of this poem as he describes the sins of gambling and whoring, while "Oh-o-oh, sinner" repeats the preacher's cry in the earlier poem as, in each, he turns his attention back to his congregant-readers. The condemnation of sin—which we now know to read in terms of the passion-driven mob that destroys the congregational community—comes, in both poems, with the invitation to step out of the crowd and repent. The saved, we learn, do not move in crowds, but "two by two they'll walk," singing together of redemption.[90]

Yet neither "The Judgment Day" nor *God's Trombones* closes on this image of salvation. Rather than the eternal (musical) life granted to the saved, the poem is structured such that it concludes with the punishment for sinners—a punishment described in language that recalls Johnson's descriptions elsewhere of the fires of lynching:

> And the wicked like lumps of lead will start to fall,
> Headlong for seven days and nights they'll fall,
> Plumb into the big, black, red-hot mouth of hell,
> Belching out fire and brimstone.
> And their cries like howling, yelping dogs,
> Will go up with the fire and smoke from hell[91]

The preacher's attitude shifts dramatically, echoing the mockery of the crowd that crucified Jesus as he goes on to taunt the future damned:[92]

> Too late, sinner! Too late!
> Good-bye, sinner! Good-bye!
> In hell, sinner! In hell!
> Beyond the reach of the love of God![93]

But while Johnson's poetry acknowledges apocalypse as one possible outcome, it does not offer it as the *only* outcome—and certainly not the preferred one. So the final lines of "The Judgment Day" offer, one more time, the possibility of repentance. *God's Trombones* ends with a question targeting its white readers:

> Sinner, oh, sinner,
> Where will you stand
> In that great day when God's a-going to rain down fire?[94]

Once more, the alternatives of apocalypse and salvation emerge through the active choices of the fallen-away (lynch) mob. White readers can either bring about their own and the nation's doom by refusing to change or return to the covenant that marks and governs this congregation. They can choose to imagine themselves as part of a public that *God's Trombones* creates, or they can choose to exclude themselves from it. Whether heard in 1927, on Fred Waring's 1962 LP, in a Syracuse church in 2015, or on this very day, Johnson calls out directly to the individual within the mob, hoping to exchange the same "quivering message from intelligence to intelligence" that had saved his life during the Jacksonville fire and that a six-year-old Louis Zukofsky accomplished by reciting *Hiawatha* in Yiddish.[95] This connection—the still, small voice of the covenantal encounter—makes possible the reestablishment of the rule of law, the expansion of political and cultural citizenship to outsiders, the restoration of covenantal community at large, just as the volume has worked to model it through its engagement with the biblical and prophetic typology of American civil religious discourse; through its prosodic form, generic conventions, modernist innovations, public performances; and through the congregation of readers that these work together to establish. Whether they—you, we—will choose to stop up their ears or to hear this voice's call is the question with which *God's Trombones* confronts its readers. The public that emerges, that we live in, depends on our answer.

CHAPTER TWO

Renewing the Covenant
Charles Reznikoff's Recitative

Three decades after James Weldon Johnson's poetic engagement with American civil religion led him to interpolate the phrases and rhythms of "My Country 'Tis of Thee" into "Lift Every Voice and Sing," Charles Reznikoff turned his attention to the song. "My Country 'Tis of Thee: Oratorical and Poetical Gestures" appeared across two issues of William Carlos Williams's avant-garde little magazine, *Contact*, in the spring and summer of 1932.[1] This poem (though it is by no means immediately apparent that it *is* a poem) represents the first published version of *Testimony*, the project at which Reznikoff would labor until his death in 1976. Like later versions, "My Country 'Tis of Thee" crafts poetry from the legal histories and case summaries that Reznikoff, a trained attorney, encountered during his work as an editor at the American Law Book Company, where, from 1928 to 1935, he edited and compiled the legal encyclopedia *Corpus Juris*. This early version of *Testimony* reveals much about the project: not merely that it critiques the United States' judicial system but how it radically revises the myths and tropes of American civil religious discourse and, just as importantly, that it challenges assumptions about poetic genre, engaging the modernist avant-garde in acts of public-creation that a covenantal readership—but not those modes of reading built to understand modernism—can perceive.

Reznikoff was born in Brooklyn in 1894 to Yiddish-speaking Jewish immigrants from Russia, and his experiences within an immigrant community and as a Jew during periods of rising global anti-Semitic violence shaped his poetry. After briefly studying journalism at the University of Missouri and receiving a JD from New York University in 1915, Reznikoff self-published two chapbooks: *Rhythms* (1918) and *Rhythms II* (1919). Their spare, Imagist-influenced verse attends to the overlooked sights and people of New York

City (beggars, sparrows, discarded newspapers) and brought him to the attention of the (in)famous modernist publisher Samuel Roth, who put out Reznikoff's *Poems* in 1920. But when Roth offered, throughout that decade, to release further editions, Reznikoff declined. He preferred to publish privately—after 1927, from the manual printing press he had purchased and installed in his parents' basement. He sold these handcrafted books at the Sunwise Turn Bookshop in Midtown, one of the major New York hubs of American modernism, where Lola Ridge (among others) was also a frequent guest.[2] Reznikoff, bespectacled and prematurely balding, possessed a desire for artistic control that could easily be mistaken for shyness. But to him, poetry was an object of both intellectual and physical craftsmanship, a link to the world of labor. To be a poet was to be, like his parents, an artisan, to resist, like them, the principles of efficiency and mass production that were reshaping New York's garment industry.[3]

"My Country 'Tis of Thee" (the song, not the poem) presents a vision of American citizenship that excludes Reznikoff at least as much as Johnson. A United States that is "Land of the pilgrims' pride, / Land where my fathers died," that is, "My native country," is not a nation that imagines immigrant populations as true citizens. Rather, it presents a civic community rooted in common ancestry. The relationship that establishes the singer's right to claim the United States as "My native country" is not the contingent givenness of where one was born or raised but indigeneity to the place where repeated prior generations have lived and died—of a nationalist intertwining of land, nation, and person.[4] So, filled with a sense of American chosenness, the song's final stanza turns to directly address "Our fathers' God," with the request that the "freedom" and "liberty" that define the nation continue unabated. This vision of American citizenship established through the blood sacrifice of ancestors remained an unofficially recognized national anthem until the year in which Reznikoff wrote. His response to its limited and exclusive vision of American citizenship builds just as steadily toward the production of a covenantal public as did James Weldon Johnson's. The results, however, look quite different: Reznikoff draws together US legal history, biblical translation, and avant-garde experimentation. Where Johnson turned to the space of the African American church, Reznikoff turns to spaces just as central to American civil religion, the courtroom and jury box. When the various iterations of *Testimony* are read as they ask to be but have not been, they emerge as more than "lyric" speech or an anti-lyric challenge but as an experiment with decidedly public verse genres. *Testimony* aims to mediate a more expansive

American public, immigration- and Depression-era complements to Johnson's Jim Crow–era labors.

Doing so leads us to situate Reznikoff's poetry differently, beyond the confines of the individual reader's encounter with the page of text. His writing is neither lyric nor epic, yet it has most often been understood not as *otherwise than* these genres but as participating in their negation, that is, as an anti-lyric or anti-epic inextricably bound up with the reading conventions and generic expectations of lyric and epic. A variety of sources shape Reznikoff's poetics: the rules of the courtroom; found texts of the historical record; practices of reading and translating biblical Hebrew; and the conventions of American musical theater. This last factor has been largely overlooked. Yet it suggests ways to reimagine the others as performative, as public and public-creating speech acts. So situated, as we'll see, Reznikoff's poetry presupposes not merely a reaction but a response: that is, it primes the audience to respond not in their world, external to the performance, but within the world of the performance and the poem itself. Whether we're reading the various iterations of *Testimony*, the magnum opus published in various iterations from 1932 through 1978 (two years after Reznikoff's death), or his biblical translations of the late 1920s, these responses enact the necessary completion of the poems.

There's a biblical parallel here, one that we'll return to in greater detail in the final section of this chapter but that, I think, it's useful to have in mind from the beginning. Biblical covenant is not merely legal-textual but performative: one upholds its terms or falls away from them not just by signing off (or declining to) but through actions. Circumcision, temple sacrifices, and the public reading of the Torah, within the world of the Bible (and beyond), are means of adhering to covenant through performance—so too with the moment in which Israel's covenant with God is enacted at Sinai. Here, a very specific kind of performance takes place: an act of witnessing. The two tablets that embody and symbolize the heart of this covenant—referred to in English as the tablets of the law or of the covenant—are, in Hebrew, the *lukhot ha-eidut*: the tablets of the testimony, of the witnessing. Reznikoff's poetry—his various works titled *Testimony*—are, in this reading, witnessed by their readers to form such a covenant. One goal of this chapter is to uncover the precise way in which this witnessing is performed rather than passively experienced.

This performance of covenant bears implications that go beyond the nature of poetics and to the ethical heart of Reznikoff's verse. Suggesting both the covenantal founding and present state of a nation offers an alternative to blood- and descent-based theories of citizenship and nationhood. In doing so, Reznikoff allows for the incorporation of newcomers and outsiders into stories and communities of national and local belonging. Yet recognizing this effect requires a very different modality of reading than we're used to applying to experimental modernists. The generic expectations of epic's national narrative or lyric's privacy—or, importantly, their avant-garde negations, anti-epic and anti-lyric—don't suffice for this purpose. Reznikoff insists that his poetry be understood as participating in a very different genre, one that's been hidden, for decades, in the plain sight of *Testimony*'s subtitle: recitative.

Recitative as Modernist Practice

Reznikoff was not the only child of New York's Yiddish-speaking Jewish immigrant community to notice that "My Country 'Tis of Thee" proposed a citizenship in which they could never fully share. Henry Roth began writing *Call It Sleep*, a masterpiece of American and Jewish modernism, in 1930 (it would be published in 1934). In a moment that scholarship has returned to often, its protagonist, David Schearl, shout-sings the song he's just learned in school as a kind of apotropaic while he descends into his tenement's terrifying cellar: "My country, 'tis of dee! Land where our fodders died!"[5] David, of course, has neither father nor forefather whose blood is in American soil: his biological father is either alive, terrorizing the apartment, or dead in Russia.[6] The work that would gain the most cultural significance during this decade, however, was George and Ira Gershwin's 1931 Broadway hit *Of Thee I Sing*. The first musical to win the Pulitzer Prize for Drama undermines the song's rooting of civic belonging in a kind of sacrificial indigeneity through satire. Presidential candidate John P. Wintergreen croons lyrics such as, "Of thee I sing, baby, / . . . / Shining star and inspiration, / Worthy of a mighty nation, / Of thee I sing!" as he aligns the virtues of his love interest with those of American self-presentation, national hymn with Tin Pan Alley songwriting.

In addition to *Of Thee I Sing*'s then-risqué parody, it was also notable for its pioneering adaptation of recitative into American musical theater—the first step toward producing the kind of folk opera that the Gershwin brothers would strive for in 1935's *Porgy and Bess*. Recitative originated as an operatic technique in which the singer, in order to further plot, deploys a mode of expository delivery somewhere between speech and song. To borrow Leonard Bernstein's example, in a scene where the price of chicken rising beyond a couple's means prompts the wife to sing a heartfelt, emotional song, there are two ways to move the plot to this point. Her husband can declare, in speech, "Dear, chicken is up three cents a pound," or, accompanied by music—a few bars from the piano, say—he can not-quite-sing it. For an example of what this *sounds* like, think of the English version of *Les Misérables* or the song "Soliloquy" from Rodgers and Hammerstein's *Carousel*. Yet "Soliloquy," though it shares recitative's aural characteristics, isn't recitative: it's closer to an aria. The difference is this: an aria's goal is to present its own emotional freight, while the goal of recitative is to prepare for the emotional expression of the song that responds to the information it provides. While an aria can be a soliloquy, recitative anticipates a response from its addressee.[7]

While later versions of *Testimony* would no longer share an explicit reference to "My Country 'Tis of Thee" in their title, they *would* include reference to recitative. In the final version, it's right there on the cover: *Testimony: The United States (1885–1915): Recitative*. Here, the term functions as an overlooked marker of genre, one with implications for how to understand the bulk of Reznikoff's oeuvre. We, the readers, like the wife in Bernstein's example, are meant to respond. Recitative signals the performative nature of *Testimony*, but the public it faces consists of addressees, not an audience. We are onstage; we share the imagined space of the courtroom with the poetic speaker. Readers of *Testimony* become more than merely that: by reading the poem, we *participate in* the act of testimony. The advocate presents his case in recitative, the necessary prelude to the verdict from the jury box that, perhaps, will achieve the status of song.

Reznikoff's "My Country 'Tis of Thee" may not yet understand itself, explicitly, in terms of recitative—but it does engage with the conventions and genres of public performance. Its subtitle—"Oratorical and Poetical Gestures"—and its visual accompaniments mark this quite clearly. In Michael Davidson's reading, these images reveal that "Reznikoff implies, sardonically, that there is a relationship between history and histrionics, between private acts and a public forum of persuasion and seduction embodied by the courtroom" in order to elaborate "on history as lived and history as embodied in its Fourth of July trappings."[8] This is correct as far as it goes, but in casting "My Country 'Tis of Thee" as "Oratorical and Poetical Gestures," Reznikoff also makes a *generic* claim, pointing toward the public recitation of history and poetry as an expression of citizenship. This goes beyond the Fourth of July ceremonies that Davidson sees: indeed, the Fourth of July would not have been the most immediately resonant context for the public recitation of poetry and history to the child of immigrants (perhaps even to most Americans) in the 1930s. Beginning in the 1890s and continuing through the Second World War, the memorization and recitation of poetry pervaded the American public school system, taking on civil religious importance. By memorizing and reciting commemorative poems such as Oliver Wendell Holmes's "Washington's Birthday" or Henry Wadsworth Longfellow's "Paul Revere's Ride," students could mark their citizenship by memorializing (in effect, celebrating) the holidays of American civil religion. (This, too, is the context from which James Weldon Johnson's composition of "Lift Every Voice and Sing" emerges, as discussed in chapter 1.) During the first decades of the twentieth century, as American schools—particularly those in cities such as New York—were tasked with educating an increasing number of immigrants and their children, memorization and recitation of prose and, especially, poetry emerged as a key strategy of Americanization: students would learn American history and values, learn to celebrate and participate in its civil religious ceremonies, and—just as importantly—learn a proper "American" elocution.[9] Roth's David Schearl has been singing "My Country 'Tis of Thee" in school to teach him patriotism through learning to pronounce "Thee" rather than "Dee." Reznikoff's poem, then, does more than look ironically or sardonically on the ways history is memorialized (though it does, certainly, do this). It revises the content of these performative ceremonies of Americanization. One becomes an American citizen, "My Country 'Tis of Thee" and later versions of *Testimony* insist, not by telling tales of Founding Fathers or singing the fiction of blood- and descent-based citizenship but by reciting the realities of the United States' legal history, its failures particularly.

Through recitative, Reznikoff's poetry continually implies the presence of a collective "you," the situational audience the poem's voices address—voices, plural, because in *Testimony* and other works, Reznikoff subsumes his own voice (or the voice of the poetic speaker) to those of others contained within his poetry. This quality Reznikoff understood as following the norms not of the stage but of the American courtroom. So, in drawing out and giving priority to the voices of history's losers—enslaved people, the propertyless, exploited laborers and immigrants, and so forth—Reznikoff rejects both the inward turn of modernist epic and the instrumental, sentimentalizing depiction of victims and victimization in Depression-era, left-leaning social documentary.[10] This distinction has led, unfortunately, to a central misreading of Reznikoff's poetry: that, as an "Objectivist," he is "objective," rendering no judgment in poems such as *Testimony*. In his introduction to the 2015 single-volume edition of *Testimony*, for instance, Eliot Weinberger highlights the fact that "we never learn how the judge or jury ruled in the case" and declares it "inaccurate to attribute any politics or reflection on human nature to" the work.[11] But when *Testimony* is placed within its historical and aesthetic context—the willingness of social documentary to sentimentalize or even objectify the victims of the system(s) it sought to critique—a different view emerges.

In a 1969 interview with L. S. Dembo, Reznikoff explained, quoting himself,

> "By the term 'objectivist' I suppose a writer may be meant who does not write directly about his feelings but about what he sees and hears; who is restricted almost to the testimony of a witness in a court of law; and who expresses his feelings indirectly by the selection of his subject-matter and, if he writes in verse, by its music." Now suppose in a court of law, you are testifying in a negligence case. You cannot get up on the stand and say, "The man was negligent." That's a conclusion of fact. What you'd be compelled to say is how the man acted. Did he stop before he crossed the street? Did he look? The judges of whether he is negligent or not are the jury in that case and the judges of what you say as a poet are the readers. That is, there is an analogy between testimony in the courts and the testimony of a poet.

And later, he continued, "I can only testify to my own feelings; I can only say what I saw and heard, and I try to say it as well as I can. And if your conclusion is that what I saw and heard makes you feel the way I did, then the poem is successful."[12] Reznikoff's objectivity is not the easy relativism that stares into the abyss of history only to turn aside and shrug off responsibility with a meek, "But who am I to judge?" Rather, the rules that govern Reznikoff's "Objectivism" and his documentary poetry are those that govern the admissibility of testimony and the roles of actors within a courtroom. As an advocate, he cannot decide the case; he can only present it. But he *is* a biased, opinionated actor and seeks to deny readers any comfort or catharsis.[13] The duty of the reader (the continuously implied object of poetic address) is not to identify with those who testify—with whom or what they do not know and have not experienced—but to judge the case on its merits and issue a verdict. Think about this, for a moment, in terms of recitative: the information it expresses is never the end in itself; it *always* serves to push the plot forward, to elicit a response from the person or persons being addressed. Reznikoff's poetry presents stories without rendering judgments or verdicts because, as the poet, as the advocate, as the performer of a recitative, this is not his role. *It is ours.*

Only by doing so can the readers of his poetry come to accept the responsibilities of their roles as actors in history.

Founding Documents and Procedures of Discovery

In *Testimony*, writes Charles Bernstein, "to found America means to find it—which means to acknowledge its roots in violence, to tell the lost stories because unless you find what is lost you can found nothing."[14] This refounding is not something that is simply written or read but is performed: first in the elocution lessons of "My Country 'Tis of Thee" and then in the developing practice of modernist recitative across later versions of *Testimony*. Precisely by taking as a target an American national anthem or hymn, Reznikoff, like James Weldon Johnson, revises the typological frameworks of American civil religion. Scholars often note the way in which Reznikoff's poetry runs against the grain of the Labor Zionism espoused by his wife, Marie Syrkin (and theorized by her father, Nahum): in its deterritorialized, denationalized cosmopolitanism, it offers the United States as a diasporic "counter-Zion."[15] Yet Reznikoff's poetry also draws on and against the tradition of a different type of Zionist rhetoric: that of the typologically charged traditions of American civil religion and nationalism: the belief, for example, that the United States could serve as a city on a hill, a sacred state and New Jerusalem that was the typological heir to the Israelite kingdom. His poetry doesn't reject these typological associations so much as it calls into question what a parallel between the United States and David's kingdom or the biblical Israelites might actually say about the modern nation.

The poems in which Reznikoff most openly explores this typological history are also, unexpectedly, the poems in which we can find the origins of his modernist recitative: "Israel" and "King David," first published in the 1929 miscellany *By the Waters of Manhattan: An Annual*. Recognizing these biblical translations as precursors to "My Country 'Tis of Thee" and *Testimony* highlights the insufficiencies in many scholarly accounts of Reznikoff's documentary poetry. In this telling, Reznikoff spent his day job as an editor and researcher for the legal encyclopedia *Corpus Juris* during the late 1920s and early 1930s confronted with immense quantities of documentary source texts: judgments, court records, and law reports ranging from the mid-nineteenth century into his present. Reznikoff, the story goes, turned to these documents with his characteristically terse, straightforward poetics, replacing Imagism's object with the document, informed by both leftist aesthetics of reportage and the innovations of Ezra Pound's ongoing *Cantos*. This account places Reznikoff within an understanding of modernist documentary as emerging from the failure (or simply the chronological passing) of Imagism, the first iteration of what Virginia Jackson and Yopie Prins term an "avant-garde anti-lyricism."[16] Imagism focused on the object in order to pare away an excessively present "lyric I," but by the early 1920s, Pound and other Anglo-American high modernists had moved away from the label. It had, perhaps, failed to escape the gravity well of "sentiment." The document-based poetics that followed were built toward the same end, simply replacing the object with the document. Reznikoff's documentary turn culminated with his largest, most ambitious, and best-known works: 1975's *Holocaust* (based on the transcripts of the Eichmann trial) and *Testimony*, at which he labored from roughly 1931 until his death in 1976 and which he published in different forms in 1932, 1934, and 1941 and over the course of 1965–78.

Yet this timeline doesn't quite fit—and, on further reflection, seems largely a product of the prejudices we, as readers, bring to Reznikoff's writing. Setting aside the expectations of lyric/anti-lyric and epic/anti-epic reading before we approach *Testimony*, however, allows us to better align our conclusions with the chronology. Reznikoff didn't begin to work for the American Law Book Company until 1928 and had already begun to explore historical narrative and the poetic adaptation of document in his verse dramas of the early and mid-1920s.[17] These plays, including *Uriel Acosta* (1921), *Meriwether Lewis* (1922), *Coral* (1923), and *Captive Israel* (1923) begin the turn toward historical verse that culminates in *Testimony*, predating the 1925 publication of Pound's *A Draft of XVI Cantos*, and reveal Reznikoff's interest in revising myths of national founding. During the same period, Reznikoff began his decades-long engagement with biblical Hebrew, teaching himself to read the language and translating from the centerpiece of Jewish literary heritage— the Hebrew Bible—to form his own poetry. The contact between these two lines of literary exploration produces recitative—a confluence first apparent in "Israel" and "King David."

These works take two possible foundational moments for a Jewish nation as their subject: the establishment, in "Israel," of peoplehood, of Israel as Israel; and the establishment, in "King David," of a Jewish state, the sacred kingdom of David's monarchy. The poems rewrite the character and meaning of these stories of national founding—and, through this, challenge and reimagine the ways American biblical typology and civil religion produce (and police the boundaries of) citizenship and national belonging. The narratives of King David and the patriarchs of Genesis, in Reznikoff's view, depict national foundings as moments of economic exploitation and political violence. Any modern nation that imagines itself as a New Israel or New Promised Land on their model, can, ultimately, only offer bloody and blood-based modes of citizenship and national belonging. But these narratives, Reznikoff suggests, are not the only model of typological imagining available. The giving of the law at Sinai offers an alternative, a consent-based covenantal community made possible (though by no means permanent) through acts of witness, testimony, and careful attention to the dry legal language and procedural mindset that come to characterize the poetics of *Testimony*.

Among the earliest of the many poems that would emerge from Reznikoff's engagement with biblical Hebrew, "Israel" and "King David" are uniquely impersonal: rather than reflect on the meaning of learning (or losing) Hebrew, of the often difficult texture of the language, as he does elsewhere with great power, these sequences represent his early documentary forays and his development of the techniques—a juridical "Objectivism"; recitative as modernist poetics—that would come to define *Testimony*. In retrospect, the contents of the collection in which they first appeared, the 1929 *By the Waters of Manhattan: An Annual*, provide a cross-section of Reznikoff's evolution as a writer and signal an aesthetic turning point. The bulk of the miscellany was prose: a series of short stories, some previously published in the *Menorah Journal*, which he would revise into the second half of following year's novel, *By the Waters of Manhattan*; and "Early History of a Seamstress," a family memoir written either by or in the voice of his mother, which would be lightly revised to serve as the first half of the novel.[18] The third portion of the collection, under the heading "Editing and Glosses," offers the two narrative poems developed from biblical source material.

Just as Reznikoff's short, ambulatory poems of New York's neighborhoods and streets function by drawing the reader's attention to that which they might have otherwise overlooked (whether unnoticed beauty or human suffering obscured by city life), his biblical counterhistories draw out the stories and voices suppressed by the originals. "Israel" and "King David" eschew the Bible's third-person narrative. Nor is Reznikoff's recovery of voices concerned with the authorial layers uncovered by textual criticism (e.g., the Yahwist, the Elohist, the Redactor). Rather, his focus remains with the voices of the actors themselves—especially those who do not stand at the center of the biblical narratives. "Israel," tracing the history of the Hebrews between Jacob's theft of his brother's birthright and the revelation at Sinai, is presented through the perspectives of Rebecca, Rachel, Laban, Joseph's older brothers, Potiphar's wife, Pharaoh's cupbearer, Joseph, the collective voice of Israel enslaved, and Pharaoh. The major figures of these narratives appear only in situationally dependent roles: Isaac, only in dialogue with Jacob and Rebecca; Jacob, in dialogue with Laban, Esau, and his father (only briefly on his own); and Moses as he interacts with Pharaoh and delivers the legal code that is revealed at Sinai.

Although these figures continue to reside at the center of events, they are testified *about* rather than offering testimony of their own. The opening stanza of "Israel" immediately marks a distinction between those whose voices offer first-person narrative and those who appear only in dialogue with others:

> Our eldest son is like Ishmael, Jacob is like you;
> therefore, you like Esau better:
> because he is a hunter, a man of the fields,
> ....
> but Jacob who is like you, a quiet man, dwelling in tents, is the better.[19]

The first half, framing the story of Jacob (and the entirety of "Israel") provides Rebecca's perspective: her subjective perception of the family's dynamics anchors the narrative. The scene of deception that follows, drawn from Genesis 27:20–27, is presented "objectively," a record of dialogue: witness and then evidence: "My father, sit and eat of my venison. / How is it that you have found it so quickly?"[20] The notable changes made by Reznikoff's translation are of omission. He deletes all third-person narration, including that which offers otherwise-absent characterization of Isaac. The old father's perceptions, central to the biblical narrative, fall away: the effect is that of a deposition read aloud or entered into the record. Rebecca's explanation of the sons' natures (and Isaac's attitudes toward each) is entirely Reznikoff's interpolation. This characterization takes the place of the deception in explaining *why* Isaac believes that Jacob is Esau. In Genesis, the tangible senses ultimately prove decisive over the evidence of voice; here, where voice is all that can be trusted, the implication is that Isaac believes the deception because he *wants* Esau to be present at his bedside: he will believe because he longs to be kissed by his favorite. Likewise, the remainder of the story of Israel is told through the voices and from the perspectives of those who are not necessarily outsiders but who, in the biblical narrative, are peripheral or merely instrumental. When otherwise-central figures appear only in dialogue, they are presented as Rebecca is in the Bible: figures who are important to the story but whose perspectives or perceptions do not really matter.

This radical decentering of ancient Israel's national epic allows Reznikoff to reframe the story of "Israel" around economic exploitation. Jacob is "a knife," is "shrewd," and, Rebecca claims, is "like my brother Laban," who takes advantage of the "stupid" suited only to low-skilled labor as well as the infirm, like Jacob's own father. Seen through Rebecca's, Laban's, and Esau's eyes, Jacob is concerned with temporary beauty, has returned Laban's gratefulness with theft, and is an uncouth materialist. The first section of this poem ends with Jacob's sons selling Joseph into slavery; their decision-making process, like their father's, is businesslike. They do not kill him outright because, "What profit shall we have in the death of our brother?"[21] The pattern continues throughout the generations. Joseph is seen as others see him: never a captive but a powerful man with "a gold chain about his neck" who "ride[s] in the second chariot and all cry out before him, Bend the knee!" Reconciling with his brothers, he offers wealth: "I will give you all the good of the land of Egypt. / I will establish my people like a pyramid, / no longer to be blown along like sand."[22] Being Jacob's children as well, the brothers accept and exchange the iconography of Abraham's covenant, in which his descendants will be as numberless as the sand, for that of Egyptian wealth and power.[23] The compression of Reznikoff's poem emphasizes the details that are retained. So it is notable that, during the Exodus, the Hebrew slaves are depicted taking "the jewels of silver and the jewels of gold, / the fine clothing [they] have borrowed from the Egyptians," and that the time they spend on the accumulation of wealth is directly contrasted with their rushed preparation of food for the journey.[24] None of this is to say that Reznikoff depicts Jewish history as the history of greed or economic manipulation. It is one of oppression and high ideals—but also of a people that is no less prone to failure than any other.

This depiction, of course, runs decidedly counter to the concept of chosenness, particularly when applied typologically to the United States. In Reznikoff's telling, the Hebrews are a chosen people only insofar as they possess and acknowledge an ethical ideal that they repeatedly fail to actualize. This, rather than the "errand into the wilderness," "shining city upon a hill," or "light unto the nations," would be the typological quality of American chosenness: chosen not in the absence of failure but in the recognition that these failures *are* failures, that there is a higher ethical standard to strive for. And this, in turn, runs counter to the typologically charged language of American political rhetoric during Reznikoff's lifetime, the vision of the United States as a chosen nation on a quest to "make the world safe for democracy."[25]

"King David" turns to the concept of the sacred state. The Davidic kingdom fails to achieve the ethical standards for economic and social justice presented at Sinai. The fault lies not in the nature of these ideals but in the very nature of political power. The state—even the sacred state—is unable and, more often than not, unwilling to separate itself from violence. Reznikoff signals this in his epigraph, which quotes the biblical passage in which God prohibits David from building the Temple because of the blood he has spilled. *This*, says "King David," is the model for your sacred state: one in which David is not, in fact, the triumphant poet-king ushering the golden age of Jewish national existence but a tragic figure who, by doing more than any other to create the state that might actualize the radical economic justice called for in "Israel," has also stood in the way of achieving it. The failure to achieve holiness is directly connected to the violence committed in its pursuit.

In depicting a nation of casual violence, "King David" prefigures the content of *Testimony*—so, too, with its formal construction, which begins to approximate the retrospective testimony offered in a courtroom. Rearranging the order in which events are narrated (though not in which they are said to have *occurred*) so that their presentation enhances Reznikoff's brief, he assumes the role of poet-advocate in this poem, calling Saul, Jonathan, Ahimelech, Ish-bosheth, Abner, Joab, minor military and court figures and messengers, the residents of Jabesh-gilead, and the leaders of non-Israelites (the King of Gath, Philistines, Doeg the Edomite, ambassadors from Hamath) to testify against David.[26] Reznikoff calls his witnesses to narrate past events straightforwardly, without the extrapolation that, in his interview with Dembo, he insisted had no place in his poetry because it had no place in the courtroom. The voice of a third-person narrator occasionally intervenes, like that of an attorney, to introduce a new event or situation. By recovering these forgotten voices and arranging them as testimony, "King David" highlights the trauma that the civil war between Saul and David would have caused. David's voice is minor, almost absent, with the exception of a few snatches of dialogue and a psalm of thanksgiving, presented near the poem's end, where it can be read only with the deepest irony.[27] Cast in typological terms, this is the poet-prosecutor as the prophet Nathan appearing in David's court to condemn the king (2 Samuel 12). Formally, it mirrors that which he will later call recitative.

Michal, David's first wife and Saul's daughter, offers the most important and poetically powerful testimony. Her words alone have no origin in the biblical source but are merely extrapolated from what can be gleaned from it about the events of her life, her reactions, and her relationship with David. If the role of "Editing" is the arrangement and highlighting of voices already present in the text, then the function of "Glosses" is, perhaps, what Reznikoff accomplishes with Michal: the recovery of the testimony of a major figure whose voice has been entirely suppressed by a monologic source text.[28] Indeed, the details of her life that become most central to her character in "King David"—that she had five children with Paltiel during the civil war and that David hanged them in order to end a famine caused by Saul's sins—are themselves extrapolated from a textual crux: the puzzling reference to the five sons of Michal and Adriel, deemed impossible by Jewish tradition because he was also her brother-in-law.[29] Of the editions Reznikoff is known to have read, Luther's German translation reads, "die fünf Söhne *Merabs*, der Tochter Sauls, die sie dem Adriel *geboren hatte*"; the KJV, on the other hand, refers to "the five sons of *Michal* . . . whom she *brought up* for Adriel" (emphasis, in both cases, added). One, that is to say, denies Michal's role entirely; the other says that she was in fact the mother, rather than the guardian, of the children David hanged.[30] Reznikoff rejects this papering over of Michal's suffering: she does not hate David, as the Bible insists, because he danced drunkenly and exposed himself before the Lord (2 Samuel 6:16) but because she holds him responsible for the death of her father, her brothers Ish-Bosheth and Jonathan, her nephews, and her five sons.

The recovery of Michal's voice and suffering coincides with a rejection of the biblical statement that she died childless and that this was caused by her condemnation of David's dancing naked before God (2 Samuel 6:20–23). The words of the biblical narrator are given to David, who sneers at her toward the poem's end with no regard for syntax: "God— / Who chose me rather than your father and all his house / to be king of Israel; / but you shall die childless." In "King David," however, she is not childless because of *her* sins but because of David's quest for power, his jealousy of her happier marriage with Paltiel, his rejection of his own responsibility for the civil war, blaming it instead on "Saul and his bloody house." She is childless, she retorts, only "After you have hanged my sons, / from the eldest who was as tall as I / to the youngest who had not yet learned to walk." Michal casts this poem explicitly as a counterhistory of King David's Israel. The poem's closing lines see the future clearly: "Your scribes will write me down a cold, proud woman, / wandering about the garden of the king, / and you a glorious king, a glorious king."[31]

On Not Knowing Hebrew

The case of Michal exemplifies the dialogic recovery of voices throughout Reznikoff's poetry. This emerges from more than just a multiperspectival or decentered narrative structure. Rather, his poetry is dialogic in the strong sense of the term that Jahan Ramazani proposes, pushing back against Bakhtin's insistence that poetry is, in fact, monologic: it "is infiltrated by and infiltrates its generic others."[32] "King David" reveals how translation operates as the means for this intergeneric infiltration—and, further, how translation serves an integral role in the recovery of suppressed voices and plays a foundational role in the "objective" courtroom in which Reznikoff's poetry situates itself. Like the other witnesses called in "King David," Michal is limited to testimony concerning her own experiences with David or under his rule.[33] Hers is emotionally stirring and, as the last voice heard in the poem, the climax of the case, the final witness toward whose testimony that of the others has been arranged to build, to whom the jury responds. The role of the translator, this is to say, resembles that of the advocate in court who can arrange testimony to construct the strongest possible case but cannot speak in place of others and cannot sentimentalize or instrumentalize them or their experiences. Counterhistory, for Reznikoff, is translation—and translation is counterhistorical, but only to the extent that each mirrors the practice of an idealized legal system in which the voices of the marginalized are recovered and placed on an equal level with those of the powerful.

This alignment of translator, poet, and advocate develops out of Reznikoff's long and ambivalent engagement with Hebrew—a relationship that, channeling Virginia Woolf, might be best described as an active process of "Not Knowing" Hebrew. Although Reznikoff was raised by Yiddish-speaking parents, it is unclear whether his childhood provided him with any degree of *literacy* in a non-English language. His parents (also fluent in Russian, though they ceased to speak it after immigrating) followed a deliberate course of Americanization and committed to raising English-speaking children: Yiddish was limited strictly to conversations with grandparents.[34] Reznikoff's childhood Hebrew education was nonexistent. He recalled visiting, with his mother, the traditional Hebrew-school environment of a *kheyder*; both were appalled by its darkness, its disorganization, and its casual corporal punishment.[35] In his poetry and recollections, Reznikoff associates Hebrew with a grandfather who had been a *melamed*, or Hebrew teacher, in Russia. The destruction of this grandfather's Hebrew-language poetry (fed to the fire "a few sheets every morning") recurs throughout Reznikoff's writing and serves, writes Stephen Fredman, as "the primal scene of poetry" in his work.[36] Hebrew language, Reznikoff declares, was "lost— / except for what / still speak[s] through me / as mine."[37] Scholarship, understandably, has focused on the first word—on the loss of Hebrew.

Yet this loss occurs alongside continuity.[38] Reznikoff himself recollected, "I began to pick it [Hebrew] up when I was in my twenties": that is, sometime in the 1910s or 1920s.[39] His accounts always imply that he was self-taught (though his poetic and fictionalized accounts should by no means be taken as definitive); he used Modern Hebrew's Sephardi pronunciation, not his grandfather's Ashkenazi. How he studied it at this time, or with what intensity, is also unclear: Marie Syrkin's recollection of his reading, each evening before bed, several pages of the Bible in Hebrew with English and German translations open beside it dates from later decades (they met in 1927 and married in 1930, after his study began). It is not until 1927's self-published *A Fifth Group of Verse* that he turns his attention to the process of learning Hebrew; "Israel" and "King David" were his first published translations from the language.[40]

Even more than as expression of ambivalence about Jewish identity or nationalism, Reznikoff's relationship to Hebrew is perhaps best placed in dialogue with the works of twentieth-century European poets who took up minor, vanishing dialects and vernacular of which they did not have native knowledge at precisely the moment such languages began to disappear from everyday life—as, that is, a decidedly modernist literary and linguistic practice. Outlining this phenomenon in Irish literature, Barry McCrea draws a distinction between "native" or "vernacular" Irish and "revivalist" or "national" Irish: between the disappearing Irish language of the countryside and the simultaneous yoking of Irish language study with the nationalist project of postindependence Ireland.[41] Poets, he observes, favored the disappearing Irish over the living but politicized iteration. "As they fell out of the speech of everyday life," he writes, "these declining vernaculars [Irish, Italian vernacular, patois French] became unlikely repositories for a host of modernist dreams, expectations, and disappointments about what language could or should do," a way to combat alienation from tired or degraded major languages, to inject these with "new life."[42] We might say that Reznikoff's preference for a biblical Hebrew rather than a modern or Zionist one mirrors this contemporaneous preference for "native" or "vernacular" Irish over "revivalist," "national" Irish. Rather than bound inexorably to "a wider discourse of nationalism, patriotism, or nostalgia," Reznikoff's Hebrew, through its quest for new and "distinct lyrical possibilities," undermines nationalist discourse by appealing to the same set of typological associations.[43]

Hebrew and Irish were on different trajectories during the 1920s and 1930s, with the latter fading rapidly even in its last enclaves and recovered only as a secondary language for schoolchildren, and the former continuing to expand both among a growing Jewish population in British Mandatory Palestine and among a Hebraist literary elite in the diaspora. And Reznikoff, of course, never *wrote* in Hebrew. The ambivalence he maintains in his writing *about* Hebrew and his translations *from* it continually expresses a skepticism of his own knowledge that resembles Virginia Woolf's stance of "not-knowing" Greek. The translator or writer engaged with "not-knowing" a language differs markedly from the translator who merely does not know a language. Reznikoff, Woolf, and Pound all demonstrate a disinterest in reading or translating primarily for equivalences between vocabularies; all grasp for "the sense" rather than literal translation—but whereas Pound does so from a position of intellectual self-confidence unto arrogance (he does not *need* to know Chinese to translate from the language), Reznikoff, like Woolf, foregrounds the limitations of his own knowledge. Reading or translating "for the sense" is necessary not because literal translation is unnecessary but because the distance between our situation and the situation of the original text makes it impossible. Woolf, in "On Not Knowing Greek," argues that we can only approximate knowing Greek because its natural, living embeddedness in everyday life eludes moderns. One can know *modern* Greek, perhaps, but not *Classical* Greek.[44]

The relationship of Hebrew to the everyday likewise shapes Reznikoff's active practice of "not-knowing" Hebrew. In a 1927 poem, Reznikoff laments the language's difficulty:

> even the Hebrew for *mother*, for *bread*, for *sun*
> is foreign. How far have I been exiled, Zion.[45]

Precisely Hebrew's separation from the everyday is what creates its difficulty for him, but Reznikoff deliberately and doubly foreignized his Hebrew, eschewing not only the modern language for the biblical but also the familiar, traditional Ashkenazi pronunciation for the Sephardi pronunciation that the modern ("revival," "nationalist") language adopted.[46] The linguistic "exile" in which he finds himself, moreover, is the same concept that, in the poem "Joshua at Shechem," enables an exiled and "scattered" Jewish people to become "citizens of the great cities, talking Hebrew in every language under the sun."⁴⁷ Hebrew, not capable of being the language of the everyday, remains cut off from the mundane. It is not, and can never be, a *mame loshn* (or mother tongue) because it must remain *loshn koydesh* (a holy language). In Reznikoff's Hebrew's stance otherwise than (perhaps in opposition to) the everyday, it mimics the distinction between spoken dialogue and the not-quite-song of recitative. This sacredness, born of separateness, is what Hebrew can offer to—inject into, perhaps—other, major languages.

By "talking Hebrew in every language under the sun" (or at least in English), Reznikoff solidifies his poetics' opposition to the sacrificial indigeneity expressed by patriotic hymns like "My Country 'Tis of Thee." The prophetic, sacred valence that Hebrew provides English necessarily stands in tension with idea of a "native country" possessed by later generations by virtue of its being the "land where my fathers died." To not-know Hebrew is to encounter the language as perpetually foreign—as perpetually Other. But this relationship of humility and subordination is not directed toward the text itself—Reznikoff's translations are not in the service of the "original" text— but toward the subjectivity of others contained within it.⁴⁸ The encounter between Hebrew and English, between translator and text, is freighted with the demands of ethics; the translator's voice does not have the right to take priority over those contained within the original—but at the same time a final, finished original *also* does not make a claim on the translator's fealty.⁴⁹ Reznikoff's concern as a translator is always with those voices that are contained within the original text but that have been subordinated to that of author, redactor, or final form.⁵⁰ His translational practice is as skeptical, this is to say, of the agenda and priorities of that which sits before him, focused into a monologic text, as of his own ability to know the language. The task of the translator is to break down the dominant voices of the monologic original and to arrange those of the ignored and the marginal into a dialogic array of narrative perspectives. This arrangement reflects the motivations of the translator and poet, whose roles are aligned not with David the Psalmist but with the prophet who, like Nathan, storms into the king's court to indict him.

Testimony, Typology, and Translation

Testimony, we might say, represents Reznikoff's effort to write "Hebrew in every language under the sun"—or, at least, in American English. This goes beyond the poem's design as a decentralized counterhistory focused on the orphan, widow, and beggar. *Testimony* shares more than this applied structure with Reznikoff's work in "King David" and "Israel." They also share *found* structures: the rhythms, forms, and literary qualities of the Hebrew Bible serve Reznikoff as documentary sources much as those of the King James Bible do for James Weldon Johnson. His seemingly "objective" legalisms, on the level of poetic form, emerge from translating and adapting biblical poetry into English. So, much as Johnson embeds the readerly expectations of public speech acts into the prosody, rhythm, and soundscape of *God's Trombones*, Reznikoff embeds the typological expectations of his modernist recitative into the formal features of *Testimony*. These formal structures, in turn, provide the prophetic charge and typological inversions that allow each page to "speak Hebrew." Together, content and form produce and enable a mode of poetic readership that might best be described as covenantal.

Like "King David," *Testimony* casts its readers into the position of judge and jury, while the poet acts as a prosecuting attorney, calling and arranging the testimonies of witnesses. Instead of offering an identifiable narrative of American origins or national founding (or even a clear, identifiable parody), each iteration of the poem presents a series of discrete, individual narratives. Its decentralization is more extreme than that of "Israel" or "King David," which nonetheless continue to present a single, unified, and familiar narrative—even if turned on its head. Taken together, the individual narratives of *Testimony* present an image of the United States between 1885 and 1915. But individually, they can make no such claim. The narrative of American history is not merely decentralized but dissolved; in its place, one finds a composite snapshot. The lives of Americans, it implies, are not lived through its national story. This sets Reznikoff apart even from a pluralism as multitudinous as Walt Whitman's. The expansive democratic embrace of Whitman's voice "contain[s] multitudes" within an "I": Reznikoff's America does not—cannot—speak as one. Indeed, his poetry expresses deep skepticism of such speech.[51] Even if well intended, monologic poetry suppresses voices by merging, blending, and holding them together. The ideal is not *e pluribus unum*, out of many, one, but *ex uno plures*, out of one, many.

Those whose voices are most likely to be suppressed—and whose testimony Reznikoff's poetry likewise seeks to highlight and recover—are precisely those with whom the biblical prophets were most concerned: orphans, widows, beggars, and wanderers.[52] The 1941 "Testimony" distills their centrality to the project's indictment. In this version, the national story (such as it is) accumulates in the aggregate from the lives of day laborers hired to unload a steamer trapped in darkness as the boat wrecks against ice and begins to fill with water; of Amelia, "just fourteen and out of the orphan asylum; at her first job—in the bindery, and yes sir, yes ma'am, oh, so anxious to please," whose hair is pulled from her scalp by a bookbinding machine; of Madelina, an Italian immigrant who is raped and (the poem implies) forced into prostitution after the murder of her husband; and how, "Once upon a time (the best beginning!)," a rich woman grew tired of the beggar who came to her door every day and conspired to poison her.[53] Although scholarship makes the point that *Testimony* highlights the ways in which the legal system has failed these figures from the margins, this system is not the only, or even primary, target of its reproach. Instead, *Testimony* highlights the ways in which a variety of mediating institutions have failed in their obligations to the orphan, widow, beggar, and immigrant. In the expansive 1978 version, for example, a nonexhaustive list of these institutions would include US courts but also the industrial economy, spreading railroads, shipping, mining, intracity transit, gambling halls, marriage, the police, neighborhoods and neighbors, property law (wills, divorce, prenuptial agreements), the Jim Crow regime, schools, and even organized labor.

Because of *Testimony*'s scale and its resistance to narrative unity, it is often referred to as an "anti-epic." But just as avant-garde anti-lyric ultimately calls forth modes of lyric reading, so avant-garde anti-epic calls forth modes of epic reading: that is, the generic conventions of epic continue to define readerly expectations. Yet epic reading, like lyric reading, can only partially account for the poetics of *Testimony*. Attending to the role of biblical poetics in *Testimony* allows us to understand how and why this occurs. "Perhaps the greatest peculiarity of biblical poetry among the literatures of the ancient Mediterranean world," writes Robert Alter, "is its seeming avoidance of narrative."[54] By contrast, an inexorable narrative thrust defines Classical epic.[55] Each version of *Testimony*, likewise, dismisses narrative progression—in fact, a far more radical move than the manner of decentralization of multiple perspectives offered in his biblical poetry of the late 1920s, which offers a kind of cubist narrative, given from multiple perspectives but still following familiar tracks.[56] Yet in both biblical poetic forms and Reznikoff's *Testimony*, this avoidance is only "seeming": biblical poetic form contains, rather than denies, narrative progression, sharply delimiting it within smaller poetic units. Such is the case with the biblical formal technique of parallelism, in which the parallels "are approximate equivalents but prove to be, on closer inspection, logically discriminated actions that lead imperceptibly from one to the next."[57] This progression lays the foundation for the technique of *intensification* through parallel repetition, a heightening of emotion, strength of language, and the reader's awareness of these qualities.

Stephen Fredman has observed that Reznikoff's language and that of biblical Hebrew share an affinity for "grammatical compactness," "condensation and terseness," observations reinforced by what Alter refers to as the "reticent" nature of characterization in biblical prose.[58] But the parallels go beyond—and run deeper than—this Imagist-like compactness. Syntactic techniques familiar from biblical poetry and defined by the relation to its parallelism occur in all three versions of *Testimony*. The 1941 version employs parallel intensification in its depiction of the orphaned Amelia suffering in a bookbinding factory:

> She felt her hair caught gently;
> put her hand up and felt the shaft going round and round
> and her hair caught on it, wound and winding around it,
> until the scalp was jerked from her head,
> and the blood was coming down all over her face and waist.[59]

The first three lines present repeating, interwoven actions, each inching forward temporally while increasing in urgency, detail, and strength of language: that Amelia's hair is caught, the circular winding of the bookbinding machine. First, she merely "felt" it; then she "put her hand up and felt the shaft." The development of intensification from the penultimate to the ultimate line should (one hopes) be apparent enough and not need elaboration. We can also see intensification in phrases within lines, as Reznikoff's repetition of words to intensify and highlight an action mimics the repetition of a root or lexeme in biblical Hebrew, which is at times manipulated to develop a poetic leitmotif: "the shaft going round and round"; "wound and winding around it." Elsewhere, Reznikoff's poems utilize this technique but end with a break from the parallel, rather than an intensification of it. This is the focused turning of the reader's attention to a final image that, in the context of Reznikoff's sequences of short verse, Charles Bernstein refers to as "Reznikoff's nearness," a poetic method that, we can now see, is also dependent on those of biblical Hebrew.[60]

Similar techniques appear even in the ostensibly prosaic 1934 *Testimony*:

> It had stopped raining. He was walking home with his brother. There was a
> puddle of water on the sidewalk, shining in the afternoon sunlight, and when
> he came to it, he slapped his brother on the arm and said, "See, there is money,

can't you see? I will make money out of that. That is the biggest thing in the world to make money out of."

   In the middle of the night it was raining and thundering again. His wife woke up and found that he was gone. She didn't know where he could be. She got up and lit the lamp and waited an hour or so. At last she heard him on the attic stairs; he came into the room, dripping wet, the water running from his hair, and his nightgown pasted to his flesh. He had been up on top of the house. He said it was very nice on top of the house when it rained and the lightning flashed; he liked it.[61]

The two paragraphs of this prose-poem function together much like two versets in biblical poetry. Each presents the man's reaction to the rain—though the second, both in the length and detail of action it provides, intensifies it. While these paragraphs do not offer a true narrative, the juxtaposition and descriptive and emotional development from one vignette to the next does express a kind of progression of the relationship between the man and the idea expressed in the title of the sequence of which this poem is a part: "Depression." The depression that drives a man to seek to monetize rainwater develops into that which drives him to drench himself (and his nightclothes) in it. The juxtaposition also compares two types of depression: economic (in the first, the man is fixated on money, whether his attempt to profit from puddles is sincere or ironic, rooted in greed or desperation) and psychological (the man who cannot sleep at night sitting drenched on the roof of his house, watching a thunderstorm, because *this* might allow him to feel the peace he desires).

The qualities of biblical prose also reveal themselves in Reznikoff's verse, particularly the syntactic and thematic repetitions of biblical narrative. Consider, for instance, the repetitive yet progressive parataxis of the first stanza of the first poem in the 1978 *Testimony* (first published in 1965):

> Jim went to his house
> and got a pair of plow lines
> and then into the stable
> and put one on the jack
> and led the jack out
> and tied him to a fence;
> and put the noose in the other line around the head of the jack
> and began to pull.
> The jack began to make a right smart noise.[62]

This passage, demonstrating the compactness of language for which both Reznikoff and biblical Hebrew are notable, develops through the simultaneous brevity of its actions and the development of keywords and images through their repetition. The verbs—"got," "put," "led," "tied," "put," "pull"—are all verbs of Jim's hands, which, though never described, develop through them into a trifold leitmotif: of human *techne*, of human power, and of human cruelty. This, in addition to the passage's reliance on repetition rather than elaboration, marks it as closer to biblical parataxis than Homeric—even though the style is that of biblical prose rather than poetry. What is important is not whether biblical narrative is prosody—it isn't—but that Reznikoff found a poetic source within it nonetheless.

These qualities of poetic formalism are inseparable from the legal meaning of *Testimony*: they are "how the law means," to borrow a phrase from the legal theorist Richard Weisberg. Weisberg, drawing on the opinions and theoretical writings of Reznikoff's contemporary Benjamin N. Cardozo, whose service included the New York State Supreme Court (1914), the New York Court of Appeals (1914–27), and the United States Supreme Court (1927–38), argues that "it is the language used in the opinion, and only that language, that perfectly constitutes the 'doing'—the holding—of the opinion."[63] In opinions and essays published from the time Reznikoff began law school through the time he began work on *Testimony*, Cardozo makes much the same case—especially in *Law and Literature*, published in 1931, as Reznikoff was at work on "My Country 'Tis of Thee." I don't mean to say that Reznikoff was reading Cardozo—though, as a Jewish attorney interested in legal writing far more than the practice of law, it seems not improbable that the second Jew confirmed to the Supreme Court held his interest to at least *some* degree—but that an understanding of law as literature was emerging from pivotal, mainstream, and quite decisive venues as Reznikoff studied law, worked on *Corpus Juris*, wrote "Israel" and "King David," and began to develop the long-term project of *Testimony* at the same moment, that is, in which Reznikoff was developing his own understanding of law as literature and then putting it forward in modernist little magazines and books published by the Objectivist Press, which he founded with Louis Zukofsky and George Oppen. In *Testimony*, legal meaning emerges from the plain sense of the words—but also from their presentation as poetry. In its difficulty, dryness, and violence, *Testimony* uncovers the ugliness and unaesthetic nature of unjust law and legal outcomes. On one level, what appears to be the failure of poetic aesthetics in *Testimony*—

it's long, it's a slog, it often reads like a legal brief, which means (frankly) that it's sometimes quite boring—points toward a failure of *justice*.

So, what do we do with the underlying qualities of biblical poetics that we've just uncovered running throughout the iterations of *Testimony*? They don't contradict the way in which Reznikoff's poetics make a legal argument— indeed, they deepen it. "A legal tradition," writes another legal theorist, Robert Cover, is

> part and parcel of a complex normative world. The tradition includes not only a corpus juris, but also a language and a mythos—narratives in which the corpus juris is located by those whose wills act upon it. These myths establish the paradigms for behavior. They build relations between the normative and the material universe, between the constraints of reality and the demands of an ethic.... The normative meaning that has inhered in the patterns of the past will be found in the history of ordinary legal doctrine at work in mundane affairs; in utopian and messianic yearnings, imaginary shapes given to a less resistant reality; in apologies for power and privilege and in the critiques that may be leveled at the justificatory enterprises of law.[64]

Although by "corpus juris," Cover simply means its literal meaning—the body of law—the term allows us to apply this reading of legal *reality* to Reznikoff's creation of legal *poetry*. *Testimony* creates a legal tradition; this tradition includes not only the source of the cases and histories that comprise it, *Corpus Juris*, at which Reznikoff was at work during business hours, "but also a language and a mythos"—a mythos, we might say, *through* the language: by deploying biblical poetics, Reznikoff embeds the mythos of "Israel" and "King David" within this legal tradition by incorporating its language. This mythos, in turn, is the necessary context in which to understand the relations among individual actors, the context that establishes the very means to adjudicate not whether the law was upheld (though it may do this) but *whether that law was itself just or unjust*.

This should sound a great deal like the role of biblical typology in American civil religion. They are analogous processes and, in *Testimony*, operate simultaneously—indeed, inseparably. The critique of American civil religious discourse with which this chapter began, as embodied in the song "My Country 'Tis of Thee," depends on *both* the biblical mythos embedded into the project *and* the legal critique it engenders. *Testimony* applies typology to more than the American people and their history—to American language and American law as well. Poetics and language serve as simultaneous vectors of legal and typological critique: by translating the nature of the Hebrew language, Reznikoff frames contemporary failures of the legal state within the failures of its biblical predecessors. Yet the way in which Reznikoff "speaks Hebrew" in *Testimony* does far more than critique and condemn. It is also the means through which the poem opens the potential for constitutional reparation through covenant, more specifically, through a covenantal poetics of recitative.

A Covenantal Poetics

When *Testimony* is read as it asks to be read, as recitative, it is speech that presupposes that its addressee will respond—that its readers, cast as they are in the position of jurors listening to an advocate's brief and the testimony of witnesses, will pronounce a judgment. This is a critical role, to be sure, one that does not give the nation a pass for its past or present. Yet it is also a fundamentally reparative act, in much the same way as Nathan's condemnation of David or Elijah's of Ahab and Jezebel. These are moments, in their way, of covenantal return opening the possibility of national refounding. The public that *Testimony* creates is not simply defined by the courtroom; any such reading is correct but incomplete. Rather than a merely legal relationship among poet, poem, and audience, it seeks to (re)establish a covenant among them. The aesthetics of the courtroom, perhaps, are necessary for this covenantal readership: "A nation under covenant," in one understanding, "is not a nation under contract but a nation under *judgment*."[65] In biblical narratives, those who proclaim the judgment are prophets. But in the secular, disenchanted twentieth century, who can play such a role? The poet, perhaps, and, too, the actors in the American courtroom. Much as formal qualities of biblical poetics are, a covenantal readership is embedded into the text of *Testimony*. To see this fully, we must turn back to Reznikoff's biblical translations one last time.

"Israel" and "King David" depict two possible ways of understanding the foundation of a Jewish nation: in "Israel," of peoplehood (marred through economic exploitation); in "King David," of statehood (marred through political violence). Yet there is a third option, offered in the final pages of "Israel": the covenantal refounding of the people of Israel through the giving of the Torah at Sinai. Such a covenant operates through appeal not to "blood descent" but to a shared and agreed-upon law.[66] A covenantal nation is not founded once and for all time but continually founded and refounded through the renewing and renewal of this covenant. Such a society is thereby able to incorporate immigrants and other outsiders into both its national story and its concept of citizenship—which, perhaps, goes a long way toward explaining the time period Reznikoff settled on for the final version of *Testimony*: 1885 to 1915, mapping quite neatly onto the period now understood as the United States' "immigration era." The moment of discovery becomes the foundational moment; America is refounded, again and again, during the period of mass immigration that brought Reznikoff's parents (and millions of others) to its shores.

Reznikoff's translation and retelling of the giving of the commandments and divine law at Sinai constitutes the final third of "Israel" and functions as the pivot to "King David." In fact, this moment, not *Testimony*, represents the first time that Reznikoff crafted verse from legal code and court reports: it prefigures the dryness of much of the later poem and similarly focuses on the details a reader might expect an attorney or jurist, rather than a poet, to be drawn to. Reznikoff's Torah is highly redacted, focusing primarily on laws of jurisprudence, economic ethics, land use, neighborliness, and the radical economic regulations of the sabbatical and jubilee years. The language of this section, not surprisingly, resembles *Testimony*. For example,

> The land shall not be sold forever: the land is God's,
> you are strangers and sojourners before Him;
> you shall grant a redemption for the land;
> but if the land is not redeemed,
> it shall stay with him who bought it until the jubilee,
> and in the jubilee he who sold it shall return to his possession.[67]

This passage challenges Jahan Ramazani's argument that poetry's "impatience" with the law's "binary logic, linearity and formality, and argumentative single-mindedness" necessarily results in a "friction" between the two modes of writing and thinking.[68] The dry legalese of this scene, its "linearity and formality," its clear binaries of positive commandment and interdict—these are what characterize the covenantal nationhood that the scene establishes. Just as the formal poetics of the Hebrew Bible embed the narratives and critiques of the typological model into Reznikoff's legal history of the United States, so too does the *legal* style of this passage—in writing as in thinking—work to embed its covenantal potential into the language and texture of *Testimony*.

Reznikoff's revelation at Sinai presents an expansive view of citizenship and belonging: adherence to the law, not the inheritance or spilling of blood, determines civic boundaries. As Johnson's preacher might have phrased it, "Anyone, from anywhere, can belong to this congregation." This is a striking alternative to the foundational moments of peoplehood and statehood found in "Israel" and "King David." Perhaps more importantly, this also implies a rejection of the particularity of the Sinaitic covenant as established in both the biblical source text and its reception across Jewish history and thought. It's not that Reznikoff shucks off particularity altogether. He just changes what it means. This comes through most clearly in his presentation of the Ten Commandments. On first glance, there are only nine; Reznikoff has excised the first two-thirds of Exodus 20:2, which Judaism recognizes as the first commandment in its entirety: "I am the LORD thy God, who brought thee out of the land of Egypt, out of the house of bondage."[69] In cutting this verse, Reznikoff removes one of the signal, repeated refrains of biblical law, often used to connect commandments to the memory of enslavement. The ethics of metaphorical memory—so far, so good. But in Reznikoff's poetics, they contain the seeds of something rather more problematic: a historically defined peoplehood. This nation is limited to those who were slaves in Egypt and brought forth from it and their descendants—just another version of "Land where my fathers died."

So this excision implies something more: a re-creation of meaning through Reznikoff's signature redaction and compression of source materials. Immediately preceding this Decalogue are two lines derived from Exodus 19:6: "You are not to be like other nations; / you are to be a kingdom of priests, a holy nation."[70] At first glance, their new juxtaposition with the Decalogue is simply the by-product of cutting excess material. But these lines, highlighted at the beginning of a new stanza, also assume the role formerly performed by "I am the LORD thy God, who brought thee out of the land of Egypt." They provide the theological foundation for the commandments that follow. Reznikoff doesn't simply cut the first commandment, traditionally understood, but *replaces it with a different commandment*: to be distinct, priestly, holy. This, not historical experience or descent, defines the boundaries of citizenship. The derivation of the first half of the commandment ("You are not to be like other nations") only intensifies the effect, linking the commandment in Exodus 19:6 "to be unto Me a kingdom of priests, and a holy nation" with the repeated prophetic condemnation of the later Israelites when they proclaim, "We must have a king over us, that we may be like all the other nations," and "We will be like the nations, like the families of the lands, worshipping wood and stone."[71] This new Decalogue demands both a break from the past—

ancestors who worshipped material products and profit, metaphorically and literally—and the future kingdom of David. National history, the political institution(s) and power of the state, it insists, do not establish a "holy nation." The commandments that follow do.

This connection runs through Reznikoff's consistent translation of the Hebrew word *tzedek* as "righteousness," a term that binds the concept of a holy people or nation, the Ten Commandments, and economic regulations. Between the second and third commandments (against idolatry and false oaths), he interpolates a clause that does not appear in the biblical source, "By righteousness you shall serve God."[72] Here, thinking back to Reznikoff's deployment elsewhere of parallel construction and intensification, we can see a focusing of the opening "you are to be a kingdom of priests, a holy nation" to service not through Temple sacrifice but through acts of *tzedek*, of "righteousness." To be a holy people, then, is determined not by descent or chosenness but by behavior, by adherence to covenant. We see this as well at the end of Reznikoff's Ten Commandments, which flow immediately into the subsequent commandment (drawn from Leviticus 19:15, rather than Exodus 21), "In righteousness shall you judge your neighbor."[73] Laws of jurisprudence, economic ethics, neighborliness, dietary restrictions, harvests, gleanings and tithes, treatment of animals, treatment of strangers, and the sabbatical and jubilee years (with an emphasis on fields, property law, slavery, credit, and lending) follow: the legal thinking toward which poetry, Ramazani argues, is impatient and often opposed. Yet these lines come to define the concept of righteousness and therefore what it means to be a "holy people," again, not through descent or the spilling of blood but through adherence to an ethics of community: how you and your community behave toward the poor, the defenseless, the wanderer, and debtor determines whether you have fulfilled your covenantal duty and chosen to stand within the civic community by behaving righteously.

These commandments, moreover, reflect the rejection of individual(ist) and national(ist) narrative that informs Reznikoff's poetry generally. They are not interested in the relationship between humanity and God (except insofar as the worship of false, materialist idols, the preference for profit over prophecy, is to be avoided) or ethics on the level of nation or history. These are commandments that order the ethical structuring of the intermediary institutions on which *Testimony* will turn a critical eye in American history. Reznikoff's rewriting of Deuteronomy 6 (adapted into Jewish prayer as the liturgically central affirmation of faith, the *sh'ma*) concludes the poem. The biblical lines govern the inner life of a Jew: to "love the Lord your God with all your heart and with all your soul and with all your might," to establish both the love of God and the fact of God's oneness within the household understood both as the building itself (its door frames, its gates) and as the family (through teaching this truth and love to children, through reciting it upon waking and upon going to sleep—in moments of noncommunal life particularly).[74] Reznikoff retains portions of this passage but radically revises the famous opening ("Hear, O Israel! The Lord is our God, the one Lord"):

> You are not to do each what is right in his own eyes:
> the words of this day shall be upon your heart,
> teach them diligently to your children,
> talk of them when you sit in your house,
> along the way, when you lie down, and when you rise up,
> bind them upon your hand,
> they shall be frontlets before your eyes,
> you shall write them upon the door-posts of your house and upon your gates.[75]

Excised are the central affirmation of faith and the commandment to love God—the traditional antecedents to "the words" that must be remembered, taught, spoken of, bound as frontlets and doorposts. Instead, Reznikoff draws on the language of Judges 17:6 and Proverbs 21:2, which condemn idolatry, greed, and wealth while making clear the necessity of an ethics oriented around communal, rather than individual, good. In the place of the monotheistic faith in the God of Abraham, Isaac, and Jacob, who brought the Israelites out of Egypt to be their God, Reznikoff inserts a one-sentence summary of the legal code that the poem has just outlined. These laws, in both entirety and summary, proclaim the existence of an objective justice, an all-pervasive ethics: not "each what is right in his own eyes" but what is right according to ethically oriented legislation.

This is a crucial moment for Reznikoff's poetics, one that sews together his use of recitative with concepts of covenant. Like recitative, the Sinaitic revelation was speech that required a response. So too with Reznikoff's poetic reimagining of Sinai: *Testimony* casts readers into the position of the jurors whose judgment is never heard in the text but toward which it builds; "Israel," at its end, casts readers as Israelites at the foot of Sinai, whose assent or rejection of the terms of the covenant is never heard in the poem but is, ultimately, required by the covenantal speech act itself. The terms of the covenant—legal speech rendered as poetry—produce recitative. The use of recitative elsewhere carries with it echoes of this moment of covenantal founding just as Reznikoff's deployment of biblical poetics carries commentary on biblical narrative.

Recitative *does* channel the moment of covenantal founding and response into *Testimony*, the project's very title makes clear. It has a twofold meaning. On the one hand, there is the obvious: drawn from court records, *Testimony* presents the testimony of those whose voices it recovers, arranged by Reznikoff in the role of poet-prosecutor. Yet *Testimony* also refers to the name of the two tablets of the covenant received by Moses at Sinai—in Hebrew, the *lukhot ha-eidut*, literally, the tablets of the *witnessing*, of the *testimony*.[76] This is the covenantal testimony presented by the poet-prophet. According to Jewish tradition, the covenant was established not merely by the giving of the law or the tablets on which the Ten Commandments were engraved but by the communal act of witnessing that event, to which the *lukhot ha-eidut*, housed in the Ark of the Covenant, gave testimony. For Reznikoff, God is excised: the covenant, whether that of the Israelites or the United States, is one that is continually established through the act of testimony. *Testimony*, this is to say, has a dual function: it highlights, condemns, and prosecutes the nation for its failures, both real and typological. And through this very action, it performs the second: the ongoing creation and re-creation of that very covenant through testimony and the readerly response anticipated by recitative. To title these works *Testimony* is, in many respects, to title them "The Covenant." The poet, poem, individual reader, and communal audience all participate in the giving and witnessing of this testimony. In so doing, they are all bound covenantally—and this covenant is renewed with each reading, each witnessing, of Reznikoff's *eidut*, of *Testimony*.

PART II

CIRCULATING MODERNISM

CHAPTER THREE

Immigrant Publics
Lola Ridge On and Off the Page

The December 1929 publication of *Firehead*, just in time for Christmas, marked the crest of Lola Ridge's literary reputation. This strange, book-length retelling of the New Testament's crucifixion narratives is the least characteristic of all her work in scope, setting, and form. Written over six furious, amphetamine-fueled weeks that summer at the Yaddo artists' colony in a self-created competition with an oblivious Robinson Jeffers (whose similarly themed *Dear Judas* nonetheless preceded hers), *Firehead* juxtaposes sprawling passages of Whitmanian free verse with others that push to the limits of formal conventions.[1] Energized by a prophetic exuberance, the final product resembles nothing so much as what might have happened had, defying the laws of time, William Blake and Allen Ginsberg come together to rewrite the gospels. In her fifty-sixth year, Ridge had long been an established presence within American modernism and labor activism. Yet this work seemed something altogether new.

Firehead's reception on publication contrasts sharply with its reputation today. Across sixty national reviews, doubling the total of her previous three volumes, critics placed her work on par with that of Countee Cullen and Edna St. Vincent Millay.[2] The *New York Times* offered glowing praise: "forceful and beautiful, a work in which imagination and intelligence fuse in a white flame," *Firehead* stands out in a time of "generally circumscribed lyric accomplishment in poetry" and demonstrates "more poetic daring than is usual with modern poets."[3] (Note, however, that this two-hundred-page poem is referred to as a "*lyric* accomplishment.") Ridge's poems were lauded, selling, solicited for anthologies. In 1935, she was awarded a Guggenheim Fellowship and received the Poetry Society of America's Poetry Guarantor's Prize; the next year, its Shelley Memorial Prize. After her 1941 death, the same organization established a Lola Ridge Memorial Prize. (Louis Zukofsky would be among its winners.) The prize was only awarded for ten years. Its last, 1952, marks the beginning of the abrupt forgetting of Ridge's poetry, literary networks, and social activism. Despite multiple efforts to recover her reputation—among feminist critics in the 1970s and 1980s; among efforts, such as Cary Nelson's *Repression and Recovery*, to rehabilitate Depression-era Left modernists in the 1990s and 2000s—Ridge remains at best marginal. Even that might be an overstatement. Unlike Millay or Stephen Vincent Benét, Ridge doesn't even garner the lingering memory of a poet who, once upon a time, was widely read.

Lola Ridge presents us with a question worth investigating: *Why?* Why did this widely read, well-connected, and often accessible American modernist, a poet who built her reputation in avant-garde little magazines *and* popular fora, fall so quickly out of favor? She would, after all, hardly be the most historically obscure (or most tendentious) poet in any of the Norton anthologies. Why, too, have multiple efforts to rehabilitate her reputation failed—even as the critical movements that hailed her succeeded in changing the practices of literary scholarship? Her partisans have, to date, offered versions of two answers: because she was a woman and because she was a leftist. There is truth in these. Ridge appears as a bit player in the memoirs of modernist publishers and poets, always as an obstacle to be overcome, her stubbornness only admirable when placed in defense of Sacco and Vanzetti—never aesthetics. A deep vein of misogyny characterizes these accounts. And, indeed, Ridge's poetry and politics were intertwined, and her works were caught up in the great forgetting of Depression-era leftist writing that was institutionalized after World War II.[4] And yet. We've recovered—in part due to the success of books that *also* make the case for Ridge—the politically engaged, leftist version of Langston Hughes that he himself deliberately suppressed and edited out during the McCarthy era. Feminist scholarship has helped raise Nella Larsen as a key figure of the Harlem Renaissance. The reputation of Muriel Rukeyser, outspoken as both a leftist and a feminist, has waxed and waned (and waxed again) over the decades—but her poetry has never been as forgotten as Ridge's.

I want to suggest a different answer: that Ridge's poetry rests at best uncomfortably within twentieth- and twenty-first-century expectations and norms of poetic reading. The success or failure of her poetry depends, to a degree not true of James Weldon Johnson or Charles Reznikoff, on the specific ways in which it is situated and circulates. Those ways most conducive to her work are neither the modes in which modern and contemporary poetry primarily circulates (the book, the magazine) nor the modes most central to building and maintaining posthumous reputation (the anthology, the classroom, the close-reading assignment). By contrast, Ridge's poetry succeeds when set in the contexts of labor and immigrant solidarity, not just because political activism was central to her life and writing but because these contexts allow for the emergence of the relationship among poet, poem, and public—a modality of reading—that enables the poem to flourish. Put flatly, Ridge's poetry simply does not desire to play the same game as the poetry and criticism that has taught us how to read the poetry of the twentieth century.

In this chapter and chapter 4, my approach builds on important work done by Mike Chasar in *Everyday Reading: Poetry and Popular Culture in Modern America*. Poetry, he observes, flourished in the United States in the first half of the twentieth century—but not always in ways acknowledged by literary history. "More people in the modern United States were producing and consuming more verse than at any other time in history," he notes, but the bulk of this poetry, popular or everyday rather than "literary," goes overlooked.[5] In his focus on poetry scrapbooks, radio programs, in advertising, and on billboards and other commercial signage, Chasar makes an argument not about the quality of this verse (about which he remains agnostic) but about the reading practices necessitated by the distinct dynamics of these "everyday" encounters with poetry. Ridge's work is not "everyday" in the sense Chasar describes. Yet his central focus—"how and why millions of people read the poetry they did"—suggests a way of approaching Ridge's work that might answer the question of her absent legacy.[6] How and why did readers encounter Ridge's poetry—and which situations prepare readers to encounter her poems in ways that allow for their flourishing rather than failure?

Ridge takes up these concerns in "Morning Ride," a poem from the 1927 collection *Red Flag*. Ten years after the lynching of Leo Frank, a Jewish factory manager falsely accused of raping and murdering a fourteen-year-old girl in Georgia, a young woman reads headlines about his posthumous exoneration while commuting to work on a city train. This poem marks Ridge's only foray into documentary poetics, also establishing it as the rare Ridge poem bearing visible markers associated with the modernist avant-garde. With "Headlines chanting—/ y o u t h / l y n c h e d ten years ago c l e a r e d—" the poem mimics the style of Pound's early Cantos by framing incorporated documentary material (the newspaper text) within a lyric voice that captures the sensory experience of her morning ride ("lean / to the soft blarney of the wind").[7]

Unlike the Depression-era Left modernists who would return to documentary form in the 1930s, Ridge's attempt to synthesize avant-garde documentary poetics with social consciousness and political solidarity fails. It's not that the poem doesn't succeed—it's that it *does* succeed in expressing deep skepticism both of the dominant strain of modernism (a refrain throughout Ridge's career) and of traditional modes of literary and information circulation.

While the paper's headlines may chant at the woman on the train, her attention never focuses on them. The El, by which she herself circulates through the city, provokes one turn from the event: her eyes keep wandering out the train's windows, to the "Skyscrapers / seeming still / whirling on their concrete / bases, / windows / fanged—" and the "milk-clouds oozing over the blue." The newspaper itself guides the second, more troubling turn: its structure suggests not outrage or labor solidarity after reading a news headline but that she allow her attention to glide to advertising headlines:

> leo frank
> lynched ten
>   say it with flowers
> wrigley's spearmint gum
>   carter's little liver—[8]

Any potential outrage or action dissipates; the energy that could have gone toward activism and solidarity pushed, instead, toward market trivialities: romantic gestures, breath-freshening gum, the little cure-all vial of Carter's Little Liver Pills (figure 7). News that circulates in newsprint doesn't produce a readership primed for anything but economic activity, much as the circulation of the morning commute also casts the woman in market terms. Both newspaper and train are, ultimately, aligned with the interests of advertisers and forces of economic and political power. These modes of circulation can produce only a distracted readership. Not until the train and the poem stop can the woman break from the reverie that the ride and newspaper induce. The train halts; the conductor's voice shouts, "Step Lively Please / Let 'Em Out First Let 'Em Out," and her thoughts turn, abruptly and at last, from the weather to the emotional power of the news:

> did he too feel it on his forehead,
> the gentle raillery of the wind,
> as the rope pulled taut over the tree
> in the cool dawn?[9]

Figure 7. Ad for Carter's Little Liver Pills

This is not quite action, not yet. But it is, at least, its predicate: the emotional resonance of miscarried justice, the production of sympathy, of what the contemporary novelist Marilynne Robinson asserts as literature's purpose, "a ghostly proximity to other human souls."[10] This can only begin to take place when the woman closes the newspaper, when she steps off the train.

There is a second turn in these closing verses—from the fragmented single-word lines and incorporated documents that, atypically for Ridge, have defined the poem's form so far. Avant-garde documentary poetics, that is, are also implicated in drawing the woman away from the fact of Frank's lynching and toward "fooling with your hair."[11] As the woman steps away from modes of circulation that lead to distracted readership, the poem moves away from the form that has been intertwined with these modes. As she rejects the documentary material provided by the newspaper, the poem rejects the documentary form that the newspaper suggests. Like the newspaper and commuter rail, the poem calls forth a mode of reading that cannot produce the kind of solidarity Ridge's poetry strives for. In aligning the three, Ridge expresses skepticism of the private, individual reading that avant-garde modernism produces, whether in baffled first takes or the ritual of close reading that grew from these experiences and through which they continue to circulate. By absorbing the news of miscarried justice, documentary and other avant-garde forms neuter its social critique—intentionally or unintentionally, the effect is the same.

But this was not limited to an Anglo-American avant-garde characterized by increasingly reactionary politics. "Morning Ride" first appeared in the March 1927 issue of *New Masses*, the leftist literary journal closely associated with the Communist Party USA. Reading this on the train, one presumes, would be a different experience than the *Times*, *Herald*, or *World*. But text and context exist in tension: with Ridge's words (which appeared on page 7) in mind, it's impossible to read the ad published on the issue's inside cover without skepticism (figure 8). When *this* young woman read *New Masses*, "a lively breeze of fresh air swept through her brain and freshened up her whole mental apparatus.... Specialists tell her that with care and a monthly dose of NEW MASSES she will someday be able to think for herself." Yet in "Morning Ride," it's *precisely* this sensory experience, as the young woman "lean[s] / to the soft blarney of the wind / fooling with your hair," that distracts her from injustice, leading her to take her eyes off the headlines and "look / milk-clouds oozing over the blue." The issue does end on a call to action—to join *New Masses* staff and readers at a March 18 "Anti-Obscenity Ball" clearly intended to fund-raise for the still-young magazine by mocking cultural reactionaries. This, too, hardly seems like the

Figure 8. Ad on inside cover of *New Masses*, March 1927

closing thought Ridge's poem would prefer. "Morning Ride" is skeptical, wary—in search of a mode of circulation that can produce solidarity and action but never trusting that the mode in which it currently circulates can or will do so.

These concerns shaped Ridge's editorial work, her vision for American modernism, and her career-long opposition to stalwarts of Anglo-American high modernism. The quarrels and the fallings-out they produced led, in part, to the posthumous collapse of her reputation. They had their roots not just in aesthetics but in questions of readership and reception. How, Ridge's career asks, again and again, should poetry circulate? In what ways does poetic circulation affect not just readership but readership understood as the way we relate to others?

Ridge's life and work testify to the ways in which the circulation of poetry and people intertwine. Born in Dublin in December 1873, she immigrated with her mother, Emma, to Sydney, Australia, in the summer of 1877. By early 1880, they had moved to the New Zealand mining town of Hokitika, where Emma (claiming to be a widow but still married to Ridge's father) wed Donald MacFarlane. Ridge began to write and publish her first poems here, as a teenager—in traditional forms, they are overwhelmingly concerned with the landscape and life of the New Zealand bush.[12] In 1895, Ridge married Peter Webster; in 1896, a son died at two weeks; in 1900, another, Keith, was born. But her family life was no more settled than her mother's had been: with her stepfather consigned to an asylum, Ridge, Emma, and Keith left for Sydney in 1903, where they stayed as Ridge pursued her career in poetry and painting until, shortly after Emma's death in 1907, Ridge and Keith set sail for the United States, arriving in San Francisco in September.[13]

In some respects, Ridge was born three times: in Dublin, as Rose Emily Ridge; in 1903, when she took the name "Lola Ridge" rather than the various combinations of "Rose," "Emily," or "Dolores" paired with "MacFarlane" or "Webster"; and in March 1908, when she arrived in New York City, entering, like a new immigrant, through Ellis Island. Ridge was alone: she had deposited the eight-year-old Keith at an orphanage in Los Angeles.[14] In New York, she would immediately insert herself into literary, anarchist, and feminist circles, contributing to Emma Goldman's *Mother Earth* and serving as literary editor of Margaret Sanger's *Birth Control Review* in 1918. She was also an editor at *Others*, *Broom*, and *New Masses* and was active in—and arrested for—agitation on behalf of Sacco and Vanzetti. Her poetry attended to revolution and unrest in Ireland and Russia as well as in the United States.

That Ridge was herself born in Ireland and raised in New Zealand did not prevent her from writing what she conceived of as a decidedly American literature. This sets her apart not only from the self-definition of expatriate modernists such as Gertrude Stein, T. S. Eliot, and Ezra Pound but also from those modernists, like Jean Toomer, Waldo Frank, and William Carlos Williams, who stayed at home and labored at what Michael North terms the "cultural project of the Americanist avant-garde."[15] Ridge's poetry offers an alternative imagining of this project. Replacing the tension between native/indigenous and colonizing/conquering with a vision of new, transient groups passing through the Americas, she presents American literary culture as, at its core, defined by the recurrent circulation of people. By placing the act and experience of immigration at the center of her poetry, it counters the claims of established American elites to control of American culture: the immigrant response to the place of the Americas *is* the defining feature of an American literature in which there are only outsiders. Revising, like Johnson and Reznikoff, the typology and rhetoric of American civil religion, her poetry re-imagines American literature as ethnic literature—cultural products of a contingent *ethnos* established as transient, immigrant populations respond to the conditions of the modern United States.

Put in very different language, immigrant and ethnic Americans stand in relation to Anglo-Americans as early (pre-Pauline, let's say) Jewish Christians did to the non-Christian Jews of the first century CE. By employing the language of supersession, I realize that I walk a fine metaphorical line. The point I seek to make—because it's the point the typological language and imagery of Ridge's poetry seeks to make—is not that "old," "Anglo" Americans are cut off from a new covenant. Rather, it is that the old American covenant was *particular*: an Anglo-American covenant, we might say, providing only for an Anglo-American community. At the end of "The Ghetto," Ridge's early and important poem of the Lower East Side, she insists that Americanness emerges "out of the Passion eternal": out of the experiences of immigrant and ethnic communities, of exploited laborers and put-upon others.[16] It's in this covenantal supersession that Ridge's concern with the circulation of people merges with her concern for the circulation of poetry—indeed, establishes it. As discussed at the end of chapter 2, assenting to and upholding (or falling away from) a covenant is a performative act; the importance of judicial procedure and recitative to Reznikoff's poetry occurs in their production of a particular generic and readerly expectation: the need to respond. Something similar occurs with Ridge's writing. She's fully aware, as we've already seen, that reading can end in complacency and distraction rather than activism. Whereas Reznikoff's poetry demands judgment and assent, Ridge's calls for solidarity.

Such a distinction further indicates how discussions of civil religion and covenant map onto the study of poetics, performance, and public. It's not that poetry that doesn't call for solidarity fails to produce some kind of covenant but that it leaves the old one—defined by particularity and *not* defined by solidarity—in place. That is, it's a poetry of and for the individual; it's read too easily, or perhaps only, through what Michael Warner refers to as "lyric conventions... automatically in place whenever we read lyric poetry." But the recognition of a text as lyric (or any other genre of speech), he notes, is a "misrecognition": "to read them as lyric, we ignore [a poem's public aspects] and reinterpret both the speaking event, the boundaries of the text, and all the figures of apostrophe in the text."[17] Producing solidarity requires a different kind of recognition: as an act of public speech, one that voices and calls for assent to the new, universal American covenant that her poetry will detail. For Ridge, public speech doesn't necessarily inhere in performance or even in its metaphorical capture. Rather, it develops from the way a poem circulates within, encounters, and is encountered by the world and its publics. When poetics and venues for poetry fail, they fail because they cannot produce solidarity: because they cast the poem as a private encounter, one not capable (or perhaps simply not likely) to escape complacency. This is the flaw she sees in the high modernist avant-garde, in newspapers, and even, she implies she suspects, in *New Masses*.

Ridge, like most humans (regardless of whether they've ever desired to write a poem), was better at articulating what she was against or dissatisfied with than articulating a positive vision of what she would prefer. So her career offers no coherent program of poetic circulation. Rather, it offers a variety of venues and contexts, which, after nearly a century, we can look back on as case studies and experiments. So we'll turn, next, to two different versions of her best-known poem, "The Ghetto": its initial publication, in the *New Republic*, and its inclusion as the title poem of her first collection later in the same year. This comparison, along with considerations of her editorial work at *Broom*, relationships with the labor movement and (anachronism and oxymoron though it may be) mainstream modernism, and her later poetry, will help us to address the mystery with which this chapter opened, of the posthumous disappearance of Ridge's reputation and the failure of repeated efforts to recover her works. Ridge herself, as we'll see, didn't always utilize the venues and modes of circulation best suited to producing a public poetics of solidarity—and that in which her poetry best succeeds in doing so is not easily transmitted across time.

Two "Ghettos"

On or about March 27, 1908, Lola Ridge arrived in Ellis Island and began to radically revise her life story. She would, on the one hand, claim to be ten years younger than she was—so convincingly that even David Lawson, whom she met in 1910 and married in October 1919, remained unaware of her true age even after her death. It's also unclear whether he was aware that, legally, Ridge was still married to Peter Webster, whom she'd left in New Zealand and falsely insisted had died before her departure. She was childless, now, too—and could devote herself more earnestly to radical activism and writing. Her immigration story itself came under heavy editing: by 1908, there were many ways to travel from California to New York, and Ridge's chosen course seems a little too on the nose. In February, she left Los Angeles on a steamer for Panama; on March 20, she set sail for New York and the immigrant processing center at Ellis Island. She then settled in the heart of the city's Jewish immigrant community, boarding in a tenement house in the Lower East Side and working intermittently as an artist's model and writing ad copy. Or maybe this, too, was just a revision: although she claimed in a 1919 interview to have lived in such a tenement, Lawson would say she did not live among Jewish immigrants—or even encounter them until years later.[18] The result, when placed in combination with the focus of "The Ghetto" and the composition of the literary and anarchist circles in which she moved, was that Ridge was at times taken not for an Irish Catholic by way of the Pacific but as a Jewish immigrant.[19]

Ridge's biographer Terese Svoboda observes that her move from California to New York allowed her to circulate with a new energy and focus among anarchists, feminists, and emergent modernists. Yet it did more than this: it allowed Ridge to gradually write herself into a specific narrative of immigration to the United States, one that wasn't, in fact, her own course. It's not that she actively pretended or claimed to be a Jew—there's no evidence that this is the case—but that, in the years after arriving in the United States, Jewish immigration seized her imagination as an embodiment of American life, culture, and ideals. She would take this up explicitly in her first major poem, "The Ghetto"—one of the earliest English-language poems to explore American Jewish immigration at length. This work, which appeared in the *New Republic* on April 13, 1918, and again as the title poem of *The Ghetto and Other Poems* later that year, emerged amid a burst of modernist-inspired creativity that saw her work land in the primary venues of the New Verse—*Poetry*, *Others*, and *The Dial*. She may have been at work on "The Ghetto" long before its publication. But if, as Svoboda speculates, Ridge wrote large portions in cities as far-flung as New Orleans, Detroit, and dozens of towns in between as she traveled the country with Lawson, this should only highlight the hold that New

York—and Jewish immigration in particular—had on her understanding of contemporary American identity. As she wrote, Ridge displayed an acute sense of how American civil religious discourse had defined citizenship—and where changes to this discourse would lead in the next several decades. "The Ghetto," in its final form, revises the meaning of American citizenship, settling on a pluralist, immigrant ideal. While this has, by now, so permeated American discourse that the phrase "a nation of immigrants" has come to be a truism even for immigration restrictionists, it was by no means widely accepted at the time of Ridge's writing.

Yet the precise nature of this revision depended on the modes in which the poem circulated among readers. In both versions, "The Ghetto" describes the lives and struggles of immigrants (mostly, but not exclusively, Jewish) in the city's crowded tenements, speaking through the voice of a boarder in the Sodos family apartment, on or near Hester Street. Opening with a depiction of city life that recalls the visual and sensory focus of T. S. Eliot's early verse, the poem depicts technological modernity and human physicality intersecting in surreal imagery. "Cool, inaccessible air is floating in velvety blackness, shot with steel-blue lights" but is blocked by "The heat. . . . . / nosing in the body's overflow, / Like a beast pressing its great steaming belly close."[20] (Ellipses are a distinguishing characteristic of Ridge's writing; all those included in quotations from her poetry, unless set aside in brackets, are original to her work.) After the first two stanzas, however, the two versions of the poem take markedly different courses. Its final version divides "The Ghetto" into nine sections; the magazine publication, not surprisingly, is shorter—only three. These are also arranged differently. So, the beginning of the *New Republic* version omits (or Ridge had not yet written) four stanzas describing urban residents in greater detail and merges sections I and II: instead of a panorama, the poem moves, immediately, into the declaration, "I room at Sodos' with Sadie and her old father and her mother."[21] This shapes the poem to follow, producing a work more specifically focused on a single family than on the lives up and down Hester Street that the longer version details. Likewise, this version does not include three stanzas from the end of section I, describing the upstairs neighbors, Sara and Anna; an entire section (section III) describing a parade of children; the meetings of radicals in a café (section VI) and an apartment (section VII); and, importantly, the nine closing stanzas, which we'll examine at greater length. (Until that explicit return to the final, book version of the poem, I'll be referring to the April 13, 1918, text from the *New Republic* unless otherwise noted.)

As printed in the *New Republic*, "The Ghetto" is a feminist poem published as the US House and Senate debated and voted on the Nineteenth Amendment; a proimmigration poem at a moment when nativist sentiments, intensified by World War I, were building toward the 1924 Johnson-Reed Act; and a politically progressive poem, giving voice to the rallying cry "Forward!"— and in an ambiguous Yiddish/German, no less: "Vorwärts ... Vorwärts ..."— in an issue that began with unsigned editorials against lynching, calling for the expansion of the federal administrative state, celebrating precedent just established on behalf of collective bargaining and union membership by the Labor Policies Board, and expressing cautious support for Woodrow Wilson's postwar agenda (the creation of a League of Nations).[22] It even included the text of a recent lecture by Thorstein Veblen, the economic theorist increasingly critical of capitalism, "A Policy of Reconstruction," which called for "disallowance of anything like free discretionary control of management on grounds of ownership alone" and for the government to "take over and administer as a public utility any going concern that is in control of industrial work which has reached such a state of routine, mechanical systematization, or automatic articulation that it is possible for it to be habitually managed from an office by methods of accountancy."[23]

But this version of "The Ghetto" is decidedly *not* three things: it is not a politically radical poem, it is not a poem that engages meaningfully with American civil religious discourse, and it is not a poem that mediates the same kind of covenantal public as Johnson's or Reznikoff's works do. All three are true of the final version. There are practical reasons for some of the differences between the two: even a magazine devoted to publishing poetry, not highbrow, technical political programs, would have trouble finding space for the entirety of a twenty-four-page poem (its length in *The Ghetto*). And Ridge appears to have continued revising the text between the two publications: it simply isn't clear which sections omitted in April had already been written— or, if written, whether Ridge had yet settled on them as part of the "complete" work. But the modes of circulation also shape the differences in the poem— and, indeed, the textual history can't easily be read apart from them.

The most politically radical sections of "The Ghetto" do not appear in the *New Republic*—a leading journal of progressive opinion, yes, but one that was stridently opposed to radicalism and that took great pains to separate its policies from socialism. Its editorials suggest that Wilson's policies might enable the Democratic Party to absorb socialist support, blunting the possibility of too-radical reforms or elected officials; accuses conservative opponents of an expanded administrative state of "materially obstructing the prosecution of the war"; and celebrates incremental, institutionalized labor reform; while Veblen casts his policies not as socialism but as a democratic alternative: "Current events in Russia," he concludes, "attest that it is a grave mistake to let a growing disparity between vested rights and the current conditions of life over-pass the limit of tolerance."[24] His point and that of the editorials (most likely written by the magazine's founding editor, Hebert Croly) is clear: the *New Republic* is progressive, yes, but progressive reforms are the only way to stave off revolution.

So it perhaps shouldn't surprise that the two scenes—parts VI and VII of the final poem—depicting meetings of radicals and anarchists aren't printed in the *New Republic*. Even the Lola Ridge who circulates in this magazine differs from the Lola Ridge of her published volumes and literary reputation. Her biography stands out among the contributor notes on the penultimate page: she avoids, or can't commit to, the laconic irony of Croly, Veblen, and H. G. Wells ("Everybody knows") (figure 9). So we read, "An Australian who came to America about twelve years ago. For a while she contributed short stories to popular American magazines, but soon tired of this work, and has published nothing for several years."[25] It's worth noting what Ridge omits here: she hasn't been unpublished for half a decade only because she grew weary of writing but because she committed those years to radical activism.

Contributors

to this Issue

H. G. WELLS—Everybody knows.

THORSTEIN VEBLEN—Economist; Author of The Theory of the Leisure Class and The Nature of Peace.

HENRY HAZLITT—New York financial writer; Author of Thinking as a Science.

W. A. NORRIS—A young Harvard graduate.

LOLA RIDGE—An Australian who came to America about twelve years ago. For a while she contributed short stories to popular American magazines, but soon tired of this work, and has published nothing for several years.

Figure 9. "Contributors to This Issue" (*New Republic*, April 13, 1918, 335)

Ridge, far from the radical firebrand who would become known for not giving ground as mounted police charged protestors on behalf of Sacco and Vanzetti, appears here as that other period type: the disaffected, alienated artist. The "popular magazines" are wearisome—too trite, too commercial, the educated readership of the *New Republic* might conclude. No true artist wants to write for the world's Babbitts.

The poem mirrors this version of Ridge. Without the meetings of radical cells, it loses its most hopeful, forward-looking passages—so, too, with the omission of the liberated upstairs neighbors, Sara and Anna; the parade of children in part III; and, above all, the rhapsodic closing of the final version of the poem, which finds vibrancy and life, not despair, in the ghetto. Instead, the poem closes as its narrator returns to her room at dawn. She shuts her door and observes,

> Out of the Battery
> A little wind
> Stirs idly—like an arm
> Trailed over a boat's side in dalliance—
> Rippling the smooth dead surface of the heat,
> And Hester Street,
> Like a forlorn woman over-borne
> By many babies at her teats,
> Turns on her trampled bed to meet the day.[26]

All of these words are present in the final text of the poem. But their meaning changes when they are given the last say. In place of radicalism, or the birth scene of the future America among its impoverished immigrants, we get loneliness, abandonment, and isolation. Let's go a step farther and consider these qualities as they circulate among readers of the *New Republic*: What characterizes the Lower East Side? Not the birthplace of change enacted from the ground up, by the residents of the neighborhood themselves, often through radical means, but the kinds of problems that can be resolved by top-down, technocratic reforms: precisely the approach promulgated in the editorial and review columns surrounding the poem.

The version of the poem published in *The Ghetto and Other Poems* from its beginning resists such a reading. In its expanded opening section, life on the Lower East Side remains on the level of abstraction; individuals are transformed into metaphorized masses:

> The street crawls undulant,
> Like a river addled
> With its hot tide of flesh
> That ever thickens.
> Heavy surges of flesh
> Break over the pavements,
> Clavering like a surf—[27]

This opening, however, only establishes a premise that the remainder of the poem works to reject. The figures in her poetry retain their individuality—their status as subject. "The Ghetto," in this printing, ultimately presents urban modernity as an experience that *heightens* subjectivity, rather than abstracting and alienating the individual into objecthood. As the poem's closing litany proclaims, it is the site of *"Life, / Articulate, shrill, / Screaming in provocative assertion, / . . . / Electric currents of life, / Throwing off thoughts like sparks."*[28]

More than just the inclusion of stanzas about radicalism creates this change. Shorn of one circulatory context, the single-author volume grants Ridge the ability to frame "The Ghetto" and the poems that follow it as a kind of poetic communion. This begins almost as soon as one opens the book, with the dedicatory poem "To the American People," which appears between the copyright page and table of contents:

> Will you feast with me, American people?
> But what have I that shall seem good to you!
>
> On my board are bitter apples
> And honey served on thorns,
> And in my flagons fluid iron,
> Hot from the crucibles.
>
> How should such fare entice you![29]

At once dedication and epigram, these lines cast the entire collection as part of an invitation. To continue reading is to accept, to agree to eat the "bitter apples," "honey served on thorns," and "flagons [of] fluid iron." The dedication instructs the volume's readers to see themselves not simply as individuals interested in poetry but as members of a wider American people about to be confronted with the reality of their country: not a land of milk and honey but one of bitter fruit, of torture. This feast of horrors doesn't just produce awareness or sympathy, however. The language—"thorns," "crucibles"— begins to recall the language of Ridge's Ur-myth: New Testament accounts of Jesus's crucifixion, which function in her poetry much as the tale of Odysseus does for many high modernists. A parenthetical on the first page of "Three Men Die," from her final volume of poetry, expresses her use of the story succinctly:

> (old myth
> Renews its tenure of the blood
> Recurrently; in a new way
> Reforms about an ancient pith
> With all the old accessories)[30]

This feast is a kind of communion, and just as the blood and the body of Christ give life beyond death to those who consume them, so the "Life" that emerges from the Lower East Side's "Passion eternal" isn't limited to those who have endured it any more than the new covenant established through the crucifixion is limited to the one who endured it or the few who witnessed it. Reading Ridge's poems marks an act of communion: of entering into this covenantal readership.

Both versions of "The Ghetto" depict the circulation of people, immigrants to the United States moving within the city and neighborhood. But the changes made for *The Ghetto and Other Poems* transform these movements to produce a poetic covenant that, like those of James Weldon Johnson and Charles Reznikoff, revises the discourse of American civil religion. In this telling, the residents of the Lower East Side are, despite their seclusion, poverty, and foreign speech and customs, fundamentally *American* in a way they are not in the *New Republic*. Section III, omitted in its entirety from the *New Republic* version, describes a Fourth of July on Hester Street:

> The sturdy Ghetto children
> March by the parade,
> Waving their toy flags,
> Prancing to the bugles—
> Lusty, unafraid ...
> Shaking little fire sticks
> At the night—[31]

They celebrate, that is, just as any American child might. Nor are they totally assimilated: despite the flags and bugles, they speak Yiddish and continue to gaze "Out of the shadow of pogroms / Watching... watching...."[32] Even the children retain the memory of other, very different nighttime marches and torches targeting Jews. Yet the historical experiences of eastern European Jewish immigrants do not keep them outside of Americanness or render them only partially fit. Rather, these memories and the wariness to which they give birth are simply taken as an unquestioned part of what it means to be American, to celebrate the Fourth of July.

Elsewhere, the experiences of the immigrant poor are aligned specifically with the mythology of American nationalism. Amid the crowd of children, Talmud scholars, peddlers, and mothers with infants on Hester Street, the poem singles out a "young trader" at his cart who

> Looks Westward where the trade-lights glow,
> And sees his vision rise—
> A tape-ruled vision,
> Circumscribed in stone—
> Some fifty stories to the skies.[33]

His talent and ambition as a merchant direct his gaze in a refiguration of Manifest Destiny's defining slogan—to "Go West, Young Man." Rather than gazing westward at the open frontier, he gazes toward downtown Manhattan, where skyscrapers are beginning to rise, and imagines himself going a few blocks west to erect his own. On one level, this is Manifest Destiny for the twentieth century, in which capitalism has replaced the frontier as the seat of desire. On the other, it situates a recent immigrant—a peddler hawking goods on a street corner—as driven by a quintessentially "American" desire and casts him in the role of pioneering American frontiersman.

Jewish immigrants, in Ridge's telling, come not to destroy some old, Anglo-Protestant America by their presence but to fulfill its promise, flung "Like an ancient tapestry of motley weave / Upon the open wall of this new land."[34] Sections included only in the later version of "The Ghetto" make their Christ-like supersession clear—and focus it specifically within the radical and anarchist circles absent from the *New Republic*. So, in section VII, a group of activists meets in a tenement house recast as a Nativity scene, "this room, bare like a barn," "this shut-in room, / Bare as a manger."[35] This meeting of immigrant youths and section VI's depiction of older radicals in a tea room transform the lone Christological moment shared across the two versions, the moment when

Lights go out. . . . .
And the great lovers linger in little groups, still passionately debating.
Or one may walk in silence, listening only to the still summons of life—
Life making the great Demand. . . . .
Speaking in that strange, portentous voice. . . . .
Calling its new Christs. . . . .[36]

In the poem's initial publication, there is no indication of what these lovers are debating, nothing to lead one to suspect it's political. In the final version, however, the earlier scenes of young radicals contextualize this moment: these are young lovers debating social action and revolution.

Indeed, only by including the previously omitted closing stanzas and sections VI and VII does the image of these young lovers as "new Christs" develop beyond a striking but meaninglessly ambiguous image. After the picture of Hester Street as a worn and tired nursing mother with which the first publication closes, the second pivots into a nine-stanza, italicized celebration of "LIFE!": *"Startling, vigorous life, / That squirms under my touch, / And baffles me when I try to examine it."* This, indeed, is what the personified Hester Street nurses into being. Through *"the black and clotted gutters," "the pushcarts," "Long nights argued away / In meeting halls / Back of interminable stairways— / In Roumanian wine-shops / And little Russian tea-rooms . . ."* where young lovers and old men sit and plot revolution comes the *"Bartering, changing, extorting, / Dreaming, debating, aspiring, / Astounding, indestructible, Life of the Ghetto . . ."* It is a *"Strong flux of life"* that emerges *"Like a bitter wine / Out of the bloody stills of the world . . . / Out of the Passion eternal."*[37] Life—that which is promised by the covenant that emerges from Jesus's crucifixion and the act of taking communion—emanates not from moments of historical note or from the city's elite neighborhoods but from the mundane, everyday details of urban poverty, of peddlers' capitalist ambitions, of parents crushed by the piling up of life's minor disappointments, of children waving toy flags on the street, of heavy summer heat, of furtive sex, of tearooms, sweatshops, and radicals talking of Marx and Lenin.[38]

Grounding American biblical typology in immigrant experience, Ridge explores, we might say, the immigrant (rather than Puritan) origins of the American self.[39] The presence and experiences of new immigrants, particularly Jews on New York's Lower East Side, fulfill, renew, and expand a national covenantal promise—but only in "The Ghetto" as it circulates in the volume put out by B. W. Huebsch, the modernist publisher who was himself the son of Jewish immigrants and whose press was best known for the first authorized American editions of James Joyce and D. H. Lawrence. In this iteration, "The Ghetto" extends beyond the act of poetic speech to a Eucharistic performance. In the "bitter apples" and "honey served on thorns" that Ridge would serve to the American people, we might read, "This is my body, which is given to you"; of the flagons of fluid iron, "This cup that is poured out for you is the new covenant in my blood."[40]

Broom's American Encounters

"The Ghetto" offers no explanation why Ridge associates immigration or Jews particularly with the fulfillment of an American covenant. There's plenty on which we might speculate: affinity between her own immigrant experience and this larger community's; time spent in anarchist circles with Jewish immigrants like Goldman and Berkman; the inescapable fact that the demographics of American life, and New York in particular, were being remade by mass immigration. The most concrete grounding, tied to Ridge's own words and works, emerges from a more surprising place: the year she spent, from 1922 to 1923, as the American editor of the modernist little magazine *Broom*. In this role, she articulated a distinctively American vision of modernist aesthetics—one that, like "The Ghetto," insists that the ideas of America and American literature emerge through the circulation of people and the immigrant encounter with place. In doing so, Ridge's modernism resists easy classification within the bifurcated camps of her contemporaries: expatriate cosmopolitanism (though Ridge was herself an expatriate cosmopolitan) and an Americanist avant-garde interested in indigeneity. At *Broom*, as Ridge's beliefs about the circulation of people and the circulation of poetry grew intertwined, her rejection of expatriate high modernism grew more strenuous. No less than a clash over the merits of Gertrude Stein led to an acrimonious break with Harold Loeb, *Broom*'s publisher. Its ramifications still echo: Loeb's 1959 memoir, *The Way It Was*, helped produce Ridge's reputation as little more than a nagging troublemaker, more talented as a secretary than as a poet.[41]

Together with Alfred Kreymborg, Loeb founded *Broom* in 1921. The cash—$9,000—was Loeb's: he came from a German-Jewish family that was well established in New York's financial circles and no strangers to supporting literature and the arts: Peggy Guggenheim was a cousin on his mother's side; on his father's, James Loeb would endow Harvard's green- and red-bound Loeb Classical Library. Yet the decision to publish from Rome, not New York, distanced *Broom* from the financial support of Harold Loeb's family. When Loeb bought out Kreymborg's share of ownership in January 1922, he further strained the magazine's finances. The publication that Ridge joined the next month was on deeply insecure footing despite three successful issues. Expanding the magazine's circulation was her first priority. She developed a mailing campaign of over ten thousand addresses; offered sample issues for the cost of postage; solicited advertisers in New York and Chicago; found art shops and museums willing to stock the magazine; recruited submissions; stood on street corners handing out fliers; and secured what Loeb himself could not: an additional $5,000 in support from his mother.[42] By late March, she was optimistic enough to assure him, "I believe that we are going to make it pay this side"—that *Broom* might run in the black, at least in the United States.[43] By that summer, the magazine's finances appeared stable.

This success came at a cost. From the beginning, Ridge strained to assert that she was more than an office manager, laying out three conditions for her work in a letter of February 1, 1922: "(1) My name on BROOM as American editor. (2) Full authority and power of veto on this side. (3) All American MS. drawings etc to come to this office."[44] Yet in a letter detailing her resignation a year later, Ridge complained that Loeb had treated her less as an editor than as a first reader of slush, sometimes opening "a new BROOM to see some shivering bit of mediocrity" she had rejected "cheeping feebly out of the pages" because an author had, on receiving her rejection, contacted Loeb directly.[45] The conflict came to a head over aesthetics. The problem was twofold. Loeb preferred to publish established voices, typically connected to his own expatriate set; yet the result, in Ridge's eyes, was that "'Broom' has published such rotten stuff by men who have done good work." Rather than taking what *The Dial*, for instance, would not, Ridge preferred "to have 'Broom' discover, lead not follow."[46] She looked for the young and the unknown—preferring writers who had stayed in the United States and were interested in examining it: she was among the first to publish and a strenuous early advocate for Kay Boyle, Jean Toomer, and Hart Crane.

Ridge believed that the study of America was the next great frontier in art. "Spiritually America makes me think of the dawn of creation," she tried to explain to Loeb; "all the essentials are there—great sprawling oceans and uninhabited prairies waiting for the faintly stirring life that must take for and come up out of those deeps and none other." *Broom*, she implored, should be "the early visible symbol of this new birth."[47] So, from the beginning, she pushed for a periodic "all-American number," an issue of *Broom* that "would present an unbroken contour of American art to Europe."[48] Although Ridge's correspondence with Loeb reveals him dragging his feet, Ridge's persistence won out: the January 1923 issue of *Broom* would be an "American number."

Without this issue, there would be little reason to remember *Broom* (which, in any event, may well have folded in early 1922 had Ridge not come aboard). Scholarship has long recognized its importance: Michael North, for instance, reads it as marking the arrival of the "Americanist avant-garde" that he examines at length in *The Dialect of Modernism*.[49] The issue brought together Jean Toomer's "Karintha" with William Carlos Williams's "The Destruction of Tenochtitlan" and the second part of Hart Crane's "The Marriage of Faustus and Helen" (as "The Spring of Guilty Song"), all solicited or encouraged by Ridge, along with works by (among others) Marianne Moore, Kay Boyle, and Kenneth Burke; associate editor Matthew Josephson's ambivalent review of *The Waste Land*; and, to Ridge's fury, Gertrude Stein's "Wear," a poem that Stein herself never saw fit to republish.

The bulk of Ridge's resignation letter consists of a withering denunciation of Stein—and, by implication, any editor (such as Loeb) so in thrall to literary celebrity that he'd publish her rather than just about *anyone* else. Stein, in Ridge's view, is "a tricky craftsman whose highest attainment is an occasional flippant cleverness of presentation"; "her literary reputation—a bladder blown up by many breaths." "I object to her work in BROOM," Ridge declared, "not because of the missing substance in her work, not because she merely plays with words, but because she does not do it well enough. If you must play with words, as such, with no impetus or passion behind, then you must do it skillfully as a swordsman plays with rapiers—as Marsden Hartley, Amy Lowell, Wallace Stevens have done it. G. Stein's words—house-wife's canning plums—peanuts rattling in a straw hat—at best, corn popping in a skillet."[50] Stein stands directly in the way of discovering new American voices (she has been established far too long for Ridge's taste); she is insincere, passionless—the direction that following French literary fashions will lead American culture: "What real growth shall we foster if we squeeze the feet of this giant child into a French shoe?"[51] Loeb, to her mind, had gone over her head one time too many, overriding her veto to publish Stein in her American issue. So Ridge resigned. Four issues later, *Broom* folded.

These objections from Ridge's letters offer a kind of photo negative of her vision for American literature that we can illuminate with "The Ghetto" and the December 1922 advertisement for the forthcoming American number. Read together, they reimagine the relationship between national culture and immigration. The ad, strikingly designed, occupied a full page of *Broom* (figure 10). North reads it as the "manifesto" of the Americanist avant-garde, an "effort toward an indigenous American cultural renewal" that was nonetheless hobbled by "a persistent inability to understand how race fit into its conception of modern America, or how the language of African America fit into its conception of 'plain American.'"[52] North's critique, with its focus on the quest for multiracial American indigeneity, is defined by the visions of Frank, Toomer, and Williams at the expense of that actually depicted in Ridge's advertisement and editorial labor. Indeed, he all but ignores the first, pivotal paragraph of this manifesto/ad: "The Art of the Mayas was the earliest American Art. Conceived some ten centuries ago, it remains the magnificent expression of one of the noblest races which inhabited America. Since then, many races, many cultures have come and gone. All but the topography of North America has been altered. But the new races which populate the transformed continent are also creating a new art which mirrors as faithfully the astonishing environment they have made for themselves. Why not read them now?"[53] The point is not to assert that American culture and literature are or must be indigenous—but something rather the opposite, that none of the "many races, many cultures" that have made up and continue to make up America and the United States can claim to be indigenous. They "have come and gone"; they are "new races"; "All but the topography of North America has been altered." The "American" quality of such writing is defined not by the author's claim to be indigenously "of" America but by the work's (im)migratory response to the place and situation of the Americas. As a network in which art is embedded and of which it must be aware, circulation is inextricable from literature's creation and assessment. The Mayans serve as a model or starting point for American modernism because of the example they offer for original, sincere, and decidedly new responses through art and culture to the experience of circulating within the Americas.

The contrast this idea strikes with William Carlos Williams's Americanist vision, as articulated in *In the American Grain* (six sections of which appeared in *Broom*), is instructive. For Williams, quintessentially American figures achieve this status by rubbing against the American grain—by choosing to assert themselves as outsiders within their own country. Yet Williams's work establishes, in essence, an aristocracy of outcasts that at best collapses but more likely subsumes the democratic into the aristocratic, "as," he writes, "an aristocracy is the flower of a locality and so the *full* expression of a democracy."[54] So we find that, counterintuitive and revisionary though it may be, why not read them now? why not read them now? why not read them now? why not read them now?

The Oldest and Newest Art of America
in the January Broom

Maya Sculpture and
Architecture

Contemporary American
Prose and Poetry

The Art of the Mayas was the earliest American Art. Conceived some ten centuries ago, it remains the magnificent expression of one of the noblest races which inhabited America. Since then, many races, many cultures have come and gone. All but the topography of North America has been altered. But the new races which populate the transformed continent are also creating a new art which mirrors as faithfully the astonishing environment they have made for themselves. Why not read them now?

BROOM from old Europe will present in the JANUARY number an array of AMERICAN writings such as no magazine in America has yet ventured. Why not read them now?

PRIZE CONTEST

Which prominent American does this portrait-statue represent.

PRIZES for best answers!

1st. PRIZE
Subscription to
B R O O M
for Life.

2nd. PRIZE
One year's
subscription to
B R O O M

3rd. PRIZE
One year's
subscription to
B R O O M.

BROOM has never lacked faith in the Artistic future of America. Here are **new writers**, some known, most unknown, whose work is as varied, as fertile, as powerfully muscled as anything being written in England France or Germany. Here is Comparative Literature. Here are writers who will be studied in Courses in Comparative Literature twenty years hence. Why not read them now?

KAY BOYLE	MARIANNE MOORE	KENNETH BURKE
ROBERT SANBORN	MALCOLM COWLEY	GERTRUDE STEIN
MARGARET EVANS	JEAN TOOMER	CHARLES GALWEY
	WILLIAM CARLOS WILLIAMS	

and others who are not to be had in book form, not to be found on library shelves. In them is the clamor of a young culture. The JANUARY number of BROOM is a challenge to Americans to recognize a national art as profoundly American as

BASEBALL   **THE CINEMA**
THE JAZZ BAND   **AND THE DIZZY SKYSCRAPER**

while fundamentally in harmony with the Art of the ancient Mayas. The best way to be sure of reading them now is to

SUBSCRIBE AT ONCE Five Dollars ($ 5) to BROOM
3 East Ninth Street, New York.

why not read them now? why not read them now? why not read them now? why not read them now?

Figure 10. Advertisement for the forthcoming American number of *Broom* ("Prize Contest," *Broom* 4, no. 1 [December 1922], 74)

Williams retells the history of America through the familiar historical aristocracy of its "great men": Red Eric, Columbus, Cortez, Ponce de Leon, Sir Walter Raleigh, Cotton Mather, Daniel Boone, George Washington, Benjamin Franklin, Aaron Burr, Abraham Lincoln.

The central dynamic, throughout, remains the tension and violent encounter between the native and indigenous, on the one hand, and the colonizing and conquering impulse, on the other. This plays out in expected forms: Cortez's defeat of Montezuma, as described in "The Destruction of Tenochtitlan," which appeared in the *Broom* American issue. Yet it also inheres in the struggle between the outcast's self-assertion and the subsequent hatred of "the whole crawling mass": the native, indigenous self under colonizing assault by the mass. Washington, "the typical sacrifice to the mob," stands in simultaneous alignment with both Montezuma and Cortez, "courageous almost beyond precedent, tactful, resourceful in misfortune, . . . a man of genius superbly suited to his task" nonetheless "traitorously attacked [by Velasquez] from the rear," a man whose "own captains would have deserted him, so hard was he to follow."[55] Williams aligns the assertion of oneself as an American outsider with both nativity and aristocracy: to be an aristocrat is to remain outside the mass of the local community in which one resides—hence, perhaps, the significance of Montezuma, both native and king.

Encountered as part of *In the American Grain*, "The Destruction of Tenochtitlan" participates in the ongoing exaltation of an American aristocracy central to Williams's search for an indigenous genealogy of American identity and culture: that is, the standard account of the Americanist avant-garde as embodied, alternately, in the works of Williams, Toomer, Crane, and others. Yet as it circulates within and as part of *Broom*'s "American" issue, Williams's piece—like Toomer's "Karintha" and Crane's "Marriage of Helen and Faustus"—participates in a different kind of encounter with the Americas, one we might imagine somewhere between the "Americanist" approach and what Harris Feinsod terms "the meditation on ruins," the encounter prominent in North, Central, and South American poetry of the 1950s.[56] None of the works in the issue gaze or meditate on ruins. Nor do readers—even as they gaze on the photographs of Mayan architecture and statuary interspersed throughout or the pen-drawn illustrations of Mayan figurines and designs that accompany almost every piece of writing. These are, for the purposes of the issue, no more "ruins" than the love poetry of Shakespeare or Sappho are. Just as earlier explorations of romantic and sexual love are not ruins simply because they are earlier, so too, the earlier explorations of the encounter with the place, space, and history of the Americas are not ruins simply because they are old, weathered, or even partially collapsed. Ridge makes no claim that Mayan statuary laid the aesthetic foundation—or provided any influence whatsoever—for her own poetry or that of any of the issue's contributors. Rather, she makes the claim that they all participate in the same act of encounter and creation. We don't have to believe that Sappho "influenced" Shakespeare to read her fragments and his sonnets as participating in different temporal iterations of the same genre ("lyric," "love poem," "poem of loss," and so on). Here too, they engage, synchronically, in shared or overlapping genres. As a whole, the issue expands the temporal and geographic boundaries of American history, literature, and culture. There's an alienating effect, looking for genres shared not with the cultural history of Europe but with the Americas. The result, perhaps, is the ability to gaze on American art and landscape anew: to encounter them as an immigrant might. The one outlier, of course, is Stein's "Wear," which stands gallingly out of place. "January," Ridge lamented, "will not be the brilliant number that I could have brought out, but it will be good."[57]

"Stone Face" and the Situations of Poetry

Even as Ridge engaged in the writer's work of editing magazines, creating and maintaining extensive literary networks, hosting salons, and seeing her verse into print, she never stepped away from her commitment to political activism. This is apparent in numerous poems—on Sacco and Vanzetti (Italian immigrants convicted, in 1921, of homicide and executed after much protest in August 1927), Emma Goldman, Alexander Berkman, and the Irish labor boss Jim Larkin, among others. So too in her actions: during a protest shortly before the execution of Sacco and Vanzetti, multiple accounts insist, she stood firm when mounted police charged protestors; she was active in the Writers League against Lynching; on a visit to Gallup, New Mexico, in 1935, she organized fund-raising for the defense of striking miners.[58] Even from today's perspective, a century later, after the New Criticism's separation of the political and the poetic has long since been abandoned by both critics and practitioners, these seem like separate spheres of circulation. We find poetry, past and present, seeking to change consciences within the pages of little magazines, major literary journals (*Poetry*), and highbrow mass publications (the *New Yorker*, the *New Republic*). Writers don't hide their political convictions, instead taking to the pages of the *New York Times* to explain that these are no longer separate subjects.[59] None of these modes of circulation differ substantially from those explored so far in Ridge's career—or, if we're being totally frank, from each other. They are different in tone, reach, and limit, yes: but all are modes of bound, print circulation that are, in important respects, fundamentally *literary*.

For Ridge, however, the inseparability of activism from art wore down barriers, however imagined, between the modes of circulation natural to each. Although she never abandoned methods of literary circulation—she is at once skeptical of magazines, big and little, and optimistic; critiquing them, trying to change them, and continuing to publish in them; she would continue to publish books with mainstream publishers, reaching wide readership—she never limited herself to them. Indeed, political circulation may have been a more ideal venue for much of her verse. One of Ridge's twenty-first-century champions, Daniel Tobin, a poet and critic who has edited two recent volumes of her poetry, highlights the many failures of her later work. It is "highly romanticized," "melodramatic," "operatic and hieratic," and "baldly didactic."[60] Invoking W. B. Yeats's oft-quoted distinction between poetry and rhetoric, he deems much of her political verse failures: "Despite her passionate convictions, or perhaps because of them," he writes, she "gradually substituted the hyperbole of political and religious rhetoric for the genuine quarrel with self by which a poet advances both in the craft of making and in the achievement of a sensibility that continually tests itself against its own convictions."[61] Tobin, in fact, offers two lines of critique in these descriptions: some of her late poetry fails because it is too political, and some of it fails because it is too stylized (and, on occasion, both at once).

I want to suggest that we can think of these failures as products of circulation—where the way in which the text is transmitted and encountered doesn't enable it to produce its fullest meaning. In the cases of Ridge's too-stylized poetry, literary circulation has, in a sense, led her astray: her final two volumes, *Firehead* (1927) and *Dance of Fire* (1935), were her most widely circulated. While *Firehead* contains moments of formal virtuosity and brilliance, at others, it is overwritten, difficult to follow, or simply not engaging. It reveals the first step toward a deeply hermetic and inaccessible poetics, increasingly dependent on a return to traditional forms, best encapsulated in the opening sonnet sequence to *Dance of Fire*. Other poems, simply, are too political: within the context of print circulation, they appear too much like "rhetoric" rather than like "poetry"—not that we *have* to accept Yeats's dichotomy here, but insofar as his essay and thought like it continue to shape the reception of poetic meaning, we have to account for it. It's not the goal of

Ridge's most political poetry to prompt her readers to tetchily dismiss it as propaganda. She wants to move her readers—passion, emotions, and action are paramount in her descriptions of her poetics.[62] Many of these poems call for a mode of circulation built not for the quarrel of self with self of the lyric conventions that Yeats and Mill simply call "poetry" but of what Yeats deems "rhetoric": the quarrel of self with others. The key insight of historical approaches to genre and, especially, lyric has been that the expectations we, as readers, bring are what prevent or allow us to recognize it as poetry or participating in a particular genre. The same work, depending on how *we* situate it, can appear to be rhetorical propaganda or can circulate as poetry.

As the discussion of *God's Trombones* showed in chapter 1, examinations of publication history don't exhaust the story of a poem's circulation. At times, they can even foreclose access to the ways alternative modes of circulation create meaning and establish communities. But we shouldn't rest satisfied in the too-easy dichotomy of print and performance. While, on the one hand, I've been encouraging readers to reject their separation, even this rejection of contrast can mislead: performative modes of circulation are not the only alternatives to print. Or, I should say, they are not the only alternatives to *literary* circulation—the modes of circulation that establish a work within the supergenre of "literature": little magazines, poetry journals, book publication, anthologies, and textbooks.[63] These were the initial contexts of Ridge's "Stone Face": a first printing in the September 24, 1932, issue of *The Nation* and then inclusion in her final collection, 1935's *Dance of Fire*. Its readers since 2001 have disproportionately encountered it within a work of literary counterhistory, as one of many "Modern Poems We Have Wanted to Forget" in Cary Nelson's *Revolutionary Memory*. But it also circulated within, and as a part of, Ridge's political activism: in mailers, on broadsides, at labor rallies. These, indeed, would have been the circulatory routes by which the poem encountered the largest number of people—*readers* seems too limiting a term here—and met in this way, rather than on bound, glued, or stapled pages, her poetry flourishes, transforming literary liabilities into the means of solidarity.

"Stone Face" takes as its subject the imprisoned labor activist Tom Mooney. Perjured testimony led to his conviction for the 1916 San Francisco Preparedness Day Bombing that killed ten people and injured forty more. Despite public statements from the trial judge, jurors, and a federal commission that the conviction was in error, and despite support even from President Wilson, California governor James Rolph merely commuted Mooney's sentence from death to life imprisonment. Until his release, in 1939, Mooney served as a rallying point and important symbol for American and global labor activism; a 1935 survey found that, after Franklin Roosevelt, Charles Lindbergh, and Henry Ford, Mooney was the fourth-best-known American in Europe.[64] "Stone Face" met its largest audience not speaking *about* this cause (as a reading in *The Nation* or *Dance of Fire* would have it) but as *part of* the effort to secure his release: as one side of a large poster used at rallies on behalf of Mooney as he prepared to appeal his conviction to the California State Supreme Court. The poster was over two feet tall and nearly three feet wide (twenty-eight by thirty-four inches), and both sides presented images of Mooney. One demanded "FREE MOONEY," proclaiming him "A CLASS WAR PRISONER FOR 19 YEARS" and a "VICTIM OF MONSTROUS CAPITALIST FRAMEUP"; the other, under the heading "LABOR MARTYR IMMORTALIZED IN POEM," presented the full text of "Stone Face" (figure 11).[65]

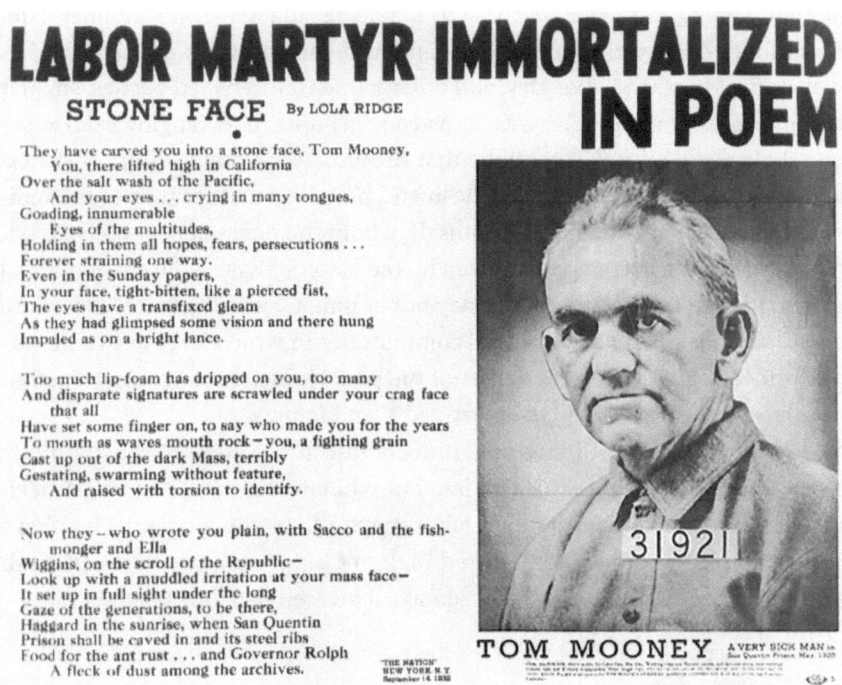

Figure 11. "Labor Martyr Immortalized in Poem, 'Stone Face,' by Lola Ridge, with Photo of Tom Mooney," poster (*Radical Responses to the Great Depression*, University of Michigan Special Collections Library and University of Michigan Library Digital Collections, Ann Arbor, MI, accessed April 24, 2017, http://quod.lib.umich.edu/s/sclradic/x-sce00669/sce00669.tif)

Recognized through the conditions and expectations of this context—public, collective, political—"Stone Face" quite clearly strives to establish solidarity among the individual members of its audience (and, perhaps, between its different audiences). The mechanism that produces this solidarity requires a mode of reading different from that of the encounter with the poem that circulates as a literary text. Virginia Jackson observes that the idealized lyric of mid- and late-twentieth-century criticism, in its total independence from history and society, was "perhaps not intended for public reading at all."[66] Nothing could be further from the case with "Stone Face." As with Johnson's *God's Trombones*, Ridge situates her poem outside the confines of isolated, silent reading. (That a 1927 publicity mailing for Viking Press advertised *God's Trombones* in a full-page ad adjacent to one for Ridge's *Red Flag* looks far less surprising in this context.) Distributed by organizations ranging from the Tom Mooney Molders' Defense Committee of San Francisco to the Chicago Federation of Labor, the poster was used as a fund-raising mailer for Mooney's defense fund, displayed in union halls and at demonstrations on his behalf as well as for May Day, Labor Day, and other parades. Interested parties, smaller text indicates, could purchase the broadside in bulk orders ranging from ten to one thousand copies.[67] The public that this broadside publication constructs and participates alongside—real, flesh and blood—is neither that of the individual reader nor Tom Mooney himself, whom the poem appears to address. "Stone Face" speaks to and is spoken by the labor activists who carried it and surrounded it, talking not *to* Mooney but *of* him, turning its voice, as well, to the larger local, state, and national communities in which its activist role was performed as the shared encounter of the poem joined these groups together in solidarity as they beheld the martyred Tom Mooney.

This encounter continues and, indeed, fulfills the goals of the distinctly American modernism that Ridge laid out while working on *Broom*'s American number. Through Mooney's labor martyrdom, she writes, "They have carved you into a stone face," "lifted high in California / Over the salt wash of the Pacific." This "face tight-bitten like a pierced fist" is "clenched" and

> set up in full sight under the long
> Gaze of the generations—to be there
> Haggard in the sunrise, when San Quentin
> Prison shall be caved in and its steel ribs
> Food for the ant-rust . . . and Governor Rolph
> A fleck of dust among the archives.[68]

Nancy Berke rightly notes that the stone imagery in this poem aligns Mooney with "the rocks worked by San Quentin prisoners."[69] Yet there's something more going on here: he's not merely transformed into broken rock but a stone face made permanent, one that will still stare out onto America long after the passing of the United States, when, as the *Broom* ad put it, "many races, many cultures have come and gone." Future generations will look on images and descriptions of Tom Mooney's clenched stone face as Ridge encouraged her own to look on the stone faces of Mayan statuary that populated *Broom*'s American issue (see figure 12). In looking on him now (or in the future), we participate in the recurring, immigrant encounter with the Americas in which both American art and American identity inhere.

These images, particularly the right-hand figure, illuminate Ridge's poem through their resemblance to Mooney's prison photo: the slight downward angle of the head, lips pressed into a thin line, the prominent ears. But whereas the gazes of the Mayan figures turn away from the readers of *Broom*, Mooney's stare directly at the reader in, as the poem puts it, "a transfixed gleam / as

Stone Figure   Stone Head   Palenque

Figure 12. Mayan statuary (*Broom* 4, no. 2 [January 1923], between 88 and 89)

they had glimpsed some vision and there hung / Impaled as on a bright lance." This is the same language that Ridge will later use in *Firehead* to describe the crucifixion, in which Jesus's eyes are the site of his prophetic energy and the light that streams from them resembles the Roman spear that pierces his side. "Pierced like a fist," stigmata appear on Mooney's face. "Stone Face" simultaneously and doubly transforms Mooney into a quintessentially American figure: a Depression-era iteration of *Broom*'s Mayan statuary and the Christological typology of "The Ghetto."

This, then, is what it means to read "a new art which mirrors as faithfully [as Mayan art] the astonishing environment they have made for themselves." "Stone Face" is an encounter with the place of the Americas: its history, its economics, its politics, and its landscape all at once, just as "The Ghetto" is. Far from the appropriative quest for the indigenous, Ridge's use of Mayan themes and photographs of statuary and ruins in *Broom* primes us to find their echoes and recurrences in very different forms today: a poem, a photograph, a labor leader's face. The stone faces included in *Broom* are models of a kind for "Stone Face," but Ridge avoids the primitivisms of figures as varied as Williams, Pound, Picasso, or even Zora Neale Hurston. The transformation into a stone face is Mooney's "passion eternal": it is a mark, and a result, of his suffering—but it is *also* the way in which he becomes American. As those who gaze on him might, too. In his face, framed by Ridge's words, they encounter the space of the Americas, the terms of the new covenant.

Together, the varied elements of this broadside—poem, picture, headlines—combine to function as a public and public-creating speech act. "A public," Michael Warner reminds us, "is constituted through mere attention": that is, not only does membership in a public require continuing to give it one's attention, but the act of attending to discourse is inseparable from the creation of the public.[70] The *kind* of attention one pays shapes both the public and the reception of discourse. To encounter "Stone Face" on its labor broadside is different than to encounter the poem in a book—whether that book is *Dance of Fire* or the page on which the broadside is itself reproduced here. "No single text can create a public," Warner continues; a public is "an ongoing space of encounter for discourse."[71] These are three distinct (though sometimes overlapping) spaces to circulate and encounter discourse: the printed volume of poetry; the academic monograph examining the history of a poem; and the labor rally at which the poem, printed alongside a photograph and headlines on a broadside, is displayed. Because the *other* speech acts within these discourses differ from setting to setting, the meaning created by the poem differs, too. Those who carried, displayed, or mailed the broadside announced their assent to its statements: that Tom Mooney is a martyr, has been framed, should be freed. Through Ridge's poem, Mooney becomes an American symbol. This, in turn, is set within the historically specific political agenda and social context of Depression-era labor activism. Deployment becomes a speech act announcing assent and calling on those who hear the speech (who see the broadside) to do likewise.

The reader of *Dance of Fire* experiences none of this. The volume creates and participates in a discourse markedly different from that of the broadside. Among its notable works, "Stone Face" is nonetheless only one poem among many, framed by those that come before and after. On the broadside, "Stone Face" and its public engage with a discourse space unaffected by, for instance, the opening sonnet sequence of *Dance of Fire*, "Via Ignis." These poems are highly crafted—and just as hermetically private. At least in part, the sequence laments Hart Crane's death (he appears to be the poet, compared to Percy Bysshe Shelley, whom the "sea enfolds" in sonnet 20); certainly, they represent an expansion of Ridge's exploration of the symbolic meaning of light and fire, motifs throughout her career. Lines like those that open sonnet 6 are characteristic: "Come, swanly Light, all the dim continent / Turns theeward slowly, lifting up the face / Of her delighted waters."[72]

Just as there's nothing inherently wrong with antiquated or grandiose diction, there's nothing wrong with dense, difficult, heavily symbolic poetry: chapter 4 of this book, after all, turns to Louis Zukofsky's *"A"*. But what kind of public participates in and gives attention to this type of discourse? One primed for careful reading and rereading to merely grasp the plain, surface-level meaning of lines. One that does not expect this poem, as speech act, to make an *urgent* claim on one's response—how could it, when what, exactly, it says must be puzzled out? Moreover, it's a public prepared to admire and acknowledge Ridge's formal control. This incomplete description points toward a fundamental difference in the kind of attention given by its public: for "Via Ignis," it is sustained, over multiple readings of twenty-eight sonnets divided into three sections; for the "Stone Face" broadside, brief, simultaneous instants of attention: the headlines, the text of the poem, shouts from the crowd, a glance at the photograph, the remainder of the poem. There's more to *Dance of Fire* than "Via Ignis," of course, some of it more like "Stone Face" than not. And just as "Via Ignis" shapes the reception of "Stone Face," so the latter suggests political overtones for the former. But by opening the collection and constituting a full quarter of its contents, "Via Ignis" carries outsize weight in outlining the public and announcing the discourse in which the full volume circulates.

Most importantly, *Dance of Fire*'s public is not bounded by a sharply historical temporality in the same way that the "Stone Face" broadside's is. My encounter with *Dance of Fire* in the twenty-first century differs, necessarily, from another reader's in 1935; but these two encounters share far more than my encounter, in an office, with the archival document of the "Stone Face" broadside through a library website and another's encounter, in 1935, with the same document in a mailer, in a union hall, or at a rally. "Stone Face," like many of Ridge's poems, best flourishes within time- and place-bound modes of circulation, addressing temporally ephemeral publics—in ways, that is, that we can't fully, or even substantially, recapture. We can talk *about* them, but we can't experience them. The meaning remains incomplete.

Here, then, is my answer to the question with which this chapter began: the various attempted recoveries of Ridge's poetry have each failed because her poetry does not always succeed or thrive in the contexts used for scholarship and pedagogy—the anthology, the textbook, the archive, sometimes (increasingly so with late works like *Firehead* and *Dance of Fire*) even within her own collections. Certain works do—"The Ghetto," notably—but others either are incomplete or, according to the norms that these modes of circulation activate, are quite reasonably criticized for failing to meet the terms of expected speech or discourse. This doesn't mean we can't or shouldn't value Ridge and her poetry. Far from it. Ridge's works insist on asking how and why poetry should circulate, never resting convinced that a given mode can produce a readership grounded in the ways we relate to others. They lead us to ask the same questions and stand as reminders that there is no one way of reading poetry—or even a single poem. By approaching Ridge's work in this way, we grow capable of attending to the ways her typological, aesthetic, and political visions intertwine, thereby recognizing the varied publics her poetry encountered and created. We cannot always participate in these discourses. Sometimes, as with "Stone Face," we can merely stand outside them and see their shape. Though it remains partial and incomplete, such work allows us to do more than recover Ridge's poetry. We can begin, as well, to apprehend it.

CHAPTER FOUR

Louis Zukofsky and the Poetics of Exodus

When we left Louis Zukofsky many pages ago, he was still a child, harried by a gang of Italian American schoolboys, reciting a Yiddish translation of Longfellow's *Hiawatha* to ward them off. Almost four decades later, we can find him, cigarette in hand, glasses thick as his eyebrows, teaching English at the Polytechnic Institute of Brooklyn. He's also, by 1948, two decades into work on *"A"*, the "poem of a life" that Hugh Kenner once deemed (not without cause) "the most hermetic poem in English."[1] Rail-thin and gray-haired, Zukofsky is no longer the wunderkind he once appeared to be, Ezra Pound's twenty-six-year-old protégé to whom Harriet Monroe turned over the January 1931 issue of *Poetry*. He's barely a poet's poet: with a new Red Scare in the making, Zukofsky warned his close friend William Carlos Williams to be willing to dissociate from him to protect himself; Pound, indicted for treason and declared insane, now published from St. Elizabeth's Hospital. During the war years, Zukofsky had, like George Oppen and others associated with the "Objectivist" circle, lapsed into silence.[2]

Zukofsky's students, future engineers, sit with one of his books open at their desks: not the early movements of *"A"* (still uncollected) or *55 Poems* or *ANEW*, the volumes of his shorter poetry brought out by the boutique, Prairie City, Illinois–based poetry publisher The Press of James A. Decker. The cover simply declares, *A Test of Poetry*. It consists of three parts: "Comparisons," "More Comparisons—and Considerations," and "Further Comparisons." Each is exactly what it claims to be: juxtapositions of related poems or excerpts stripped (in the first and third parts) of their author, date, and all other identifying information. The book's instructional premise is that by removing a poem from the contexts in which it circulates, you can get at the truth—and the causes—of its success or failure. That's the opposite of what I proposed in chapter 3: that, in the case of Lola Ridge, it's difficult (if not impossible) to understand the successes or failures of her poetry without taking modes of circulation into account. As a classroom exercise, Zukofsky's program has great merit: history and biography often do distract from a poem's content or form. I sometimes also ask students to analyze dateless, anonymized poems. Nonetheless, Zukofsky's anthology is just another way of circulating the poems it contains: it strips them of their historicity but not of their temporality. They can't escape the present, Brooklyn, the desktops.

And Zukofsky seems to have known exactly what he was doing. Self-published under the label of the mostly defunct Objectivists Press (founded in 1931 by Zukofsky, Oppen, and Charles Reznikoff), *A Test of Poetry* has been compared to Ezra Pound's 1934 *ABC of Reading*. But whereas Pound's work is a statement of poetics in the guise of a poetry primer, Zukofsky's *Test* actually *was* a classroom text.[3] In practice, the two books are in fact distinct exercises in constructing publics. "The test of poetry," Zukofsky writes, "is the range of pleasure it affords as sight, sound, and intellection. This is its purpose as art." But the notes and comments he appends to the comparisons in the book's second section clarify that this test should not be run according to merely subjective pleasure-taking, letting us hear the lessons he used the selections to teach: "Different attitudes toward things and events are at the base of different poetic content.... Poetry convinces not by argument but by the *form* it creates to carry its content." "*The Sonnet Form* is *not* a matter of 14 lines, set rhyme scheme, 10 syllables to a line, alternating ascending accents, as the rhetoric books have it. *Sonnet* literally implies the form of the short tune, to which certain Italian poets—Dante, Cavalcanti, and others—wrote words; the form involved the statement of a subject, its development, and resolution. Dissociated from music, a *sonnet* became merely the poor versification of amateurs, without emotion or sense of the relation of the parts of a composition to the whole." "The less poetry is concerned with the everyday existence and the rhythmic talents of a people, the less *readable* that poetry is likely to be."[4] And so on. *A Test* contends that the ways poetry produces pleasure are bound up with everydayness and the inseparability of poetic thought and poetic form—neatly aligning with the various artes poeticae that recur across Zukofsky's works. "*Nomina sunt consequentia rerum, / names are sequent to the things named*," he declares in the subtitle to "'Mantis,' An Interpretation" (1934).[5] Chiefly, a poem's subject determines its form. In the "Mantis" poems, he offers a Thomist account; in "A"-6, he enlists Spinoza: both *natura naturans* and *natura naturata* (nature as self-creating and nature as passively created according to natural forms) apply to poetry.[6] By stripping poems of author, history, and context, *A Test of Poetry* in fact circulates them in the service of creating a very specific kind of public: one primed and prepared to read and appreciate Zukofsky's own poetry. And, in fact, he would guide the best of these students into upper-level seminars where they read ... the poetry of Louis Zukofsky.[7]

Zukofsky's concern with the ways poems circulate and create publics (create publics *by* circulating) was long-standing. These questions were practical as well as theoretical. For much of his life, Zukofsky struggled to find audiences, publishers, and readers—particularly for the lengthy movements of his most important project, *"A"*. A case in point is *The First Half of "A"-9*, self-published as a pamphlet in 1941. The Zukofskys mimeographed fifty-five copies (the number needed to secure copyright) and distributed them, selectively, to friends, editors, and fellow poets.[8] This may have been born of necessity, but it demonstrates a striking awareness that devising specific and controlled modes of circulation offered a way to create the ideal readers Zukofsky would need for his life's project. He knew quite clearly who needed to read his poetry today in order to lay the foundation for a broader, future public. This contrasts sharply with the perspective that, until quite recently, has shaped Zukofsky scholarship: that he wrote strictly "for the desk drawer"—that is, without a public in mind.[9] This attitude in its effect produces an ahistorical reading of Zukofsky's poetry, a neutering of his early politics filtered through a preference for his later, post–World War II work, which turned increasingly to his domestic life for content. Cary Nelson, writing of many of Zukofsky's contemporaries on the literary Left, laments that, having repressed and forgotten them, we no longer know the history of early-twentieth-century American poetry.[10] Zukofsky's case is indicative of a related but distinct reaction to the politics of Depression-era verse. By insisting that his poetry should be read as the overheard thoughts of the poet at his desk (or even the poet strolling through New York streets), we re-create that poetry as antisocial and apolitical—even while acknowledging its political statements.

But if we situate *"A"* differently, Zukofsky's poetry starts to look like Lola Ridge's: a series of experiments in self-fashioned publics. Indeed, the starting point of *"A"*, the confluence of Easter and the first day of Passover, had already been taken up by the *New York Times* as a call for the renewal and revision of the United States' civil religious covenant. On April 17, 1927, a year before the opening scene of *"A"* and the weekend of the first Easter-eve performance of Bach's *St. Matthew Passion* at Carnegie Hall, the *Times* observed "that nearly the entire population is at the same time engaged in religious observances." Protestants, Catholics, and Jews, in a prefiguration of Will Herberg's influential study of American religion, joined in an "earthly kinship" of the "basic brotherhood of man" and, more importantly, a shared Americanness. "These are festivals of deliverance and promise," the *Times* opined. "And here in America, we have special reason to celebrate both."[11] Representatives of the major religions should, therefore, agree to fix the dates of both Easter and the beginning of Passover so that they *always* overlap.

The *Times*, in essence, calls for a reimagined Easter-Passover as a decidedly *American* holiday, joining the reenactments of the religions' covenantal encounters to the celebration of the covenantal discourse of American civil religion. While this isn't Zukofsky's aim, precisely, it is revealing: he joins Easter and Passover to re-create the covenantal encounter through the poetic encounter. The covenantal publics he experiments with are, again like Ridge's, formed while interrogating modes of circulation. But for Zukofsky, *circulation* is an expansive term, encompassing the circulation of people(s) across space and language as well as the circulation of text. "The poem," Barry Ahearn announces in his introduction to the 2011 New Directions edition of *"A"*, "is full of things in motion, from the very beginning": a harried and hurried Bach, the speaker's perambulations, trains, road crews, the history of immigration to the United States—Zukofsky's family story in particular.[12] These, in turn, blend into the formal experiment that guides the poem's structure, to answer the question posed at the end of "A"-6: "Can / The design / Of the fugue / Be transferred / To poetry?"[13] Etymologically, a fugue is a form of motion as well as a form of music: both the Italian *fuga* (its direct antecedent) and the Latin *fugere* refer to acts of running away, of flight. A fugue, then, can be understood as a specific form of motion captured in and expressed by music.

A fugue's flight, though, is not simply *away* but *around*, recurring, circular. So as Zukofsky seeks to write poetry that naturally expresses itself in this form, the poem's fugal structure merges with the covenantal reenactments that, once we listen for them, recur at the poem's center and its margins, beginning with the two, twined in the pages of both "A"-1 and the *New York Times*: Bach's *St. Matthew Passion*, which the poem's Zukofsky-like speaker attends, and his family's Passover seder, which he does not. Despite that absence, the Exodus represents a central, understudied structural and thematic element of the first ten movements of *"A"* (those written before Zukofsky's wartime silence), a motif moving in fugal counterpoint to the crucifixion of

Bach's *St. Matthew Passion*. The movement of people and peoples, cast in the language of Exodus, merge with covenantal history.

This chapter begins by examining that Exodus, first as the theme is established in "A"-1 and then as it recurs, in fugal variation, in "A"-6 and "A"-8. Situating *"A"* within moments of covenantal recollection and reenactment defines the public it seeks to create and casts the world-historical crisis described by "A"-10—the outbreak of the Second World War; the fall of Paris to the Nazis—as a crisis of *poetry* that, perhaps, can shed light on the poet's wartime silence. Poetry, *"A"* contends, can help to repair covenants damaged by history's horrors—but only by translating the contemporary audiences for art (like Bach's *Passion*) from an indulgent, self-flattering formality into the chaotic, "motley" audiences for whom it was first performed. In the New York of the 1920s, '30s, and '40s, this means the city's Yiddish press and literary scene. For Zukofsky, the very circulation of poetry is a covenantal act. But circulation, like any other term in his verse, can appear in a multitude of forms.

Memory and Metaphor

"When you were 19 months old," Zukofsky writes at the beginning of his essay "Poetry / For My Son When He Can Read,"

> your ability to say "Go billy go billy go billy go ba," much faster than I could ever say it, made me take some almost illegible notes on poetry out of my wallet. The time had come for me to fill the vacuum I abhorred in my life as much as you had filled it in yours. Though I was not too agile then, I hope you will sense reading me why I had forgotten my notes—had stopped speaking while I was not writing poetry. Three months were to pass before the atomic bomb was used that ended the Second World War.[14]

This twisting together of domestic life with world events and the creation of poetry suggests the direction that *"A"* would follow once Zukofsky returned to it after this three-year hiatus he references: the period when the United States was at war with Germany. Paul Zukofsky was nineteen months old in May 1945; V-E Day was May 8, precisely three months and one day before the bombing of Nagasaki. Not war's end, precisely, but the fall of Nazi Germany allowed work on *"A"* to resume—just as its rise had led Zukofsky to put the poem aside. To understand why this was the case requires us to think about the role of publics—how they are created, what they are for—and, ideally, what they should look like.

The answer begins on that scrap of paper in Zukofsky's wallet. Those "almost illegible notes" were by then eighteen years old. Somehow, after all those years in Zukofsky's wallet, they're still intact, at the University of Texas's Humanities Research Center. I've seen them; "almost illegible" is just about right: his handwriting was small and cramped; here, as in his correspondence, he made use of every corner of a page before turning to a new one. But part of the illegibility seems almost by design: he's layered ideas over one another in a visual record of the development rather than erasing or starting anew. As palimpsests, these notes and jotted plans begin to form notes in a musical sense, the ideas that will recur in combination and recombination as the chords of his fugal poem. Among these nested scrawlings, one note stands out: the words "an Exodus" in clear, bold handwriting.[15]

So we shouldn't underestimate the importance of the announcement, near the midpoint of "A"-1, that "It was also Passover."[16] From the beginning, the poem meant to set this Jewish narrative in dialogue with the New Testament's crucifixion story—and not just the narrative but the ways Exodus and crucifixion enter into the holidays of Passover and Easter. Both the passion play (of which Bach's *Passion* is a controlled, elegant, high-culture iteration) and the Passover seder are communal speech acts that create publics through the reenactment of the moments when covenants were first established. Uttered as the poem's speaker-protagonist—a more or less autobiographical version of Zukofsky—leaves an Easter-eve Carnegie Hall performance of the *St. Matthew Passion*, the declaration also serves as a reminder of what this speaker's family sits doing that evening as he strives to enter the sacred chambers of Western culture. As he listens to Bach, his religiously observant, Yiddish-speaking immigrant family reads from the Passover Haggadah on the holiday's first evening.

These settings are, culturally, quite different: Christian and Jewish, Carnegie Hall and the Lower East Side, and (importantly) the secularized space of the performance of Bach against the still-religious setting of the seder. Indeed, an evening performance in this secular space places Bach's *St. Matthew Passion* (at least in 1928) squarely within the much-earlier tradition that Regina Schwartz calls a "sacramental poetics": a response to a Reformation Eucharist without transubstantiation (Bach, keep in mind, was a Lutheran), itself part of the broader early-modern disenchantment of the world. Schwartz identifies two responses to this loss: to mourn it or "to displace their [the poets'] longing for that sacred world onto other cultural forms, to accommodate sacramentalism to modernity."[17] The sacrament—bread and wine as *in fact* the blood and body of Christ—displaced to representation (*as if* the blood and body) becomes sacrament*al*: a mode of signification. Schwartz finds this mode not only in the Anglican communion but in Shakespeare, Milton, Donne, and Herbert, whose works "interrogate why and how the impulse that informs the ritual could govern the poetry, how the spiritual cravings for communion with divinity addressed so fully by the Eucharist could also be addressed in poetry."[18] This 1928 Easter-eve performance of Bach's *St. Matthew Passion* functions, in New York City, in relation to the actual Easter Mass much as an Elizabethan performance of *Othello* would the Sunday Mass with which it competed and in some ways replaced: "a space where a community recalled, represented, and remembered sacrifice but did not endure it."[19]

The performance that Zukofsky attends on the first night of Passover creates a public through the shared act of recalling, representing, and remembering a covenantal sacrifice. Though (as we'll see when discussing "A"-4) *this specific* moment of covenantal public-creation seems to have failed in Zukofsky's reading—it does not propel the wealthy to care for the poor around them—it *does* contain the potential for a transformation of the Passover seder from "sacrament" to "sacramental" by displacing its reenactment of the Exodus onto poetry. Let's think about this, for a moment, by considering what it would be like for secular (or Jewish) audience members to attend the *St. Matthew Passion* and participate in its sacramental performance. God—in the form of Father, Son, or Holy Ghost—is absent, except as a performative fiction (and, perhaps, longing). In God's place—the cause that drives the public's creation, that stirs and moves emotions within the audience, that joins them in a public—stands music.

This is Zukofsky's model. Just as Spinoza, writing in the decades between Donne's death and Bach's birth, had removed the divine from philosophy and stood nature in God's stead, Zukofsky's poetry is an experiment in creating a covenantal public governed not by the divine but by poetry itself. Zukofsky does not attend his family's seder that April evening, but he transfers its design to poetry just as surely as he does the design of Bach's fugues. In the same motion: the story that *"A"* recalls, represents, and remembers is less the crucifixion (despite the *St. Matthew Passion*'s surface prominence) than it is the Exodus. People are constantly in motion: on city streets, between states, between countries, between languages, across time. Indeed, the biblical Exodus serves as a frame for both the poem and American history, recasting each as an immigration story: in Zukofsky's telling, much like Ridge's, the United States has been defined by the migration and immigration of peoples. In the historical vision of his Exodus, America is never a Promised Land or Shining City—always either Egypt itself or a harsh wilderness through which the freed Israelites wandered. This, as "A"-8 describes it, is "America's land of the pilgrim jews."[20] Like Reznikoff, Zukofsky does not reject typological readings of American history through the Hebrew Bible but insists that this means something quite different about the United States than is commonly believed. The Exodus provides a nexus in which the history and symbolism of religion, class, nation, and immigration converge, allowing "A" to examine American history as, fundamentally, the story of the circulation of its inhabitants, of migration and immigration.

For all this, Zukofsky remains outside the public created by Bach's *St. Matthew Passion* in "A"-1. There's a clear class difference: Zukofsky, the son of an immigrant pants presser, is surrounded by New Yorkers in jewels and formal wear. On the streets outside Carnegie Hall, they mingle, talking to each other—but not to him. All they can utter are banalities—even (especially) the most culturally literate among them, "Patrons of poetry, business devotees of arts and letters, Cornerstones of waste paper," whose observations can't extend beyond cliché: "Such lyric weather." The problem, of course, is that they don't *really* have any literary sensibility but just admire what they feel they're *supposed* to admire: "the sonneteers . . . / . . . / Immured holluschickies persisting thru polysyllables, / Mongers in mystic accretions; / . . . / Down East, Middle West, and West coast flaunters of the Classics and of Tradition."[21] Already, the failure of covenantal public-making is bound up with poetry and poetics.

It's not just that Zukofsky looks on these people skeptically. They look on him as an outsider. As the audience rises to depart the concert hall, an usher keeps his eye on a particular patron who seems out of place, as if he's trying to head somewhere he doesn't belong. "Not that exit, Sir!" the usher shouts—and again, four lines later, "Not that exit!"[22] The reality is more mundane: Zukofsky simply can't find his way out. It's from this recognition of Zukofsky as an outsider in Carnegie Hall that the first notes of the Exodus sound: the usher, after all, never tries to help him to an exit. Instead, he's trying to keep him *inside*. There are other oddities. As the audience rises at the end of the performance, "The lights dim[med]" and "Galleries darkened," rather than lighting the way out—so too, "blood," "bleeding," their proximity to "boys' voices" just before the poet steps into the street. As the notes of Bach's music fade, those of the Exodus begin to rise: the first, ninth, and tenth plagues; the utter darkness in which the Exodus took place; a figure of authority trying to keep a Jew from leaving.

The full description of Zukofsky's departure from Carnegie Hall only intensifies this effect:

> And as one who under stars
> Spits across sand dunes, and the winds
> Blow thru him, the spittle drowning worlds—
> I lit a cigarette, and stepped free
> Beyond the red light of the exit.
>
> The usher faded thru "Camel" smoke[23]

He does not simply *leave* but "step[s] free," following "the red light of the exit" to "sand dunes" "under stars," as the Israelites left slavery for freedom by following a cloud of smoke and pillar of fire. Both are found in his cigarette, the end of which glows red while emitting a stream of rising smoke. There's comedy in this, too: flecks of spittle, not the Red Sea, defeat his antagonist, allowing him to finally leave through the blocked exit while ignoring the usher, who, as he fades through the smoke, perishes like Pharaoh's army in the sea. This "'Camel' smoke" refers to the cigarette but also strengthens the connection to Egypt and the desert—not merely through associations that the animal carries with it. The cover of a pack of Camel cigarettes, even in 1928, depicted an Egyptian scene: a camel, pyramids, and palm trees standing on desert sands.[24] Even stepping free, Zukofsky continues to carry Egypt with him in his pocket. Like the biblical Israelites entering the Sinai, he steps into a world that hardly represents freedom. That desert wilderness swallowed the Exodus generation both literally and metaphorically, as again and again, the Israelites longed to return to the relative ease of slavery in Egypt rather than take on the task of building a redeemed world. Although the market hasn't yet crashed, the New York of "A" is in desperate need of spiritual and economic redemption. The poet's bejeweled fellow patrons grieve for the octogenarian Thomas Hardy—"he had to go so soon"—while ignoring the vision of "A tramp's face, / Lips looking out of a beard / Hips looking out of ripped trousers," that greets them at the doorway and, later, news of a strike in Pennsylvania coal mines.[25]

The images, characters, themes, and sounds that recur throughout "A" to form Zukofsky's Exodus first appear in "A"-1. The "great Magnus," who brags to other executives how he "ran 'em [his workers] in chain gangs down to the Argentine," reappears in "A"-6 conversing with Henry Ford, linking the type (a magnate) with the specific example—who is himself linked in "A"-8 with German and Italian fascists, Japanese industrialists, xenophobic congressmen, those who experiment on their workers, expelled the Jews from England, and enabled or defended African chattel slavery in the Americas.[26] If, on a Marxist reading, the Bible's Pharaoh is simply capital's embodiment exploiting labor for his own benefit, then we have found him here, during the Depression, in a constantly mutating form. Likewise, "A" ultimately casts labor as "Old Egypt's children," echoing the language of both the Passover seder and the biblical book of Exodus itself.[27] Within "A", history, like poetry, is fugal—so this Exodus repeats: in "A"-6, as the story of the American present, and in "A"-8, recurrently throughout American history from Plymouth Rock to the eve of the Second World War.

Written in 1930, "A"-6 depicts the poem's longest and clearest physical departure from New York City. Setting out, Zukofsky sees wasteland immediately:

New York, and then desolation
The steel works of Gary.
At Lake Michigan in Chicago,
Left a note he was going to Berkeley.

Desolation. Brush. Foothills of the Rockies.[28]

The voices of Pharaohs accompany him on this journey. Henry Ford holds forth for multiple pages about the economy, history, and culture: "Many people are too busy to be unemployed," "Industry itself is a part of culture," economic winners "got jobs because 'they didn't believe in Santa Claus.'" Ford is also the mouthpiece for simplistic views of poetry, the left-wing critique of the avant-garde that Zukofsky attributed to *New Masses* put in the mouth of a right-wing philistine: "I've read poetry, and I enjoy it / If it says anything, / But so often it doesn't say anything."[29]

Other voices begin, inexplicably, to stutter and stammer—to become, for a moment, like Moses's, "slow of speech and short of tongue."[30] Visions of water emerge from dry ground in a Nevada desert: "A roof, like a green sea," rises into view immediately before, in Reno, the poet is told,

You see this road thru the desert,
They call it a highway.
The Lincoln highway.[31]

This is not T. S. Eliot's "dead land"—even in the desert, there is light and life and a path to be followed. The voice of Moses persists, while the desert path Zukofsky follows is named for the Great Emancipator. The Exodus is physically and historically embedded within the United States: traveling the land recalls the past experience like musical themes, while analogies are drawn between the biblical Exodus, the history of American slavery, and the American present, in which a select few remain wealthy even while the nation's populace suffers during the Depression.

But when Zukofsky arrives in San Francisco, he doesn't find a land of milk and honey. Instead, the poem abruptly returns:

> Three thousand miles over rails,
> To adequate distribution of "Camels";
>   New York—Staten Island—
> Bay waters viscous
>   where the waves mesh.[32]

Completing the journey that maps the course of the Exodus onto the American continent doesn't achieve redemption. Instead, the cycle begins again: New York, in "A" and in Zukofsky's correspondence, is Egypt, "land of adequate distribution of Camels" and their pyramids, home to Magnus and his clothes closet.[33] But this isn't to say it ends in failure. History's structure, like the poem's, is fugal, neither strictly linear nor circular but something akin to a progressive spiral.[34] Or, as "A"-8 puts it, "History never *quite* repeats itself." So it is also (again) "Springtime when the energy under yoke freed" when Zukofsky returns to New York's Egypt: the season, that is, of Passover and the biblical Exodus.[35] The Israelites are freed by an energy—maybe their own, maybe something more than human—but this freedom comes "under yoke," the idiomatic expression of the covenant they establish with God at Sinai (that they were freed to receive the yoke of the Torah). New York—the present—is Egypt, but it is also Sinai, pregnant with the covenantal potential of that "never *quite*," of transforming the key in which the fugue's subject and countersubject recur.

In "A"-8, the Exodus repeats across American history—which, in its telling, is inseparable from the history of Jewish immigration. Indeed, Zukofsky's history of the United States begins with the 1654 arrival of the first Jews in New York (then the Dutch colony of New Amsterdam)—or, rather, the attempt by the colony's governor, Peter Stuyvesant, to expel them: "1655. All Jews are ordered to depart / From this place."[36] "A"-8 is the poem's first crescendo, threading together the notes, themes, sounds, and images of the previous seven movements over the same number of pages they, taken together, had required. The immigration story of Zukofsky's father, tales of religious persecution (early Protestant dissenters in the colonies and Europe's Jews), striking miners, and the works of the Yiddish poet Yehoash move around the dialogue between Henry Adams and Karl Marx that forms the movement's backbone, insisting that their discussion of labor and industry is also a discussion of human circulation.

As Zukofsky left Carnegie Hall in "A"-1, his lit cigarette offered both a pillar of fire and a cloud of smoke like those that guided the biblical Israelites; now, both continue to guide him throughout "A"-8. Light again and again is one of the poem's central, recurring subject-images, which the poem binds with the cause of labor, itself commanded to "Light lights in air, / on streets, on earth, in earth" at the movement's beginning and, with slight variations, in the closing line of each of the final four stanzas.[37] Labor itself, Zukofsky insists, serves as this light, guiding the people through the wilderness of history. Clouds of smoke occur in more localized instances but serve to connect labor-light with American civil religion, through the figure of Roger Williams, founder of Rhode Island, "the outspoken / Radical of his day." As Zukofsky wrote, in 1936, the state of Massachusetts had only just rescinded the 1636 decree exiling Williams for his advocacy of religious pluralism and tolerance. When "The 300 years banishment of Roger Williams / from Massachusetts" concludes, "a firm Cloud" appears in the sky.[38] Both the meteorological event and the duration of his banishment, corresponding to the length of time the Israelites were enslaved in Egypt, link Williams, like labor, to the symbolic nexus of the Exodus.[39]

So Zukofsky's father, Pinchos, in his telling, comes to "America's land of the pilgrim jews."[40] But in Zukofsky's understanding of history, characterized by the cyclical recurrence of "phases," what progress he finds in the story of Roger Williams or the constancy of light can't be the whole story. So Pinchos arrives in a country where the working class is explicitly enslaved, the people whom "The company is constantly / experimenting on"—or, in Minnesota, killing outright.[41] Another set of Pennsylvania coal miners goes on strike, eight years after the events of "A"-1.[42] History, rather than ending, spirals through new and different iterations of an Egyptian slavery from which the community continually struggles to free itself. In this account of American history, the freedom offered by "America's land of the pilgrim jews" devolves into armed conflict over African chattel slavery, echoes of which recur in the blue and gray of striking coal miners.

"You shall remember that you were a slave in the land of Egypt," Moses instructs the Israelites repeatedly near the end of his life. This is not simply metaphor but metaphor as ethics, capable of creating and renewing a covenantal public. In the absence of Moses's own commanding authority, the Israelites will continue as that public through the memory of slavery in Egypt. Through the cyclical failures and renewals of covenantal community in the Israelite kingdom, it is this memory, specifically, that is either recalled or forgotten: Josiah restores the kingdom to God from the idolatrous morass of his parents, Amon and Jedidah, by reading a rediscovered Torah scroll aloud to an assembly of the people. This isn't all five books of Moses but the last, Deuteronomy, Moses's book specifically. Josiah re-creates a covenantal public by reenacting the speech act through which Moses first established it. A different version of this speech act makes up the core of the Passover seder, in which a covenantal public is annually renewed through the recollection of having been a slave in the land of Egypt.

Through the application of the Exodus to the present and history of the United States, Zukofsky transfers this covenantal public-making to poetry, to *"A"*. He states this quite explicitly. One who "most probably will never read a line of verse" is necessarily also one "who most likely never having been to Egypt / Was 'never made blind by mummy dust.'"[43] To read poetry is to participate in the same act of moral imagination as to see oneself as having been a slave in Egypt. But not just any poetry. *"A"* notes when poetry readers fall outside this covenantal public, from the Carnegie Hall patrons to Henry Ford. What they *haven't* read—what would fail the quite different tests of poetry each applies—is *"A"*. It's worth taking a brief step back to restate what's going on here. I've been tracing the Exodus throughout *"A"* and ignoring Bach's *St. Matthew Passion*. But this isn't to say it isn't there: it is, always, right on the surface. Its importance has been clear since Barry Ahearn's 1983 *Zukofsky's "A": An Introduction*, the first monograph devoted to the poet. I don't mean to challenge this; rather, I'm arguing that the poem's transference of the *St. Matthew Passion* to the page engages in a very specific type of public-creation, one that, in fact, is quite different from what Zukofsky encounters at Carnegie Hall in *"A"*-1. The public that *this* performance of Bach creates is much more like that created by the Passover seder that Zukofsky fails to attend as the poem opens. He doesn't need to. He's got something far more ambitious up his sleeve.

Broken Covenants

On May 10, 1940, Nazi Germany invaded the Netherlands, Belgium, Luxembourg, and France. By May 15, only France still stood, but barely: Allied forces were evacuated from Dunkirk between May 26 and May 30. By the time the Luftwaffe began bombing Paris, on June 3, the result of the next week's offensive against the city already seemed inevitable. The French government abandoned Paris on June 13, and Nazi forces occupied it the next day. On June 22, Phillipe Pétain, newly marshal of France, agreed to an armistice that divided the nation. As German forces progressed, millions of French civilians took to the road, war refugees.

In New York City, Louis Zukofsky listened anxiously, angrily, for updates on *L'exode de 1940 en France*—the French Exodus of 1940—amid "baseball scores that matter / Or do not matter a damn," as Paris fell and Tours was ravaged by Luftwaffe bombs.[44] And then Zukofsky, like his government, went to work with renewed focus and energy. Franklin Roosevelt proclaimed the United States the "Arsenal of Democracy," instituting a peacetime draft, increasing defense spending, and beginning the push for Lend-Lease. At the same time, Zukofsky was spearheading the bilingual modernist quarterly *La France en Liberté*, "the review of Free France," along with René Taupin, the French-born Hunter College faculty member with whom he'd collaborated in the past. This juxtaposition is important: *La France en Liberté* represents more than a lament for Paris as the citadel of modernism; this project, though it ultimately foundered, was always more than just another "little" magazine. Beginning with the outbreak of war in 1939 and intensifying after the attack on Pearl Harbor, Jewish men across the United States threw themselves into preparations for the war that many of their fellow citizens sought to avoid until it was upon them.[45] Zukofsky was no exception, swept up with surprising intensity: the frail poet, self-proclaimed Marxist, nearing forty, applied to become an FBI translator in 1941 and, after this failed, for a commission in the US Army in the autumn of 1942. Rejected by both, he struggled to continue writing. War marked the period when *"A"* lay fallow.

La France en Liberté was an attempt—Zukofsky's first and most plausible—to join the Allied war effort. Its slogan announced its allegiance with Charles de Gaulle's London-based government-in-exile and "the struggle for free France." The magazine's clear purpose was to help rally the cultural elite behind American intervention—support that couldn't be taken for granted while Charles Lindbergh spoke to crowds at Madison Square Garden and Chicago's Soldier Field on behalf of an America First campaign that counted among its members Sinclair Lewis, Frank Lloyd Wright, Walt Disney, and the publishers James Medill Patterson (of the liberal *Daily News*) and Robert McCormick (of the conservative *Chicago Tribune*). On this front, perhaps, writers—even poets and avant-garde modernists—could meet the enemy and make genuine contributions. So the journal's Advisory Board stretched beyond Zukofsky's small circle of modernist and "Objectivist" allies: William Carlos Williams was the least-well-known figure on a list that included Yale deans, best-selling historians, Ernest Hemingway, and Albert Einstein. In London, as the Blitz raged, a newly minted air-raid warden named T. S. Eliot paced the roof of the Faber building by night and by day wrote "Little Gidding." An ocean away, Zukofsky quit his WPA job and devoted himself full-time to editing a magazine that, for reasons the records leave unclear, never appeared. He wrote "A"-10, initially under the simple title "Paris," for its inaugural issue.

This is a poem of broken covenants. Its structural inspiration, Zukofsky noted on the manuscript, was Bach's *Mass in B-Minor* (1749), and the language of the Mass ordinary peppers "A"-10 as the libretto of the *St. Matthew Passion* had earlier movements. But this is also an inverted Mass, a Black Mass: the Host is not consecrated but, as in satanic ritual, a woman's—in this case, horrifyingly, a *child*'s—body is:

> Holy
> Holy is Sylvie
>   A little girl
> Paul and Hélène's daughter[46]

This is in place of the *Sanctus* acclamation of the Eucharist: *Sanctus, Sanctus, Sanctus, Domine Deus Sabaoth; pleni sunt coeli et terra gloria tua* (Holy, holy, holy is the Lord of Hosts; Heaven and Earth are filled with Your glory). In the communion rites of a Mass, congregants then consume the Host—the bread and wine that are the body and blood of Christ. In the inverted communion of a Black Mass, the acclamation is said with the Host placed on a nude woman on the altar table; the practice is sexualized and, in James Frazer's account in that sourcebook of myth and religion for modernist writers *The Golden Bough*, connected to infanticide. It commits, at its core, the heretical act of Host desecration, the parody and violation of the covenant recalled and enacted by the taking of communion. In Frazer's account, the Mass of Saint-Secaire (the inverted Mass of the French countryside) "may be said only in a ruined or deserted church, where the owls mope and hoot, where bats flit in the gloaming, where gypsies lodge of nights, and where toads squat under the deserted altar."[47]

Such is the church in which we find, on the first page of "A"-10,

> All the people of Paris
> Mass, massed refugees on the roads
> Go to mass with the air
>   and the shrapnel for a church
> A Christian civilization
> Where Pius blesses the black-shirts[48]

The pope himself presides. In signing treaties with Mussolini's Italy (1929) and then Nazi Germany (1933) before maintaining, to international controversy, a policy of official neutrality during the war years, Popes Pius XI (1922–39) and Pius XII (1939–58) desecrate the covenant that they've been charged to transmit. This isn't simply the secular, Jewish Zukofsky criticizing what he understands as European Christianity's hypocritical acquiescence to fascism through a parody of his own creation. "A"-10 doesn't create but merely records the Black Mass, the covenantal violation, performed by the pope, the Nazis, and Pétain's Vichy government. Nonetheless, Bach's *Mass in B Minor*, among the composer's greatest achievements, continues to play in the background. Zukofsky isn't a Catholic by any means. But he *is* a poet—and a poet who loves Bach enough to place him and his music at the center of his poetics. It's not divine covenant that's been betrayed but whatever covenant art, music, and poetry at their most accomplished are capable of producing.

And, once more, it is also Passover. As in "A"-1, Sinai and Calvary play alongside each other. The desecration of the Black Mass also violates the integrity of one of the central speech acts of Jewish liturgy, the *kedusha*.[49] (The acclamation is a direct translation from this prayer's Hebrew.) Throughout the movement, the poet's eye remains firmly on those massed refugees, the millions streaming south in what the French understood, explicitly, as their nation's Exodus, the wayfarers given the resonant name *exodiens*. But the Black Mass that "A"-10 witnesses inverts the Exodus as well as Catholic liturgy. Listening to the radio in New York, the poet freezes in horror, muttering only, "The song passed out of voices / As freedom goes out of speech."[50] With the Israelites having crossed the Red Sea into their freedom, the first thing they do is stop their march and sing. They achieve freedom, that is, through musical performance that transforms them into a different kind of public. The refugees on France's roads can't perform this act of public-creation; even as they flee Nazis, their freedom evaporates.

Whereas in "A"-6 and "A"-8 America's history of immigration holds the promise of Exodus and revolution, "A"-10's fascists use forced migrations to impose their own order. Immigration promises multiplicity: of ethnicity, language, history, culture—a city, that is, always in motion. When Hitler speaks in "A"-8, he and his people are weary and desire to settle—Jews are to blame for their inability to do so. To accomplish this demands a destruction of any possibility of Exodus. They must, that is, kill Jews, throwing them "into middle Europe's rivers" or, on Kristallnacht, lynching them.[51] Hitler's speech pins the motion of Exodus on Jews alone: it is *the* Jewish condition, and one in which they attempt to immerse the world. Magnus and Henry Ford exploit laborers, but Hitler demands that humanity come to a full stop—that history end—that, motionless, nothing but death exist. Nazis are "the sailors who mistook their planet / for a light / And took the wrong soundings."[52]

The Nazis' threat manifests itself in an inversion of the symbols central to Zukofsky's Exodus. The guiding light of his cigarette, for example, becomes part of their "lightning attack" while civilians huddle "in the blackout" in fear of "the / stringed lights of the bombers."[53] Likewise, fascists do not simply prevent an Exodus into freedom but seize and transform it into its opposite. "Battered France halts her railroads / To freeze the flight south of her millions," while in Germany, "Feet trap all / Air traps all."[54] Escape is impossible because the borders are controlled—but also because the direction of migration is forcibly reversed: "Return return," proclaims Pétain's government. "Men women children of France / ten million / Troop back to your occupied north." Germany's war strategy is more than just blitzkrieg:

> Driving both aliens and citizens under dive bombers
> Herding peasants into firing onslaught of tanks
> Plotting plebiscites migrations
> Hunger for all but themselves
> Moving entire cities to certain death[55]

The Nazis do not merely kill—they deliberately drive, herd, move, and force migrations of people *from* freedom into "Slavery Penury Ruin."[56] Nazis first reverse the flow of immigration, from freedom now *into* slavery; then they seal borders, freezing people in place. They see Jews as the embodiment of the freedom of motion; they therefore kill Jews. In the context of the alignment in *"A"* of Exodus with American history, the diabolical anticovenant that the Nazis produce threatens to effectively unmake America.

Throughout *"A"*, Zukofsky has drawn on the communal, public-making speech acts of Judaism and Christianity as superstructures for his poetry—the representation or reenactment of Jesus's sacrifice and the recollection of the Exodus from Egypt at the Passover seder, which entails its own kind of transubstantiation: we, too, were slaves in the land of Egypt. Mapped onto the histories of labor and immigration, particularly as they guide the American experience, these Jewish and Christian communions operate as ways to produce a corporate public, whether the *corpus mysticum* of the Church or Judaism's *am Yisrael*. In a modernist iteration of the early-modern transformation from sacrament to sacramental, from actual to representative performance, these recollections and reenactments create a public—as with Ridge's poetry, a strikingly, surprisingly, decisively *American* public—through the focal sacrifices of labor and public-defining moments of circulation. Reading poetry, "A"-8 insists, is akin to declaring on the first and second nights of Passover, "This is what the Lord did for *me* when *I* went out of Egypt." Those who read poetry have "been to Egypt," where they were "made blind by mummy dust." That is, the public created by Zukofsky's refiguration of American history transforms the meaning of the typological image, "America's land of the pilgrim jews."[57] The true meaning of being a chosen people is not greatness, power, or election but to take one's place among the demeaned, marginalized, and oppressed, to think of oneself as a slave in Egypt—and not just in Egypt. Circulating as a thrust on the cultural front of the fight for a free France, "A"-10 would have engaged in a particular, specific kind of public-creation: a readership established through its rejection of the Black Mass, yes, but also through the typological imagination. Zukofsky has transformed the French into refugees, *exodiens*—which is to say, into "pilgrim jews," into Americans. "A"-10 is an urgent call for a historically isolationist nation—and, perhaps, the Anglophone literary movement that was too sympathetic, at least initially, to fascism's rise—to recognize itself as part of the same public that was physically threatened by the Nazi blitzkrieg and race laws.

And yet. "The poet stopped singing to talk," Zukofsky declares as "A"-10 moves toward its close, a silence he references again in the opening paragraph of "Poetry / For My Son When He Can Read." Only the poetic rhythms and sounds of his son's early speech in days following the official surrender of Nazi Germany allow him to break this silence. He didn't stop writing poetry completely. Though his pace slowed markedly during the war years, he continued to work on a handful of short poems. The pause, which he alternately refers to as either the cessation of song or a lapse into *total* silence, was limited to *"A"*. I've tried—hopefully with success—to outline the ambitious vision the early movements of *"A"* propose for what poetry is and should do. Zukofsky is not merely a Poundian or a Marxist. He's also a Spinozist. Spinoza, faced with his inability to believe in the God of Abraham as either a personal God or the God of history, stood nature in place of the divine: *natura naturans, natura naturata*. In place of nature—perhaps as just another way of imagining it—Zukofsky offers poetry. Poetry can create publics, joined in covenant, and govern those covenants.

Nazi Germany, particularly as depicted in "A"-10, challenges this claim. I want to be very careful here not to engage in armchair psychologizing. The metaphor I would like to use is that the poet, unable to sing or speak, has suffered a crisis of faith: that his poetry might be just as unreal as his father's God. To do so, however, would be to read not Zukofsky's mind but my own, in which the two are deeply intertwined. So I will limit myself to this characterization: across the Atlantic, there was, as Alan Jacobs has narrated, a crisis of Christian humanism among major English and French literary figures.[58] Those he surveys in *The Year of Our Lord 1943* responded with a tendency to overproduce—and to produce excellence: Eliot's *Four Quartets*; Auden's "For the Time Being," "The Sea and the Mirror," and *The Age of Anxiety*; fifteen books by Jacques Maritain; Simone Weil's brief, flaming burst of an oeuvre. Zukofsky, on the other hand, produced very little, much of it minor. Both the crisis of Christian humanism and Zukofsky's silence emerged from the same event: the war that threw not just the survival but the very purpose of poetry into question. The world that "A"-10 sees being established in Europe is not just a world without Jews, a world without mercy, but a world without poetry—a world in which humanity is wholly, totally alone, with nothing to bind and obligate us to one another, governed not by the perfect, self-creating, self-created laws of Spinoza's nature but by Tennyson's "nature red in tooth and claw."

Circulating Yiddish

Yet *"A"* is hardly a poem of despair. The conflagration of the 1940s may represent a covenantal break, but covenants are not mere contracts. When broken, they are not discarded but repaired, restored, and renewed. From its very first pages, *"A"* found itself faced with this challenge. As we've seen, its Exodus narratives don't present the United States as any kind of nation in which the covenant is fulfilled. Rather, the poem starts from the most basic step: to create a readership that recognizes itself as part of a covenantal public.

Consider that, for all the structural importance of the *St. Matthew Passion*, for all Zukofsky's idealization of Bach, the opening page of "A"-1 expresses deep dissatisfaction with the piece: not with the music or the performance itself but with the kind of public this evening has created. Wearing diamonds and formal evening wear (the "Black full dress of the audience"), the concert-goers ignore beggars and the pressing social issues of the day. They don't even seem particularly moved by the music once they step outside Carnegie Hall—unlike Zukofsky, who spent much of the rest of his life turning it over and over in his poetry. They're not likely to be a public receptive to or capable of recognizing the music of the Exodus. They don't even seem to understand the crucifixion. Certainly, they aren't the kind of public that first gathered to hear Bach's *Passion*, the "motley"

> Country people in Leipzig,
> Easter,
> Matronly flounces, starched, heaving,
> Cheeks of the patrons of Leipzig—
> "Going to Church? Where's the baby?"
> "Ah, there's the Kapellmeister
>   in a terrible hurry—
> Johann Sebastian, twenty-two
>   children!"[59]

Harried, poor, wearing whatever they had been wearing—this "motley" public bears more in common with the working poor of Zukofsky's Lower East Side childhood than with the wealthy of a "Dead century."

Such publics, in fact, gathered regularly in Carnegie Hall during Zukofsky's childhood and early adulthood: not only the home of the New York Philharmonic and the nation's most prestigious venue for classical music, it also hosted major events for New York's Yiddish literary culture. The most famous of these took place on June 17, 1916, when the memorial service for the Yiddish writer Sholem Aleichem (best known as the creator of Tevye the Dairyman) packed the main auditorium to capacity. "There were no jewels to be seen in the tier boxes," the *New York Times* wrote the next day. "And there were few limousines in front of Carnegie Hall last night," for the mourners "were not aristocrats, but plain folk." Physically, they make for quite a contrast with the concertgoers around Zukofsky in "A"-1: "The hats that were put on in respect to Sholem Aleichem at the beginning of the funeral hymn 'El Mole Machemin' [sic] . . . were dusty hats that showed the signs of long journeys in the rain. The hands that lifted them were stained, too, and they shook. The seats that were filled first in the hall were the cheap seats, seats that sold for a dime. . . . Few were able to get seats in the more expensive sections that were finally thrown open to all."[60]

Of course, this was a memorial service; and there's no evidence that the twelve-year-old Zukofsky was present (though he may well have been among the several hundred thousand who, a month earlier, lined his neighborhood streets as the famous author's funeral procession passed). But the setting is not nearly as different from *"A"* as it may seem at first glance. The *St. Matthew Passion*, after all, laments a death—and there's mourning aplenty in the earliest movements of *"A"*, those to which Zukofsky worked before turning outward, toward national and class history. In "A"-3, it's his friend Richard Chambers; in "A"-5, his mother; and in "A"-4, the Yiddish poet Yehoash, author of the translation of Longfellow's *Hiawatha* that Zukofsky once recited from memory to ward off schoolboy gangs and among the most prominent and ambitious figures in American Yiddish literature. Yehoash, too, had sold out Carnegie Hall: in December 1913, as he prepared for an extended trip to British Mandatory Palestine, a crowd gathered to celebrate his works. The "Yiddish Milton," as the *Times* described him, received a fifteen-minute standing ovation when he tried to slip in, late and unnoticed. The celebration included readings of his poetry, sometimes set to music—by a violinist, the *Times* noted, and by a sixty-person children's choir that tempts comparison to the twenty-two-child chorus that Bach herds along in "A"-1.[61]

As *"A"* sets out to re-create a public that resembles the Leipzig crowd that attended the *St. Matthew Passion* in 1727, Zukofsky draws forward Carnegie Hall's history as a focal point for Yiddish culture—a literature, even at its most experimental, read and created by people like him, the immigrant poor and their children.[62] "Publics," Michael Warner writes, "are essentially intertextual, frameworks for understanding texts against an organized background of the circulation of other texts, all interwoven not just by citational references but by the incorporation of a reflexive circulatory field in the mode of address and consumption."[63] Zukofsky's avant-garde intertextual practices are *also*, simply, the ways that publics emerge: through the circulation of texts, through the intersection of different texts (and the different routes a single text might follow), and, as well, through the communal reflection on these routes. "And that circulation," Warner adds, "though made reflexive by means of textuality, is more than textual": it's physical, we might say, contained in the way that those publics themselves circulate.[64] And it's also spatial, as in the way Carnegie Hall has served as a premier venue for both the highlights of western European culture and the momentous cultural events of a small, poor, multilingual immigrant community.

Engaging with American Yiddish literary culture and, particularly, the poetry of Yehoash serves as a central, pivotal act of reparative public-creation. It's the catalyst that transforms the public of the *St. Matthew Passion* from their diamonds and evening wear into an immigrant "motley" prepared to read *"A"* by the years they've spent reading New York's Yiddish dailies. In *"A"*-4, Yiddish erupts into the poem, informing all that comes before and after. Pairing translation and immigration, it casts them as linked modes of circulation—one through space, the other through time. Here, we discover an Exodus that takes place through circulation across languages rather than physical space. Such translation stands at the core of the argument between the Jewish "elders" and "youth" at the movement's center, though only the younger generation recognizes it. The "aged" and weary elders have grown accustomed to exile and fetishize their wanderings: "Wherever we put our hats is our home," they insist. "Our aged heads are our homes." The youth, whose "Deep roots hammer lower," are at home in the United States. Onto this debate about spatial exile and rootedness, both generations transpose their linguistic differences. "We had a Speech," the elders lament; "our children have evolved a jargon," a charge they repeat immediately before the movement pivots to a series of translations from Yehoash.[65] The younger generation speaks about rootedness *through* these translations. The elders, in their exile, are linguistically settled. By contrast, as the youth of Zukofsky's generation grow more rooted in American life and culture, they grow more comfortable in motion across languages—indeed, live their lives within acts of translation.

"Jargon" isn't just vernacular. It's Yiddish, specifically—and the dichotomy between jargon and "Speech" roots *"A"*-4 in that language's history. Even its champions regularly referred to Yiddish as *zhargon*—jargon. Its detractors, on the other hand, contrasted it with a capital-*S* Speech—whether they were Hebraists in the early-twentieth-century Jewish language wars or non-Jewish German linguists.[66] Of course, both generations in this dialogue know Yiddish—so speaking jargon becomes an act of broader meaning. In doing so, the elders lament, "Our own children have passed over to the ostracized."[67]

Here, again, we find echoes of Spinoza, the seventeenth-century prodigy whose abandonment of religious orthodoxy for a secular, freethinking philosophy was lamented—but also punished with *kherem*, excommunication. Who are those who have been ostracized and cast out in the world of "A"? Jews, immigrants, workers, those who, like the bearded rag-worn beggar in "A"-1, have been politically or economically cast aside, those who are—or have been—slaves in Egypt.

And they are also the modernist avant-garde. Even as the high modernists Zukofsky admired, emulated, and challenged grew increasingly well-known, this was often as objects of bemusement, newspaper parody, or scandals of vulgarity.[68] Zukofsky, writing in their idiomatic jargon, also felt himself ostracized for the choice. This, indeed, was the original context of "A"-4's debate between elders and youth. As printed in *An "Objectivists" Anthology* (1932), the elders are clearly the editors of the *Menorah Journal*, then the nation's leading Jewish intellectual and cultural magazine (and a frequent outlet for Reznikoff's poetry). They'd just rejected Zukofsky's offer to translate selections from the best-selling novelist Sholem Asch's new book, *Di mutter*, and an essay that, as "Sincerity and Objectification, *With Special Reference to the Work of Charles Reznikoff*," would eventually become the central critical statement of the "Objectivists" issue of *Poetry*. They *did* however, take the time to print a tetchy essay by Mark Van Doren in which Zukofsky appeared as (in his versified retelling) "a pale and / Subtle poet who was not in fact / Lazy" but whose "Painfully inarticulate soul forbids" Van Doren "to use him for any purpose."[69] When he returned to "A"-4 in the first months after the United States' entry into World War II, Zukofsky's substantial revisions excised the entirety of the *Menorah Journal* complaints.

Translation, labor, modernism, immigration, the Exodus are all forms of circulation running through *"A"*, brought together through Yiddish like threads through the eye of a needle. So it shouldn't surprise us that the Exodus is present from the very beginning of "A"-4. Its opening, considered visually, reenacts the pivotal moment of the biblical Exodus, the crossing of the Red Sea. A narrow stretch of words, oriented at the center of the page, divides (provides dry land in the middle of) the page's sea of white space as Zukofsky gazes across the East River toward a carousel. The words that stream through it describe a "Tide" among a series of lights—even "Lanterns swing behind horses" as they cross the page-sea.[70] The same points of light that led him from Carnegie Hall in "A"-1 and through American history in "A"-6 and "A"-8 continue to lead the way. On the other shore, the carousel's mechanical horses repeat their journey, reviewing the city in a recurrent, circular transit. These images, central to Zukofsky's Exodus, prompt the debate between elders and youth. The latter's voices dominate the closing pages of "A"-4, filtered through translations of Yiddish poetry—specifically, a translation about a wandering samurai written by a Yiddish-speaking, immigrant New Yorker, itself probably a loose "translation" from legend or folklore.

This poem, "Shimone-san," was written by Yehoash, the pen name of Solomon Bloomgarden (1872–1927). Born in present-day Lithuania (then part of the Russian Empire), Yehoash immigrated to New York in 1890. He was in many respects a boundary-breaking transgressor, and his reputation was founded on his incorporation of the foreign and "exotic" into Yiddish. Zukofsky described the arc of his career in a 1974 letter to Hugh Kenner: "starting out in the 1910's or earlier sounding like Heine, he ended up with 'freer' American forms, western subject matter & Japanese, Chinese, Palestinian travels etc (had lived in Colorado etc to cure (?) his TB)."[71] His best-known and most influential works were translations into Yiddish: *Dos lid fun Hayavata* (1910), which the young Zukofsky recited to ward off anti-Semitic bullies, and a translation of the Hebrew Bible into Yiddish, published serially in the pages of *Der Tog*.[72] Zukofsky's career as a poet began with an attempt to bring Yehoash's Yiddish into English modernism. In 1920, still a sixteen-year-old Columbia freshman, he submitted translations of Yehoash's works to *Poetry*, announcing in his cover letter that Yehoash "is, as you may know, one of the greatest Yiddish poets."[73] Harriet Monroe demurred, but these translations are among the few pieces of his juvenilia that were not eventually disowned as the work of "Dunn Wythe."[74] Instead, Zukofsky incorporates them into "A"-4.[75]

Along with "Shimone-san," a second poem, "Tsu der zun" ("To the Sun"), is also translated at length in "A"-4. They first appeared in the January 19, 1919, and September 26, 1920, editions of *Der Tog*, the Yiddish daily that Zukofsky read through at least 1928, while he was still living in his Yiddish-speaking father's home, and acknowledges as his working source for "A"-4. As was almost always the case, Yehoash's poems appeared on the paper's middle sheet, on the left-hand page typically reserved for coverage of arts and culture, set apart from the rest of the text in larger font and framed with a stylized border. The paper's editorial page and a political cartoon sat across the fold. Yehoash's poems, including those not incorporated into "A", were surrounded by works of literary criticism, political essays, and serialized novels. Luminaries of Yiddish literary culture and political activism—Avrom Reysen, Chaim Zhitlovsky, Nahum Syrkin, H. Leyvick—all appear.[76] On the days that

"Shimone-san" and "Tsu der zun" were printed, adjacent literary essays link them with the Yiddish avant-garde. A column by the writer and critic Shmuel Niger appears directly above, objecting to the aestheticism of the new *Inzikhist* movement of Yiddish modernist poetry. The *Inzikhistn* and their eponymous journal, *In Zikh*, were a decidedly American school of Yiddish modernism influenced by Pound and Eliot—on occasion, they have been compared to Zukofsky and other "Objectivist" poets.[77] One of the central figures of this movement, an editor of its journal and signatory to its manifesto, also appeared regularly in *Der Tog*. A. Glantz (known among *Inzikhistn* as A. Leyeles and alternately in scholarship as A[ron] Glantz-Leyeles) sparred regularly with Niger on questions of aesthetics and politics over the course of the 1920s. These columns appeared frequently on the same page as Yehoash's poetry— and directly below "Tsu der zun."

Looking at how Yehoash's words, well before they entered "A"-4, were originally situated within *Der Tog* lets us encounter the expansive way in which Yiddish enters "A": to ask not simply "How does Yiddish circulate *in* 'A'-4?" (that is, to examine Yehoash's translations in that context alone) but "How does 'A' circulate Yiddish?" (that is, how does translation extend *beyond* "A"-4 and inform its broader project of public creation?). Founded in 1914, in the years immediately following the First World War, *Der Tog* reimagined itself as a newspaper for educated, intelligent readers. Major literary figures were among its contributing editors. (Yehoash, Niger, and Leyeles, among others, all held the title.) High literary culture existed alongside coverage of strikes, the lampooning of tycoons, name- and off-brand product advertisements, parenting columns, children's stories, and the perpetual back-page ad for Ex-Lax, proclaiming each day to "Mames!" (Mothers!) how much easier it is to silence children at bedtime after they've been fed a spoonful.

The daily images and phrases of *Der Tog* are those that define Zukofsky's Exodus. For instance, light—a major conceptual point of reference throughout the poem as a whole and especially for its Exodus—is also an important image in *Der Tog*'s self-fashioning.[78] Its masthead at the time that the Yehoash poems translated in "A"-4 were first published offers two distinct English and Yiddish slogans. The English—"The National Yiddish Daily"—is a claim of credibility. The Yiddish, on the other hand, is an idealistic yet concise statement of purpose: "'Der Tog' brengt likht"—*Der Tog* (The Day) brings light. This guiding light recurred every day in the paper's logo—a globe bracketed by two lit torches—and throughout the poems Yehoash regularly published in its pages.[79]

When first encountered in "A"-1, this guiding light takes the form of the flaming tip of Zukofsky's cigarette. It is, notably, a Camel. The image of its 1928 packaging—a camel, a desert, and three pyramids—proliferated in ads on the pages of *Der Tog* over the course of 1919–21, as the Yehoash poems included in "A" appeared. Indeed, one version of this ad seems to presage the recurrence of Zukofsky's guiding cigarette in "A"-5, when it also contains an image of the New York cityscape: "A cigarette, / Leaf-edge, burning / obliquely urban" (figure 13).[80] In this ad, as the disarranged cigarettes peek out from the open packaging, they cast a shadow on the page. This shadow, however, does not match the even cylinders of the cigarettes: it is, indeed, "obliquely urban," looking more like a cutout of an urban skyline than an accurate representation of the shadow the package should have cast.[81] Camels, it wants to say, are a *New York* cigarette. As they were. Beginning in 1941, as Zukofsky made final revisions to the first movements of the poem, Camel's famous smoke-blowing Times Square billboard became part of the New York City landscape, its most notable ad, and "Fading thru Camel smoke," as Zukofsky puts it in "A"-1, took on a more literal meaning. In the ad's foreground, the torn foil wrapper crinkles like the desert—this is, indeed, Zukofsky's New York as Egypt, embodied in the Camel cigarettes he smokes. (The billboard stood until 1966.)

Advertisements from this period reveal that cigarettes and Egypt were firmly connected in the minds of both readers and advertisers. While occasional ads by the likes of Prince William cigarettes tried to make a pitch for the high-class elegance of British tobacco, the overwhelming majority of those appearing in *Der Tog* seek to capitalize on the exoticism of their brand—and that exoticism, no matter the origin of the company or product, seemed to be best highlighted through Egyptian imagery, sometimes taking up half a page. Consider the various ads for Helmar cigarettes, which appeared in *Der Tog* from 1919 to 1920 (figure 14). One promises, in both English and Yiddish, that these cigarettes are made from "100%" Turkish tobacco. To reinforce this fact, the company adorns the packaging with . . . the profile of a pharaoh and pillars of hieroglyphics?

Egyptian pharaohs are not the only ones depicted in this newspaper. Zukofsky's modern pharaohs are alternately critiqued and lampooned—tycoons and magnates—on the editorial pages opposite those containing Yehoash's poems and discussions of modernism, as in an August 3, 1919, cartoon, which first appeared on the page directly opposite Yehoash's "Af di khurves," which Zukofsky translated at length in "Poem Beginning 'The'" (figure 15). Here, we

Louis Zukofsky and the Poetics of Exodus   153

Figure 13. Advertisement for Camel cigarettes (*Der Tog*, November 13, 1919, 8)

see a man who might as well be Zukofsky's Magnus, the wealthy tycoon who figures prominently in "A"-1 and "A"-8. Rotund, gleeful, and bursting from his vest and suit pants, he has been placed on a pedestal so that he will be taller than Uncle Sam, even when the symbol of America stands erect. The label on his belly, "yekires," can refer to famine, scarcity, high prices, or the one who

Figure 14. Advertisements for Helmar cigarettes and Wrigley's chewing gum (*Der Tog*, June 18, 1919, 9)

Figure 15. Cartoon (*Der Tog*, August 3, 1919, 6)

insists on them—implying, in this case, that his demand for high prices has caused scarcity and hunger and that the profits have gone straight to his belly. On September 9, 1919, the same figure appears again, labeled as "koilen magnat"—coal magnate—the exact role Magnus plays in "A"-1. Meanwhile, Uncle Sam lambastes a hapless miner. Opposite the fold is the poetry of Yehoash. On the front page is news that immigrants were being arrested as "radicals" nationwide in connection with the advent of a major United Mine Workers strike.

These newspaper pages speak, moreover, in jargon. Consider the ad for Wrigley's chewing gum alongside the half-page "Egyptian" Helmar's ad in figure 14. Idyllic versions of Wrigley's ads and billboards recur throughout "A", where the "wriggly Wrigley boys" signal the transition between urban and pastoral on cross-country rail.[82] This ad depicts a grandfather holding a child in one arm and the gum in another: a product for the older, Yiddish-speaking readers to share with their American offspring. Like the scene of intergenerational strife in "A"-4, this moment of unity also occurs linguistically. The ad presents the bold-type brand name—Wrigley's—in both English and

Yiddish. But their different alphabets require that the name be transliterated as "Rigli's," a nonsense word that carried echoes of Yiddish words not for gum but for graters (*riglen*) and basting (*rigel*). The same brand name functions as both a visual and aural signifier: the shape of the English word "Wrigley's," housed within the company's logo, informs a Yiddish-literate consumer that this is the brand they're after just as much as the sound of "Rigli's" does. Its copy proclaims the company's slogan and selling point: "Der fleyvor blaybt" (The flavor lasts). *Fleyvor*, however, is *Amerikaner* Yiddish, the kind of Englishism the Yiddish literati sniffed at: *riekh* or *tam* would be more appropriate. Here we have, by the standards of "proper" Yiddish, another visual nonsense word. The result is a language held within the moment of translation, neither fully Yiddish nor fully English, suggesting an understanding of language that would shape Zukofsky's poetry: the word as object; the centrality of homophonity to meaning-making; the pun as a mode of exegesis; the ability for a word that, in one form, appears to be nonsense to still signify.

Zukofsky returns to what he already knew, implicitly, as a child: that translations are necessarily public speech acts, no matter the nature of the original being translated. Translations presuppose the existence of an audience for the work they perform. But more than this: what and how he translates creates the nature of this public—can even transform its nature. So he had done, cornered by an Italian schoolyard gang, by reciting Yehoash's Yiddish *Hiawatha*: and though there may not have been any covenant formed on that day, this recitation *did* transform the gang from the public created and defined by anti-Semitic narratives into one that listened to Yiddish poetry. Though the boys didn't know what to make of it, though they mocked him, it was lighter now, their violence contained. The same event bursts forth in "A"-4: Zukofsky pauses, turns, and recites Yehoash's poetry—this time, translated into English, rather than his translations from English into Yiddish. This presupposes a public quite different from that of the Carnegie Hall performance of Bach's *St. Matthew Passion* (and perhaps the fact that the Gospel of Matthew includes a notoriously anti-Semitic account means that the Passion itself shouldn't be overlooked here). They listen to jargon now; they listen to modernism; they listen to a language that is, quite literally, Jewish. Clad in motley, they're prepared to take their places among the ostracized.

"A"-4 not only depicts a translational Exodus but infuses this quality across the early movements of "A". An Exodus was there from the start: in "A"-1; in the outline that Zukofsky carried for decades in his wallet. But this Exodus doesn't simply circulate people from place to place. It also circulates their words among languages. And it's through this movement, through translation, that an internal movement can finally take place. By reading these lines of verse, reading, thinking, speaking in jargon, one comes to think of oneself as having been (so to speak) a slave in Egypt—whether that Egypt is today's New York, France in the summer of 1940, or any other place in American history. "A"-10's bleak reading of the outbreak of World War II seems to invert this Exodus and its parallel Mass and in so doing to uproot any covenantal public they may have formed. But the poet's silence wasn't permanent. With the fall of Nazi Germany, with his son's discovery of language, he could return to "A". And, as he would write in "A"-12—challenging either explicitly or by coincidence Theodor Adorno's declaration of the same year that to write poetry after Auschwitz is barbaric—"If it sang then / It still sings."[83]

Reading Together

The ways "A" circulated changed in the years after the war. Both its scale and its readership grew as Zukofsky completed and published its second half. It did not happen with alacrity or without acrimony, however: that New Directions put out editions of Reznikoff's and Oppen's poetry but *not* Zukofsky's in the early 1960s led to a permanent break with the latter.[84] But by 1965, Zukofsky had found, at last, a trade publisher in Random House. Even more limited runs of "A"-12 a decade earlier worked their way into the right hands: Guy Davenport used it to stave off boredom at Fort Bragg, and Hugh Kenner hailed the genius of "A" 1–12, printed by Cid Corman's Kyoto-based Origin Press in 1959, from (of all places) the pages of *National Review*.[85] Yet the scope of Zukofsky's ambition was never higher than in those first fourteen years of work. He hadn't yet settled on his late style or discovered that the aesthetic and moral richness of domestic life could serve as the foundation of his poetry—but his belief in poetry, in the avant-garde, had not yet been cowed by experience bearing out the odds against him. Experimental poetry had a mission beyond reaching just the isolated few, the university professors and their students, beyond Davenport at Kentucky, Kenner at the University of California at Santa Barbara and Johns Hopkins, beyond even Zukofsky himself, at Brooklyn Poly.

We find this outward ambition, before that middle-aged inward turn, in one of Zukofsky's fullest metapoetic works, the 1934 sestina "Mantis" and its free-verse commentary, "'Mantis,' An Interpretation." He worked on these as he labored at the early movements of "A." Their origins were unassuming.

Sometime in late 1934, Louis Zukofsky was standing on the platform of a New York subway station when a praying mantis flew onto his chest. He did what, startled by a bee, fly, or spider, almost all of us have done at some point: overreacted. But he then did what very few of us attempt (and even fewer succeed at): he transformed the incident into a sestina—and then, in response to William Carlos Williams's objection to the use of traditional form, wrote the "Interpretation" as an apologia. The pair were published the next year in *Poetry* and, in 1936, in James Laughlin's first *New Directions in Poetry and Prose* annual.

Mark Scroggins uses this fact about the poem's circulation in his biography of Zukofsky to illustrate a larger point about Zukofsky's career: "The poems were not published, however, by *New Masses*, or by any other journal associated with the Left. For all Zukofsky's concern with the plight of the poor, and for all his mastery of Marxist social and economic theory, his work was simply unacceptable to those like Mike Gold who demanded clarity and relative simplicity in writing. Personally speaking, Zukofsky was indeed a poet of the Left; but his poetry, while it addressed political and economic issues, was too deeply involved in the linguistic and formal experimentations of modernism to serve the Left's purposes."[86] Yet the poems, through their avant-garde examination of the plight of the working poor through the presence and mythos of the mantis, voiced as a sestina, reveal something much richer about where, when, and how his poetry circulated. More than just highlighting tensions between the leftist aesthetic of *New Masses* and Zukofsky's avant-garde commitments, the poems themselves offer a meditation on the decisions reflected in their publication history.

"Mantis," in its setting along urban commuter rail, its metapoetic questioning, and its concern for labor and injustice, shares much with Lola Ridge's "Morning Ride." But each poem's object lets us clearly distinguish them: in "Morning Ride," she's a young woman about whom we know very little. In "Mantis," it's the insect itself; in the "Interpretation," it's the poem. While Zukofsky's poems contain a human consciousness just as much as "Morning Ride" does—here, this serves as the poem's subject, that is, the subjectivity through which we, as readers, encounter its object, the mantis, and, then, "Mantis." This (as always) is a Zukofsky-like poet, if not quite Zukofsky himself. The first stanza establishes this relationship between speaker and insect:

> Mantis! praying mantis! since your wings' leaves
> And your terrified eyes, pins, bright, black and poor

> Beg—"Look, take it up" (thoughts' torsion)! "save it!"
> I who can't bear to look, cannot touch,—You—
> You can—but no one sees you steadying lost
> In the cars' drafts on the lit subway stone.[87]

We should be wary of assuming that the mantis itself is some kind of symbol for the poor. The "Interpretation" explicitly rejects this, declaring, "No human being wishes to become / An insect for the sake of a symbol."[88] (This is particularly pointed when we recall the rhetoric about Jews that was then rising in Germany.) Rather, the mantis announces the poet's *obligation toward* the poor. To return to Schwartz's language, the mantis is less sacramental than sacrament, the thing itself. The encounter with the poem's object prompts its subject to act—on obligation to others (the poor) and some authority announcing that obligation (the mantis), to act, that is, on the demands of a kind of covenant.

We can read this scene as a slightly comic version of the prophetic encounter. After the speaker-poet's initial fright and attempt to avoid his covenantal obligations (repeating the time-honored tradition of the reluctant prophet—Jonah, for example), he receives his charge: not to protect the subway's poor (whom he sees around him) but the mantis herself. This insect is "prophetess," both etymologically and in the poem's direct address to it; "you whom old Europe's poor / Call spectre"—clearly Marx's "spectre of Communism," the *idea* of revolution; and, through the Provencal and African folklore Zukofsky weaves through the poem's text, a deity. The mantis is a prophetess to her people; she is the prophecy itself; she is a god to her people (i.e., the speaker-poet). The speaker, in turn, finds himself bound by a threefold charge of covenantal obligations from his encounter with the mantis: to respond to the prophetess-mantis and her message; to act, himself, as a kind of prophet and spread word of the goddess-mantis's revelations; and, finally, to ensure the safety of the mantis as a fragile insect that contains the idea of revolution within its referential breadth.

To fulfill his covenantal roles, he examines modes of circulation: for words (of a prophecy or a poem), for an insect, and for people. He first turns to the press but finds it of no more use than Ridge does in "Morning Ride":

> Even the newsboy who now sees knows it
> No use, papers make money, makes stone, stone,
> Banks, "it is harmless," he says moving on—You?
> Where will he put *you*? There are no safe leaves

> To put you back in here, here's news! too poor
> Like all the separate poor to save the lost.[89]

The "leaves" of a newspaper aren't "safe" for the mantis or the message she represents: they aren't the proper means of circulation. For the insect, obviously, these leaves aren't like nature's—and the paper, folded or rolled, might just as easily be used to swat at rather than carry her. But for all that she represents, for words of poetry or prophecy, the problem is one of economics: there's "No use" in it; "papers make money." Or, as Zukofsky glosses in the "Interpretation,"

>   the
> newsboy—unable to think beyond
> "subsistence still permits competi-
> tion," banking, *The Wisconsin Elkhorn
> Independent*—"Rags make paper,
> paper makes money, money makes
> banks, banks make loans, loans make
> poverty, poverty makes rags."[90]

The newsboy, standing in for his industry, only values supposedly useful things—where use is defined as profitable, unable to see that a profit motive repeats an endless cycle of exploitation ("Rags make paper, / . . . / poverty makes rags"). So far, this is simply a more formally and theoretically complicated version of Ridge's critique that newspapers exist to sell what they advertise, not to stir their readers in response to the news. But Zukofsky goes even farther. The most proximate reason that "There are no safe leaves / To put you back in here" is because "here's news!" Ridge wants her readers to encounter poetry in spaces where they're able to recognize and be moved by the news they contain, free from distraction. Here, the poor "rising from the news may trample you"; the papers transform them into "shops' crowds." In "Mantis," news itself gets in the way. Reading the news doesn't bring people together; instead, the poor remain "the separate poor," "too poor / . . . to save the lost."

This critique of newspapers for containing *news* grows less surprising when we recognize that the poem itself is also a "Mantis." *Nomina sunt consequentia rerum*, Zukofsky insists in the subtitle to the "Interpretation." Names—titles—are, after all, sequent to the things named. (*Natura naturans, natura naturata*.) So we can read Zukofsky's charge to protect the mantis, to safely place her among leaves, as a metapoetic statement: he needs to find the proper leaves—the proper mode of circulation—for this poetry in particular and his poetry more generally. Newspapers won't do, for reasons that remain ambiguous but appear to be related to their failure to bring readers together. Maybe, if we think back to the public-creating nature of *A Test of Poetry*, it's because these readers haven't yet been prepared to read his poetry. They're a public, to be sure, but not the *correct* public. Here, the nature of that public appears surprisingly *communal*—one that approaches his work not with lyric assumptions about poetry but with the idea of poetic covenant that's emerged (in different guise) in the works of each poet considered so far: the poem itself mediates a relationship among readers, joining them in a call to action. So Zukofsky must take it on himself to fashion the "leaves" in which this "Mantis" and other poems can remain alive in the full motion of their "thoughts' torsions." And he does place "Mantis" safely among leaves: among pages of poetry, first in *Poetry* (March 1935), then in the 1936 *New Directions in Poetry and Prose*, and, finally, in Zukofsky's own collections: *55 Poems* (1941, self-published) and *ALL: Collected Short Poems* (1965, Random House).

If these don't seem like communal or covenantal ways of circulating poetry to you—or at least no more so than in the case of most modern American poetry—take a moment to consider the ways in which Zukofsky's works are, in fact, encountered. There is, for instance, *Z-site*, an online companion to Zukofsky's works. Although created and maintained by Jeffrey Twitchell-Waas, the home page announces that the site "is conceived as a collaborative project, and all additions, corrections and suggestions—however small—are appreciated."[91] The site contains an online *Selected Letters* (edited by Barry Ahearn), a transcript of the notes in the back pages of Zukofsky's King James Bible (edited by Benoît Turquety and Twitchell-Waas), commentary by Paul Zukofsky, and extensive notes to which many people have contributed over more than a decade. Likewise, the relative paucity of monographs that discuss Zukofsky has been balanced by essay collections devoted to Zukofsky and the "Objectivist" circle.[92] Even the supposedly isolated task of academic scholarship, this is to say, has been strikingly communal when it comes to Zukofsky's poetry. There's a felt need to read his works in a community of some kind—as I first did, with Guy Davenport's commentary on Zukofsky in *The Geography of the Imagination* open alongside my slim copy of Zukofsky's *Selected Poems*, while writing emails to the high school teacher, a former student of Davenport's, from whom I'd first heard Zukofsky's name. Maybe it's a classroom encounter or the loud conversation of multiple readings of Zukofsky's poetry within the same volume. In whatever situation, I want to suggest, this stems precisely from the poetry's difficulty, that extreme hermeticism that Hugh Kenner noted decades ago. Precisely because Zukofsky's poetry is so difficult, so dense, so hermetic, it is almost impossible to read in isolation. You simply have to find interlocutors—whether digital, codex, or flesh and blood. One way to assess the circulation history of Zukofsky's poetry—or at least the "Mantis" poems—is to examine whether they provided for like-minded readers prepared to encounter the poems together. Otherwise, isolated like "the separate poor," readers are bound to remain "lost." And that, as the saying goes, is a feature, not a bug.

PART III

LIMIT CASES

CHAPTER FIVE

A Covenantal Limit Case
Robert Hayden Beyond the Lyric

The crisp, vibrant blocks of color would have been a welcome break from autumn's steady, overcast gray. It was October 14, 1978, and the Detroit Institute of Arts (DIA) was opening a new exhibition—a dual exhibition, in fact. Its primary motivation was to unveil the recently completed silkscreen reproduction of Jacob Lawrence's 1941 sequence of historical paintings, *The Legend of John Brown* (the source of those panels of red, blue, yellow, orange, brown, black—almost, in their way, like stained-glass windows). Neither restorations nor facsimiles, these silkscreens had been produced over the previous four years by museum conservators and the Connecticut-based Ives-Sillman design team under Lawrence's watchful supervision. The DIA owned Lawrence's original sequence, one of the formative works of one of the most prominent midcentury African American visual artists, but couldn't safely exhibit it. Painted with a hand-mixed egg gouache on mounted paper, they suffered from severe flaking that was exacerbated by vertical display. Now, at last, it would be able to take its rightful place as one of the centerpieces of the museum's collection of modern and African American art. (The ending to this story isn't entirely happy or without irony: today, the silkscreens are on a rotating display in order to limit their exposure to the museum's lighting, which has proven damaging.)

That night, the public gathered to see it would also encounter, shown together for the first time since 1940, Lawrence's first major series: *Frederick Douglass* (1938–39) and *Harriet Tubman* (1939–40). Acquired by Hampton University in 1968, they were nonetheless advertised by the DIA as having been presumed lost until 1974.[1] That evening was the culmination of an autumn that Detroit had committed to both Lawrence and Brown. Exhibitions devoted to the painter and to the antebellum abolitionist best known for his failed raid on Harpers Ferry appeared at Wayne State University's Cultural Center, the Detroit Public Library, the Detroit Historical Museum, and Your Heritage House (a branch of the Detroit Cultural Center). Yet there was another centerpiece at the DIA's exhibition that evening—not a painting but a poem: Robert Hayden's sequence "John Brown," which also accompanied Lawrence's series in the printed exhibition portfolio. The museum had commissioned the poem from Hayden, the Detroit native and University of Michigan English professor who, since 1976, had served as consultant in poetry to the Library of Congress, the first African American to hold the post.

This is an unexpected setting for Hayden's poetry, which at first glance often seems bound to both the printed page and what has been termed a postwar lyricization of American poetry. Laurence Goldstein's and Robert Chrisman's discussion of Hayden's "near-perfect lyrics" continues in recent reframings of Hayden's work, such as Derik Smith's effort to situate Hayden not in opposition to the Black Arts Movement but in dialogue with it.[2] Smith argues that Hayden's is a decidedly "writerly poetics" and theirs a more spoken, vernacular project. This lyricized reading defines Hayden's heirs in African American verse (erudite MFA graduates) in contrast to those of the Black Arts Movement: the protest-oriented work of hip hop.[3] Such distinctions follow, roughly, Michael Warner's theorization of the differences in how lyric speech and public speech are heard: "In public speech, we incorporate an awareness of the distribution of the speech or text itself as essential to the addressee, which we nevertheless take in some measure to be ourselves. Lyric speech has no time: we read the scene of speech as identical with the moment of reading. Public speech, by contrast, requires the temporality of its own circulation."[4]

In Hayden's *Collected Poems*, lyric speech may well be the mode in which readers encounter a poem like "John Brown." But in its first incarnation, as part of a gallery exhibition and its printed portfolio, "John Brown" was inevitably heard as part of a *public* speech act: aware of and bound to the temporality of its circulation (the DIA event; the crowd assembled; October 14). When the poem is read (heard) within the bounds of Warner's understanding of a public speech act, its participation in genres that extend beyond the lyric becomes clearer: "John Brown" is an ekphrastic poem, gazing on the paintings displayed and speaking specifically of them. It's also a work of commemorative verse, designed not merely to describe the paintings but to mark the specific occasion of their unveiling, to circulate in a commemorative portfolio after the evening concludes. "John Brown," that is, creates a public—"a special kind of virtual social object, enabling a special mode of address."[5] It does so through its participation in generic conventions: the kind of poetry that its public recognizes as it enables them to recognize themselves as a specific kind of public. This public is greater than the sum of its parts: not merely ekphrastic or commemorative or art gallery, it's established as well through the topicality of Hayden's verse, which draws together these genres through his long-standing interest in covenant, both as an ideal community and as apprehended and misapprehended throughout American history.

All of this applies to more than just "John Brown." Pressure many of Hayden's poems with awareness of the temporality, historicity, and self-consciousness of their circulation and they begin to participate in genres beyond the lyric, often deploying them to establish a covenantal public. Precisely because his poems are often so seemingly, perfectly lyric, Hayden serves as a limit case that reveals how the voice of a covenantal poetics extends into the second half of the twentieth century. His poetry stands in the long and unexpected legacy of commemorative verse, extending, as we've seen, through the poetries of James Weldon Johnson, Louis Zukofsky, Lola Ridge, and Charles Reznikoff. This chapter reads three of Hayden's later poems as critical test cases for covenantal poetics, both as a modality of poetic reading and as the recognition of textual practice. Resituated in the public contexts that preceded their printing in collections of Hayden's poetry, poems as varied as "El-Hajj Malik El-Shabbaz," "John Brown," and "[American Journal]" engage readers in genres beyond the lyric as they identify and critique the mistaken, broken covenants that emerge from the rhetoric of the American Dream. Through the very act of prompting their audiences to consider what a truer, more fulfilled American covenant might look like, Hayden's poems transform these publics beyond the lyric, ekphrastic, or commemorative—into, in their own right, covenantal publics.

Hayden's earliest published work offers important contexts for reading his later, more accomplished poetry—despite the fact that, at his insistence, these "'Prentice Pieces" of the 1930s and 1940s have not been republished. The poems collected in his first book, *Heart-Shape in the Dust* (1940), evince the wide, disparate list of early favorites and models he later recalled: Langston Hughes, Countee Cullen, Carl Sandburg, Elinor Wylie, Edna St. Vincent Millay, *The New Negro*, and, of course, "Lola Ridge, who wrote *Firehead* and a book of poems called *Dance of Fire*, and *Ghetto*, and *Sun-Up* and so on. I discovered her about that time. I read *Firehead* and thought it was one of the great poems."[6] That he read deeply in and admired Lola Ridge and her covenantal poetics—that, in essence, he *apprenticed* himself to her as a young poet—will be an important factor in the readings that follow. But poets such as Sandburg, Hughes, and many of those included in *The New Negro* (James Weldon Johnson not least among them) craft poems that engage in the act of public-creation, that are indeed more "speakerly" than "writerly"—so, too, with much of Hayden's early work. Yet works like "Speech" and "These Are My People" don't simply imitate public speech acts: many of Hayden's early poems were written for and read at labor rallies during a period of growing unrest between autoworkers and management. Indeed, it was the United Auto Workers that proclaimed him the "People's Poet" spontaneously after a reading before one of its locals.

"These Are My People," an eight-page verse drama bearing the subtitle "A Mass Chant," was written for public performance. After giving voice to a full range of African American experience, it ends on a call to action for its mixed-race labor-union audience: "Take my hand / and march with me."[7] "Speech" closely mimics the preacherly effect of poems like those in James Weldon Johnson's *God's Trombones*. "I have seen the hand," Hayden announces, both at lynchings and among strikebreakers. In the third and fourth iterations of this image, it intensifies: "It was the same hand." As with Johnson's preacher, Hayden's labor speaker addresses a mixed-race audience—except he can do so explicitly: "Hear me, white brothers, / Black brothers, hear me," it begins, a call repeated until, by poem's end, Hayden need only call on his "Brothers."[8] They have become a single, shared audience. Placed again in the contexts in which the poem circulated *before* the publication of *Heart-Shape in the Dust*, at rallies and meetings of the labor groups and socialist circles in which Hayden was then active, these lines enact the creation of a shared, interracial counterpublic. On the printed page, this might seem idealistic. But imagine the audience as a flesh-and-blood crowd of autoworkers, largely from the industry's ethnic whites (Greek, Irish, Polish, Italian, etc.) who had only recently gained acceptance as "truly" white. Now the poem becomes a call for these men to maintain awareness of their historical experience of ethnic subordination alongside their present economic subordination: to imagine themselves as a public—an interracial counterpublic—established through "an awareness of its subordinate status."[9] This is not so different, all in all, from the universalist and deeply historically aware poetry of the mature, movement-skeptical Hayden.

To refer to the 'Prentice Pieces of *Heart-Shape in the Dust* differs from calling the poems juvenilia. Hayden kept an ironic distance from this early work and did not see it as fit for reprinting on aesthetic grounds. Yet he acknowledges the importance of this period for his development as a poet. An interest in the ways that poetry can mediate and enable the creation of publics—in the ways that poetry can be an act of "public speech" *as well as* an act of "lyric speech" played an important role in his apprenticeship. This influence was on display in the origins of "John Brown" but before as well: in the midst of his annus mirabilis, 1966. As an award-winning pupil of W. H. Auden at the University of Michigan, Hayden had abandoned his early persona as Detroit's "People's Poet" for the historically oriented modernism of "Middle Passage" and the baroque symbolism of "A Ballad of Remembrance." He published in major journals and anthologies, was praised by the luminaries—Hughes, Cullen, Auden—who had once been his models, and yet could find no mainstream, commercial publisher for his first three volumes of poetry. Instead, he had toiled in relative obscurity since the mid-1940s from his overworked post at Fisk University, the storied historically Black college and university in Nashville where James Weldon Johnson taught in the 1930s and where Aaron Douglas was still a member of the Art Department faculty.

Our story picks up shortly after the 1966 First World Festival of Negro Arts in Dakar, Senegal, awarded Hayden its Grand Prix de la Poesie for his 1962 collection *A Ballad of Remembrance*. (The other finalists were Derek Walcott and Christopher Okebo; the international panel of judges included Hughes.) Shortly thereafter, Hayden finally secured a commercial publisher, October House, which brought out his *Selected Poems* later that year. Between these two events—indeed, in the same month as the Dakar festival—Fisk University hosted its spring writers' conference, the event that serves as a focal point for much Hayden scholarship.[10] Here, seated next to poets who would later associate themselves with the Black Arts Movement, Hayden rejected the label of "Black poet," preferring to call himself "a poet who happens to be a Negro."[11] "You'll never make me an accident," Melvin Tolson responded. "I'm a black poet, an African-American poet, a Negro poet. I'm no accident—and I don't give a tinker's damn what you think."[12] Thus, a half century of scholarship has maintained, an irrevocable breach opened between Hayden and the nascent Black Arts Movement—whose members cheered on Tolson's rejoinder, though his poetry resembled Hayden's far more than it did their own. Yet it was at this Fisk conference that Dudley Randall, who would shortly establish himself as one of the major publishers of Black Arts poetry, developed the idea for what would become the 1967 collection *For Malcolm: Poems on the Life and Death of Malcolm X*, to which Hayden would contribute "El-Hajj Malik El-Shabbaz."

Wrestling with the Name

At the end of April 1966, fourteen months after the assassination of Malcolm X and only days after the Fisk Writers' Conference, Robert Hayden received a letter from Randall, a fellow Detroit poet whose recently founded Broadside Press would soon become an important publishing outlet for the Black Arts Movement. "Perhaps you've heard on the campus," he wrote, "that Broadside Press is publishing a volume of poems in memory of Malcolm X. If you have written one or if you write one in the near future, why not send it to Broadside Press . . . and if you have the names and addresses of any other poets that would be interested in contributing to the anthology, would you send them to me, please."[13] Despite Hayden's very much earned and deserved reputation for slow, torturous writing and revising (with drafts, by reputation, numbering in the hundreds over many years), the poem that he ultimately contributed, "El-Hajj Malik El-Shabbaz," came together, by his standards, relatively swiftly: *For Malcolm: Poems on the Life and Death of Malcolm X* was published the following year. As would be the case twelve years later with "John Brown," the initial publication of "El-Hajj Malik El-Shabbaz" places the poem in an act of public-creation that renders its participation in additional, perhaps unexpected genres legible. One of these is that of the Black Arts poem, even as a voice in dissent. As Derek Smith discusses at length, *For Malcolm* places Hayden's verse alongside works by LeRoi Jones (not yet Amiri Baraka), Margaret Walker, Gwendolyn Brooks, Clarence Major, Larry Neal, and Etheridge Knight in an important early volume by one of the movement's signature publishers. Despite the contretemps at Fisk, Hayden's public and their public, in this instance, were one and the same.[14]

More than self-conscious participation in a literary movement (the collection appeared when the Black Arts Movement was only beginning to coalesce), participation in the shared acts of commemorating the life and mourning the death of Malcolm X defines the public that *For Malcolm* creates. The collection marks and memorializes a specific occasion: his assassination. In this, the volume participates in the transformation of commemorative verse from, primarily, a genre of periodicals (especially the newspaper) to a genre of the anthology and special collection. Although commemorative verse as a distinct and regularly recognized genre has found itself largely submerged in the second half of the twentieth century, poetry's ability to establish and maintain commemorative publics did not disappear. Rather, the circulatory space of this commemorative discourse changed.[15] The same interplay between circulation and genre that we saw in the poetry of Lola Ridge and, especially, Louis Zukofsky's work on "A"-10 and *La France en Liberté* shapes the public nature of *For Malcolm*—and the poems contained within it. This context, in turn, allows us to recognize that Hayden's "El-Hajj Malik El-Shabbaz" is more than simply a lyric or even an elegy—that, in its composition and initial publication, Hayden's poem necessarily participates in the genre of commemorative verse.

The two essays by the actor and activist Ossie Davis that frame the collection help us to observe the ways in which it establishes a commemorative, rather than elegiac, discourse. The eulogy Davis delivered at Malcolm X's funeral serves as a concluding piece, while his essay "Why I Eulogized Malcolm X" is the collection's preface. Together, they frame *For Malcolm* as an act of eulogy rather than elegy, despite the ways in which many of its poems can be read as elegiac. While both genres participate in acts of mourning, a eulogy is fundamentally occasional, the genre of the funeral and memorial service, marking the occasion as such. Davis's preface explicitly notes the commemorative purpose of his eulogy. He didn't seek to endorse all of Malcolm X's political views (in fact, he highlights his own disagreements with him) but to mark the fact that *"Malcolm was a man!"* This fact, he insists, demands public commemoration. "White folks do not need anybody to remind them that they are men," Davis explains, "We do!"[16] The editors' introduction, which immediately precedes this preface, focuses on the textual and publication history of the poems: Davis's words are, in effect, the collection's statement of purpose. The preface joins the poems that follow as commemorative works that participate in the same space of discourse and continue the act of public-creation that began with Davis's eulogy.

How, then, does Hayden's poem commemorate Malcolm X as *"a man"*? Insofar as his poem does serve as a "dissenting" voice in the collection, this is because he avoids commemoration of Malcolm X as a political visionary and as a symbol of Black masculinity, two subjects about which Hayden expresses ambivalence and conflict across his career. Indeed, as the title of Hayden's poem suggests, he'd rather not commemorate "Malcolm X" at all but instead who he became, briefly, at the very end of his life: el-Hajj Malik el-Shabbaz, who left the Nation of Islam for the panracial promise of Sunni Islam, as well as the journey that he took to arrive at his final name, what the poem's subtitle refers to as the *"masks and metamorphoses of Ahab, Native Son."*[17] Various names assumed by Malcolm X organize the poem's structure: across its four sections, he transforms from "Home Boy" and "Dee-troit Red" to "Satan" to X to, finally, el-Hajj Malik el-Shabbaz. In doing so, Hayden does not simply commemorate Malcolm X as a man who changed his name or his sense of self or his political and religious views over time but as a man whose life testifies to the ongoing, partial, and never-completed apprehension of the divine and of covenant. The language of satanic evil and divine love permeates the poem's four sections. Yet they do not trace a revelation progressively revealed over time. Rather, they trace the progressive *apprehension* of the revealed, of covenant and its obligations, over time. Hayden's poem engages the commemorative public created by *For Malcolm* in the act of considering and recognizing the covenant he describes. He engages them in the same act of apprehension that he commemorates in the poem.

The instability of Malcolm X's name, performed through those "*masks and metamorphoses*," renders this apprehension legible. In the poem, as in Islam, Judaism, the Christianity of Hayden's childhood, and the Baha'i faith of his adult life, naming serves as a signifier of covenant. The renaming of Avraham (from Avram), for example, is bound up with the commandment to circumcise male offspring as a marker of covenant: this renaming serves as a verbal placeholder until the *brit milah*, the covenant of circumcision, can be performed. Something similar happens later in the Hebrew Bible with the transformations of Ya'akov into Yisra'el and of Hoshua into Yehoshua as well as in the New Testament renamings of Simon as Peter and Saul as Paul. This relationship between naming and covenant is shared across the texts of Hayden's Baptist childhood and the Baha'i faith he embraced as an adult. The John the Baptist–like figure of the Bab assumes this name when he first proclaims his role as a messenger from God; Mirza Husayn-Ali Nuri becomes Baha'u'llah (the central figure of the Baha'i religion, whom it holds as an emanation of the divine) when he announces his belief that the Bab has proclaimed a covenantal dispensation new and separate from Islam and the Quran. The shifting names of Hayden's Malcolm X don't just signal a transformation of selfhood or relationship to wider (white) American society but seal and commemorate a new or transformed relationship to a covenant and whatever authority does (or does not) govern it. The poem begins by recognizing "The icy evil that struck his father down / and ravished his mother into madness." He rejects it, "struggling to break free."[18] Yet this struggle remains incomplete. Although (as we'll see later) Hayden's poetry comes to view the stereotypical American Dream as a misapprehended covenant, the adolescent Malcolm's rightful rejection of the "cannibal flowers of the American Dream" leaves him unable to apprehend who he is or should be. He stands in relation to nothing higher, naming himself in reference to place—he becomes "Home Boy" and "Dee-troit Red"—yet travesties even the commitment to family and city by devoting himself to the pursuit of sensuality for its own sake. There is no covenant here. Taking on these monikers, Hayden writes, "he fled his name" like a Jonah fleeing his prophetic mission.[19]

In the poem's second part, the flight from naming leads to prison and the jailhouse nickname "Satan." Referring to this place as "The Hole" and "the pit," Hayden aligns it with the Tehran prison, known as the Black Pit, in which Baha'u'llah was imprisoned in 1852 and where, he later wrote, he underwent his first mystical experiences and the revelation of his mission as the messenger of God. Even as "Satan," having rejected all religion, Malcolm X, too, has his first mystical, revelatory experiences while imprisoned:

> Sometimes the dark that gave his life
> its cold satanic sheen would shift
> a little, and he saw himself
> floodlit and eloquent[20]

Although cast as a glimpse of a truth beyond himself, this vision is not of Allah or covenantal obligations but of *himself*, of his own charisma. That is, even the "shift" from darkness toward light with which this section opens prefigures that this will only bring a "black light of partial vision" that leads him not toward truth but to fall "upon his face before / a racist Allah."[21]

This initial movement toward covenant is fitting for one who had named himself after Satan, the tempter: it is a misapprehension, the temptation of his own eloquence and "prideful anger," the last property from which, Hayden writes, he still must be redeemed. So, the poem's third section announces, "He X'd his name, became his people's anger."[22] In taking the name Malcolm X, he moves away from a marker of the satanic. But the new moniker doesn't announce a relationship to the divine. It marks only an absence, naming himself in reference to himself. In the misapprehension of a "racist Allah" rather than "Allah the raceless," the X itself and the very act of naming become deeds of violence rather than redemption.[23]

Despite this misapprehension, the second and third parts of "El-Hajj Malik El-Shabbaz" *do* trace their subject's movement toward covenantal self-understanding. After Malcolm X has rejected the "cannibal flowers of the American Dream," a kind of civic covenant whose governing authority he perceives as an "icy evil," and assumed the names "Home Boy" and "Dee-troit Red," he turns inward, obligationless: a "zoot-suited jiver," "the quarry / of his own obsessed pursuit." By becoming "his people's anger," however, Malcolm X understands himself in relation to them: indeed, that relationship becomes central to his self-understanding. He is the one "would shame them, / drive them from / the lush ice gardens of their servitude." The path through these masks, metamorphoses, and names is crooked—and through this, his biography assumes the shape of the Hajj he undertook in 1964, "the ebb time pilgrimage / toward revelation." In Mecca, he proclaims *"Labbayk! Labbayk!"*—words from the talbiyah prayer, recited regularly during the hajj, that announce, roughly, "Here I am!"—and bows again, this time before an Allah "in whose blazing Oneness all / Were one."[24] Having both apprehended and proclaimed, in language shared across Abrahamic religions, his relationship to a universal covenantal authority, he assumes his final, true name, that which the poem takes as its title: el-Hajj Malik el-Shabbaz. He names himself, that is, in relation to precisely that which Hayden's poem commemorates, the "Hejira to / his final metamorphosis."[25] His very name, like Hayden's poem, becomes an act of commemoration.

By eulogizing this act of covenantal commemoration, "El-Hajj Malik El-Shabbaz" extends beyond the generic conventions of the lyric sequence or even the elegy. Hayden wrote elegiac verse, of course: "Words in the Mourning Time," "Mourning Poem for the Queen of Sunday," and "Elegies for Paradise Valley" all deploy the tonal, topical, and formal markers of elegy: compensatory mourning, melancholia-driven ambivalence, epideixis, pastoral images and themes, the pathetic fallacy, explicit discussions of grief, death, and the dead.[26] There's none of this in "El-Hajj Malik El-Shabbaz." It's hard to find grief or mourning in it at all—sorrow, certainly, but sorrow permeates Hayden's oeuvre. This distinction between elegy and eulogy is crucial to our understanding of the nature of the public that the poem creates and of the way Hayden's verse operates within the discourse of a covenantal poetics. Both commemorative verse and elegy participate in public-creating discourses, prompting readers to understand themselves as members of a public. In the case of elegy, this is a public of grief and mourning: perhaps national (as in the case of Whitman's "When Lilacs Last in Dooryards Bloom'd") or perhaps the handful of friends assembled in Allen Ginsberg's apartment to mourn his mother (as in his *Kaddish*). The public of commemorative verse, on the other hand, *commemorates*: perhaps a national event (Whitman again: "A Broadway Pageant"; or Louis Zukofsky writing of the fall of Paris in "A"-10) or something more local, such as Charles Reznikoff's jury box in *Testimony* or James Weldon Johnson's Sunday congregations in *God's Trombones*.

As with Zukofsky, Reznikoff, and Johnson, the public that recognizes itself in and through Hayden's poem commemorates—and therefore comes to recognize itself in relation to—a covenantal community.

Hayden as Baha'i-American Poet

Hayden's fascination with the path toward religious self-understanding extends beyond the content of this or any one poem: it's fundamental to his vision of poetry itself. "I also think of poetry," he stated in a 1971 interview, "as a form of prayer."[27] He expressed dissatisfaction with this formulation but soon found a better way of describing the relationship: "The making of a poem," he wrote (also in 1971), "like all other creative endeavors, is in the Baha'i view a spiritual act, a form of worship."[28] In a 1977 interview, he elaborated, "in the writings of Baha'u'llah, the prophet of the faith, it's clearly stated that the work of the artist . . . is considered a form of service to mankind and it has spiritual significance, . . . a form of worship and a form of service to mankind."[29] Hayden's understanding of the Baha'i view of art further insists "that Abdul-Baha [the Baha'u'llah] makes no distinction between 'secular' and 'religious' art," that "the creative act is fundamentally a religious act."[30]

The Malcolm X whom Hayden describes is, from this angle, an idealized universal type. Certainly, he is a kind of stand-in for the path Hayden himself may be on: from the angry Detroit childhood, the wandering among names, none of which truly fit, the progressive spiritual journey from ethnic particularity toward a universal vision of humanity.[31] When Hayden and his wife, Erma, arrived in Ann Arbor in 1941 for him to begin graduate study with W. H. Auden, he still identified (however ambivalently) with the Baptist faith of his upbringing; its sternness and reticence give shape to many of his poems, such as "Those Winter Sundays."[32] They soon met members of a Baha'i study group and began attending its meetings. First Erma converted, and after a longer period of study, Hayden too became a Baha'i. His description of his conversion involves no mystical, revelatory experience but a period of reasoned investigation, a text-based discovery: "I made some study of it, and I went to study groups and decided that it was the truth, that it answered a lot of questions that I had never had answers for up to that time. And I became a Baha'i."[33]

Hayden's faith set him apart from the other poets considered in this study: he was the most traditionally religious believer among them: James Weldon Johnson and Louis Zukofsky were openly, unashamedly secular in their beliefs; so, too, was Charles Reznikoff—though, as always, with more ambivalence: he sometimes expressed a longing for religious belief that Johnson and Zukofsky did not. "Traditional" here shouldn't be confused with "orthodox" but understood as a way of distinguishing Hayden from the idiosyncratic and highly individual Catholic mysticism of Lola Ridge. Unlike Ridge, Hayden experienced religion through its organized structures: official text study, prayer services, and participation in its cultural organizations, such as his tenure as the poetry editor of *World Order*, an American Baha'i magazine. Being a Baha'i also marks him as more of an outsider to American civil religion than the four writers discussed previously. Each poet's work translates the American trope of the nation's covenantal promise/burden into "peripheral" discourses (immigrant, African American, Jewish, Catholic, feminist, etc.). For Hayden, the fact that the Baha'i faith falls outside the midcentury triad of Americanness and American religion—Protestant-Catholic-Jew—intensifies this centrifugal effect. Far from the singular revelations of Sinai, Calvary, or the Quran, the Baha'u'llah and his successors preached a vision of ongoing, progressive revelation: Abraham, Moses, Jesus, Muhammad, the Buddha, Confucius, and others—all these were messengers of the true God, though their visions were only partial.[34] The Baha'u'llah's revelation extends (and supplants) these, while leaving open the possibility that his, too, might be extended and supplanted.

It may be useful to think of progressive revelation, at least as it informs and emerges in Hayden's poetry, in terms of apprehension and comprehension. A comprehended revelation is understood; an apprehended one is only recognized—and perhaps even then incompletely. In the example of the nineteenth-century archbishop of Dublin, philologist, and poet Richard Chenevix Trench, "we 'apprehend' many truths, which we do not 'comprehend.' The great mysteries of our faith—the doctrine, for instance, of the Holy Trinity, we lay hold upon it, we hang on it, our souls live by it; but we do not 'comprehend' it, that is, we do not take it all in."[35] So, from an early age, Hayden's Malcolm X *apprehended* covenant—but he did not, even at the time of his death, fully *comprehend* it. What sets Hayden, as a Baha'i, apart from the Anglican Trench is belief in an apprehension that deepens, grows clearer, and moves closer to comprehension over time. Progressive revelation does not lead Hayden toward the recovery of the religiosity of the past—how could it when this, perhaps, was itself a fiction and at the very least misapprehended? Rather, it leads him toward a move that, from Jewish, Christian, and Muslim perspectives, appears "postsecular" or even "inauthentic." Progressive revelation, in Hayden's account, is an ongoing, textually mediated process. Consider again his conversion experience and his further remarks that he and Erma "went to study groups—that's how you become a Baha'i; you're not born a Baha'i. You are required to learn about the faith, to study it, and then to make up your mind about whether you want to be a Baha'i or not."[36] The ability of Baha'i writings to serve this mediating role is, ultimately, not so different from a *poem*'s ability to do so—*especially* if there is no clear distinction between secular and religious art.

Hence, perhaps, the tension in much of Hayden's late work—the tension that produces its often "prophetic" feeling and charge. On the one hand, he is aware of and feels deeply the historical injustices of the United States (particularly, though by no means exclusively, against African Americans). On the other hand, as he stated bluntly, "I believe what the Baha'i teachings tell us about the destiny of America.... From the Baha'i Writings we learn that America is to become the spiritual leader of the world.... Throughout history, Americans have believed America has a purpose, a peculiar destiny, have believed in what we may call the new-world mystique. The Baha'i Faith reinforces this idea but cautions us we are going to have to be purged of our weaknesses—our old-world sickness—before we can achieve our appointed task." What we have here is, in essence, the discourse of American civil religion recast in terms of progressive revelation. Though Hayden says, "if I weren't a Baha'i, I would hardly conceive of that," there *is* truth behind the sense of a "new-world mystique," a "peculiar destiny"—that is, the sense of a covenantal national errand.[37] Yet an "old-world sickness" undermines it. This seems something more fundamental than error or sin in the definitional sense they carry of "missing the mark," of, in the Christian idiom, being perversions of love rather than its opposite. Here, the covenantal revelation itself needs to undergo a purgation—needs, that is, to attain clarity through progressive refinement. For Hayden, this is in fact a move away from American exceptionalism (whether positive or negative) and toward a simple historical fact—perhaps even accident: "as a result of having all the races, cultures, and nationalities of the world in one way or another in the country," the United States has the potential to serve as a kind of "microcosm" of the ultimate unity and oneness of all humanity.[38]

"John Brown": Ekphrasis, Commemoration, and Covenant

Back to Detroit, 1978: not literally but commemoratively—I'm sitting in my Ann Arbor office writing these words, in 2020, but the published exhibition portfolio *The Legend of John Brown* lies open on my desk. As a work of commemoration, this book and the works within it recall readers to an earlier place and moment, one that we don't need to have been present at or even to be capable of having been present at. I wasn't alive in 1978, but the portfolio, by addressing the public of the occasion it commemorates, expands that public to include its own readers. That earlier public, seemingly temporally and spatially bound, circulates into the present. The volume on my desk doesn't address me in the twenty-first century but as a member of the original public that came to view the silkscreen *John Brown* and the recently rediscovered *Frederick Douglass* and *Harriet Tubman* sequences. I mean this quite literally. The first sentence of the preface announces, "The Detroit Institute of Arts is pleased to present an exhibition celebrating the publication of *The Legend of John Brown*, a portfolio containing 22 screenprints based on the gouaches of the *John Brown* series by Jacob Lawrence in our permanent collection."[39] Frederick J. Cummings, director of the DIA, welcomes readers not to the book they hold in their hands but to the exhibition that, now, lies four decades in the past and to which the book itself—the words—were never physically bound.

We've seen how "El-Hajj Malik El-Shabbaz" transforms the eulogistic public created by *For Malcolm* into a covenantal public by inquiring how this public's individual members stand in relation to a covenant and whatever authority governs its fulfillment or violation. Hayden's "John Brown," first published in the exhibition's portfolio, performs a similar act, transforming an ekphrastic, commemorative public into a covenantal one. These two adjectives—"ekphrastic," "commemorative"—are also the two genres that work together in Hayden's act of public-creation. They are, in fact, the forms (genres) of attention that enable its creation.[40] As *The Legend of John Brown* addresses me in 2020 as if I were present at the 1978 exhibition, it extends these forms of attention, to the same object (Jacob Lawrence's paintings), across space and time.

In addition to commemorating the event marking the unveiling of the silkscreens, the portfolio book frames Hayden's poem itself as a second object of commemoration: Detroit wants to celebrate one of its own. In the same breath, however, it casts his poem as itself an important act of ekphrasis and commemoration focused on the silkscreens themselves. Set immediately after a black-and-white reproduction of the original *John Brown* sequence, Hayden's "John Brown" offers the portfolio book's most extensive commentary on the images. It isn't only discussed by Cummings's preface and the introduction written by Ellen Sharp, the museum's curator of graphic arts, but also joins the task of these art-world professionals: to direct and guide the gathered public's attention as they view the sequence. Even the photograph of Hayden that precedes his poem suggests this duality. Whereas readers see Lawrence head down, surveying one of the new screenprints of the *John Brown* series,

Hayden turns to the camera, aware both of his status as object of attention and of our expectation that he will speak. Seated at a small, wooden secretary with pen still in hand, Hayden has paused in his work: in a suit vest, he's jacketless; his collar is open and his sleeves rolled to the elbows. Yet, like the narrator or host of an early public-television documentary or period-piece adaptation of Dickens or Austen, he doesn't look startled. He's been expecting us. He's our museum docent, our guide. Reading the poem that begins on the facing page, we hear his deep, resonant voice guiding us through the exhibition.

The genres that emerge from the poem's original contexts locate it within discourse publics that are not immediately evident in its later publications, first in the posthumous *American Journal* (1982) and, later, in the *Collected Poems* (1985, 2013). In these volumes, "John Brown" is one of Hayden's historical sequences, composed of five short lyrics. When, in the poem's final lines, the speaker turns to "these haunting stark / torchlight images," the vision is self-referential, a turning back on the very images that Hayden himself has constructed and deployed throughout the poem.[41] Generically, it isn't so different on this reading from the lyric speech of Hayden's historical and documentary poems: "Middle Passage," "Runagate Runagate," or "Frederick Douglass." As an ekphrastic, commemorative poem, however, "John Brown" participates in modalities of public speech. Filtering the historical figure through Lawrence's interpretation, Hayden explores the way in which Brown has been transformed from a man into the symbol and embodiment of a covenant, the visual marker (like Noah's rainbow) of its terms. The pages that follow offer three linked readings of "John Brown": first, as an ekphrastic poem creating an ekphrastic public; then, as a work of commemoration; and, finally, how these produce a covenantal poetics, one that aspires to create a covenantal public. This movement mirrors that which takes place both within the poem itself and within the assembled public it addresses: the oscillation between apprehension and comprehension. John Brown, as historical figure, can be comprehended, known and understood. But as both Lawrence and Hayden present him—as the sign of a covenant that binds a public across time and space (2020 with 1978 with 1859)—he can only be apprehended: seen but only partially perceived. The incompleteness of our understanding resembles that of John Brown himself or of Malcolm X in "El-Hajj Malik El-Shabazz," joining the poem's public in their shuffling uncertainty as they stand in relation to covenant.

There's one rather striking difference between the exhibition portfolio and the exhibition itself: the portfolio reprints the original gouaches, not the silkscreens. Partly, this speaks to the way in which the silkscreens, standing in for fragile originals that can't be publicly displayed, themselves perform an act of commemorative visual art that parallels Hayden's. The portfolio reproduces the original—not the silkscreen commemoration—in a different but linked iteration of this commemorative project. This also aligns with the composition history of Hayden's poem. Hayden had struggled for years with the idea for a poem about John Brown but had been unable to complete a work that took the historical figure as its locus. His breakthrough came, Ellen Sharp recalls, when the DIA gave him special access to the flaking originals. "He studied the gouaches closely," she writes; "somehow this aided in resolving his difficulties with the subject."[42] The portfolio itself invites its readers to gaze on the paintings both as Hayden did when writing and as his poem does. Like the poet, readers are directed toward the originals, not the silkscreens, still unfinished as Hayden wrote. Like the poem, the portfolio book doesn't start at the beginning and proceed in sequence but opens quite near the series's end. The full sequence is produced in black-and-white images—with the exception of two, each printed a second time in full color. The first of these, following the title page, is also the first image at which Hayden's poem gazes. This is the penultimate painting from the series, depicting the moment when (as Lawrence's caption reads) "after John Brown's capture, he was put to trial for his life in Charles Town, Virginia (now West Virginia)."[43]

In this painting, Brown is an isolated figure. There's not even a setting, just a murky yellow background. Shrouded in a black cloak, he bows his head beneath his shoulders, and long, straggling, white-streaked hair conceals his face. Between his hands, he clasps a blood-red cross. This description is one approach to ekphrasis: describing the colors, body language, and pose. Hayden's poem does none of these things as it captures the essence of the image: the isolation of the prophetic figure whose raid has failed—who, at the climax of antebellum debates over slavery, may have seen his mission fail:

> Loved feared hated:
> aureoled
>   in violence.
>
> Foredoomed to fail
> in all but the prophetic
> task?
>   Axe in Jehovah's
> loving wrathful hand?[44]

In the poem's reading, the course and ending of Brown's life give meaning to each other simultaneously. We can only grasp the importance of his actions in Kansas and at Harpers Ferry by beholding him, shortly before his death, in failure.

Hayden's symbolism derives its visual motifs from those that Lawrence's paintings deploy. Brown's "life," Hayden writes in the first poem, "has the symmetry / of a cross."[45] This is an elegant way of stating one of the visual arguments of Lawrence's paintings. In the first image presented in the portfolio, Brown's crucifix stands in stark relief against the yellow backdrop. The first image of the series goes even further, making a claim in visual grammar as explicit as Hayden's poem: *John Brown* begins with a painting of the crucifixion, in which a larger-than-life Christ hangs from a massive, black cross against an empty, apocalyptic landscape. As blood streams from the wounds in Jesus's feet, a young John Brown leans against the base of the cross, head turned down in sorrow. From this beginning, crosses recur throughout the series, a shape that patterns the composition as much as Lawrence's signature early affect does: a limited, controlled, and recurring color palette. Sometimes these crosses are as obvious as the crucifix hanging on the wall above Brown's head in painting 4, sometimes as subtle as the position of the two rifles Brown holds in painting 6 or the positioning of his arms as he leans, conspiratorially, across a table in painting 7. Hayden transfers this visual symmetry to the poem itself through his arrangement of words and white space on the page. Each section of the poem appears as a narrow, vertical column (just as in the preceding quoted passage). By frequently avoiding left justification and making liberal use of indentation as stanzas break midsentence or midimage, the poem forces its readers' eyes to dart back and forth *horizontally* on the page at the same time that it highlights a beam-like vertical. Although they aren't concrete poems, traditionally construed, and don't take the literal shape of the cross, they nonetheless guide the physical act of reading: the sharp horizontal movements produced by white spaces and indentation while the eyes move down the page's vertical take on, like Brown's life, "the symmetry / of a cross."

Working in conjunction, the poem and portfolio create an ekphrastic public: one that gazes on the paintings while hearing—and being directed by—Hayden's poetry. Such a public can recognize prophetic, covenantal meaning that is not immediately available from the words in isolation: the ways that "John Brown," like "El-Hajj Malik El-Shabbazz," takes the nature of covenant as its subject as much as the historical figure at its center. The fourth poem of the sequence opens,

> fire harvest: John Brown
> and his Chosen
>   at Harper's Ferry:
> fury of The Word made pikes guns
> swords:[46]

This opening "fire harvest" and its recurrence in the twelfth line appear to refer, specifically, to the battle between Brown's men and federal troops under the command of Robert E. Lee at the Harpers Ferry arsenal—the spilling of blood with which the poem creates a visual and syntactic parallel. Yet a return to painting 21 in Lawrence's sequence suggests another definition. Here and in other paintings, Brown's hair appears in the shape of a flame. Read the image upside down, and his head is concealed not by hair but by the crackling of black and white fire. So while "fire harvest" can refer to gunfire, Lawrence's paintings indicate that we should also associate these images with Brown himself, that *he* is what the fire harvests. Hayden's poem bears this out. The middle two lines of the poem ask and answer a question: "Who sent you here, John Brown? / None in human form."[47] Brown, the poem reminds us, understands himself as a prophet of God chosen for a divine mission. Whereas Moses heard and recognized the voice of God from a bush that burned but was not consumed, in Hayden's verse and Lawrence's paintings, Brown himself is aflame but unconsumed. To gaze on the image of John Brown is, the poem insists, to gaze on the way he stood in relation to covenant. Like Malcolm X, he contains ambivalence: a figure of sacred order and a figure of violence. And again like Malcolm X, this ekphrastic act of public-creation allows the public to, in turn, recognize themselves in relation to a covenant.

But "John Brown" goes further than "El-Hajj Malik El-Shabbaz." The later poem develops a distinct visual and poetic syntax that facilitates the physical act of gazing that will, in turn, establish this ekphrastic-covenantal public. This operates through one of the poem's most idiosyncratic features: Hayden's liberal use of the colon. While he had never understood himself as bound to any one poetic form, style, or structure and his poetry on the whole is not regularly bound to either the presence or absence of punctuating for standard syntax, his style in "John Brown" is distinctive.[48] There are nineteen colons in the poem, and each acts as more than a marker of pace, pause, or reference (as they do, for example, in Ezra Pound's *Cantos*). Rather than a marker of written syntax, they punctuate and mark the syntax of looking on— of beholding—these new silkscreen prints. As Hayden blends written and visual syntax, he draws together the generic expectations and publics of ekphrastic and commemorative verse. Colons turn the reader's gaze mentally and visually, moving the eye from one image, concept, and print to another, as in the opening and closing lines of the first section. Its final lines read,

>   the life
> has the symmetry
> of a cross:
>   John Brown
> Ossowatomie   De Old Man.[49]

A line-ending colon marks multiple visual and conceptual turns: from object to person, from the symbol of the cross to the human form, and—if we're still gazing on the painting with which the portfolio book opens—from the object in Brown's hands to Brown himself, tilting one's head slightly to refocus.

This syntax is a crucial component of the imagery and meaning of the "fire harvest: harvest fire:" that the poem's fourth section posits as central to Brown's prophetic self-understanding (that is, how he stands in relation to a covenant). Ten colons—more than half those contained in the entire sequence—appear in this section's twenty lines. They work to twine the visual act of beholding the still images of Lawrence's sequence with Hayden's movement among historical, ethical, and religious concepts. In places, this is as simple as the direction from still image to still image, as with lines like "bloodburst: bloodflow:" where the colons signal a turn from the burst of blood as a bullet strikes a body to the flow of blood from one of Brown's men, now lying wounded on the floor, as they struggle to hold the arsenal at Harpers Ferry.[50] They also redirect readers swiftly among Lawrence's paintings. So the poem's opening lines instruct us to shift our gaze from the abstract, prophetic imagery of "fire harvest" to the paintings that will allow us to understand the meaning it bears:

> fire harvest: John Brown
> and his Chosen
>   at Harper's Ferry:

First, we are directed to paintings 19 and 20 in Lawrence's sequence, where Brown and his men march to the arsenal. The following line turns to "fury of The Word made pikes guns / swords:" focusing gazes on the bayonets prominent in painting 19, an image that Sharp recalls that Hayden was especially drawn to, and the image of their own stockpile of weapons in painting 18.[51] The following lines, Brown's instructions to his men in preparation for the raid, continue the poem's reverse course through history and Lawrence's images. They bring the audience to paintings 16 and 17, in which (in the words of Lawrence's captions) Brown first "liberated twelve negroes from a Missouri plantation" and then "remained a full winter in Canada, drilling negroes for his coming raid on Harper's Ferry."[52]

Progressing through Lawrence's series while *also* returning to the images of the poem's opening section, "John Brown" prefigures the visual syntax of its own ending. The line "bloodburst: bloodflow:" returns the audience's gaze to the combat depicted in the twentieth painting of the series. The poem then turns explicitly to Brown's prophetic calling, asking, "Who sent you here, John Brown? / None in human form," and introducing the repeated, unstable image, "Fire harvest: harvest fire."[53] Earlier, I discussed these lines in the context of painting 21, reprinted in full color at the beginning of the published exhibition portfolio. Here, the poem again directs our gaze toward Brown's flame-like head, unconsumed, "spent forlorn colossal / in that bloody light."[54] Taking up roughly half the canvas, the bowed image of Brown is the largest of the series. Alongside this "colossal" representation, his physical and emotional (spiritual?) exhaustion are apparent in his "spent forlorn" posture. To move forward through the paintings is also a motion of return, the progressive spiral of covenantal time.

In the fifth and final section of "John Brown," Hayden speaks within two, simultaneous public encounters: as a member of the paratextual team of writers who work together in the exhibition portfolio to guide the public through Lawrence's paintings and *also* as one present at the physically real and decidedly new encounter of the silkscreen unveiling. In doing so, he renders explicit the poem's participation in this earlier public and in extending it temporally and spatially. And now, he begins,

> these mordant images—
> these vibrant stainedglass
> colors, elemental shapes
> in ardent interplay
> with what we know of him
> know yet fail to understand[55]

The poem steps back and asks its readers not only to view themselves as members of the extended public of the silkscreen exhibition but to actively gaze on and consider—to, in effect, commemorate—themselves as they view these images. They (you, *we*) see what remains of John Brown over a century after his death: not the historical figure but an image, a symbol. Like Hayden's idiosyncratic colons, Brown's meaning—what he symbolizes—coheres in a visual grammar, here one of shape, color, and light. From these, contained in the paintings at which Hayden directs our gaze, Brown becomes a symbol, commemorating what he represents: his—and our own—relationship to a covenant. As with Malcolm X in "El-Hajj Malik El-Shabbazz," by considering Brown's relationship to a covenant, by considering the covenantal obligations he symbolizes, the ekphrastic and commemorative discourses grow to include a covenantal discourse, all three merging in the poem's act of public-creation.

The final image to which Hayden's poem turns, John Brown condensed to symbol, is the final painting of Lawrence's sequence:

> Hanged body turning clockwise
> in the air
>   the hour
> speeding to that hour
> his dead-of-night
> sorrows visions prophesied:[56]

In Lawrence's rendering, Brown's body is thrown against the sky like the rainbow Noah beheld after the flood. "Shall we not say he died / for us?" Hayden's poem asks. Christ-like, his slack body marks and seals a new American covenant. As its symbolic image, Brown transforms from a historically bound prophetic figure to one who speaks to us, as well—in 1978 or in our present-day encounter with the poem. Speaking to those who gaze on Lawrence's prints, John Brown's body warns that "the hour"—in which *we*, the public the poem creates, exist—is "speeding to that hour." Just as the Civil War followed the inability of Brown's generation to change its course, conflict and sorrow, "bloodburst: bloodflow:" loom as a covenantal threat that might recur at some point in the future—the twinned pole to covenantal promise, a marker of biblical covenant that we've seen in the verse of James Weldon Johnson and Charles Reznikoff.

Unlike "The Judgment Day," the final poem of Johnson's *God's Trombones*, Hayden does not end on the threat of the horrors to come should this covenant be violated. Rather, he ends—where else?—with a colon:

> And now,
>   these haunting stark
> torchlight images:[57]

After framing John Brown as a covenantal symbol, Hayden's poem asks its readers to turn their gaze back to the beginning of both sequences, painting and verse, and reconsider all that they have seen and read in light of what they now begin to apprehend. In essence, Hayden stands behind his podium at a gallery opening and, commenting on the final images of the series, now spreads his arms wide to encompass all twenty-two—to consider, that is, the nature of the covenant that Brown symbolizes. This is uncertain, ambivalent. Turning back to the beginning, we bring the "ardent interplay" of Lawrence's shapes "with what we know of him / know yet fail to understand." Apprehending and comprehending the symbol of the hanged John Brown are different things: Brown, like Malcolm X, is at once a figure of racial and American justice and of violence, anger, and death. Hayden may, as a Baha'i, believe that (to borrow from the title of his poem and collection) a "Mourning Time" is the necessary prelude to the peaceful world order prophesied by Baha'u'llah and his successor, Shoghi Effendi—but that doesn't mean he *welcomes* this period of suffering. This circling, uncertain return, from end to beginning, clarifies the discourse of public-creation in which this poem engages: a discourse of and about covenant, how to apprehend it, how to stand in relation to it. In "John Brown," different verse genres converge to produce this reflective, self-conscious consideration of covenant, to mark Lawrence's images of Brown as its symbols, and to wonder in both hope and dread at its terms and its consequences. Hayden offers no vision of the United States' future here. But a covenant, after all, is more like a contract than a prophecy—not a vision but a set of obligations.

Aliens in America

One more limit case, the final one. After all, maybe the exceptional nature of these historical sequences makes them just that, exceptions. Perhaps Hayden's poetry thinks about history in terms of covenant, but what about works that don't depend on the reader's prior knowledge of a historical figure? Does the covenantal poetics that emerges in poems like "El-Hajj Malik El-Shabazz" and "John Brown" when attention is paid to the histories of their composition and publication extend to works that don't share these textual histories? "[American Journal]," the final poem in Hayden's final, posthumous collection, suggests that it does.

Finality weighs heavily on this poem. Its location in the 1982 *American Journal* (and, later, as the final poem in the *Collected Poems*) makes it tempting to understand the work as a closing summation of all the writing that came before. There is no use in denying it: there *is* something to this. The poem draws together the themes, observations, and attitudes that pervade Hayden's career and, in particular, his mature work: examinations of American ideals, character, hypocrisy, and history; the alienation and outsider status of the poem's speaker, both from Americans in general and from his own, smaller community as well; an educated, elite figure's distanced observation of a vernacular culture he nonetheless feels deep, abiding affection for; the listing of various personae that Hayden's poetry has taken on, wearing "their varied pigmentations" and performing "in bankers grey afro and dashiki long hair and jeans / hard hat yarmulke mini skirt."[58] Here, you want to declare, is a metapoetics. Here, Hayden's mask is deliberately thin and acrylic, the stuff you'd find in an aisle of children's Halloween costumes.

The poem shares, as well, the seemingly lyric voice that includes but extends beyond this genre. The poem's engagement with personae—both those it lists and that which it performs, a space alien surveying Earth—signal this: it's a kind of dramatic monologue, certainly; it's also a Space Age poem (a topic and genre to which Hayden was drawn) and, indeed, a science-fiction poem.[59] (Here we find, perhaps, the move from "literary" poetry *into* "genre" poetry, to borrow from the language of prose fiction.) It isn't a commemorative poem, though—and only an ekphrastic poem if you squint, tilt your head until your neck stiffens, and risk expanding the definition of "ekphrasis" beyond recognition to include simply cogitating on historical sights. Nonetheless, it engages in the kind of public-creation found in Hayden's earlier poems and in the works of Johnson, Zukofsky, Ridge, and Reznikoff. Though the word "covenant" is never mentioned, "[American Journal]" offers perhaps Hayden's most explicit and sustained meditation on the relationship between the United States—its history, its present, and its future—and covenantal community. By drawing the reader into this act of self-conscious reflection on the nature of American character and American covenant, "[American Journal]," like "El-Hajj Malik El-Shabbaz" and "John Brown," situates its readers within the selfsame covenantal public it examines and describes.

"[American Journal]" is the diary of a space alien who has been sent to Earth by his community's leaders. Unlike the "reports" that, we learn in the first stanza, he regularly sends, this is a private journal, not meant for his superiors, as he attempts to come to terms with what he observes. The ultimate purpose of his observations is unclear, though the tone, certainly, is scientific, that of the ethnographer or anthropologist. Picture one of those many *Star Trek* episodes in which the crew disguise themselves to go among and learn about a more primitive society, their intentions (mostly) governed by goodwill toward all—this, it strikes me, is the approach of Hayden's alien. So, we learn, he disguises himself "in order to study them [humans] unobserved." Though this study is interactive, it is, nonetheless, a detached, scientific process: America, he states, is like "an organism that changes even as i / examine it." This metaphor of the scientist in his laboratory signals what the alien's observations and attitudes *should* be like and contrasts with his secret affections for them, that he is "curiously drawn unmentionable to / the americans," perhaps one reason for his worry that he will be judged a failure.[60] While Hayden's alien has been sent to study Americans in a detached manner, he finds himself the Space Age equivalent of Lola Ridge's immigrant: the alien who becomes American by *beholding* the space and community(ies) of the Americas. This is unintentional and puts the alien's mission in jeopardy.

The covenantal is precisely that which Hayden's alien observes in "[American Journal]," much as the covenantal is ultimately what "El-Hajj Malik El-Shabbaz" and "John Brown" come to consider as symbolized in their title figures. The notes the alien records for himself trace the ways Americans themselves imagine, gaze on, and relate to the higher, governing authority of their covenantal community. Americans, Hayden's alien observes, "it appears worship the Unknowable / Essence the same for them as for us but are / more faithful to their machine made gods." Hayden's alien worships a manifestation of the same divine authority that Americans do—and yet he can announce, "we are an ancient race and have outgrown / illusions cherished here," namely, the individualist manifestations of liberty and freedom of which Americans sing in lyrics like those of "The Star Spangled Banner" and "My Country 'Tis of Thee."[61] The turn to "machine made gods"—apt as though the complaint may feel to some people in the twenty-first century—is not about turning away from American ideals but the most recent manifestation of a turn away from the divine *already embodied in those ideals*. Despite the Unknowable Essence having made Itself manifest to Americans (who, at least in word, acknowledge It as their true God), they nonetheless persist in a studied misapprehension of the relationship to the divine that true worship of the Unknowable Essence would establish. The alien is confused, then, because Americans recognize that they exist in some kind of covenantal community. They are even aware, to some extent, of the higher authority that governs that covenant. Yet they are incapable of correctly stating to themselves the terms of that covenant, which they seem to misstate as "something they call the american dream."[62]

A man in a bar explains the terms of this covenant to the alien: "whats good could be a damn sight / better," "every body in the good old u s a / should have the chance to get ahead or at least / should have three squares a day." Put slightly otherwise, the terms of the American Dream are that "irregardless of the some / times night mare facts we always try to double / talk our way around," an American will be able to say, "as for myself / i do okay." "i / fear one does not clearly follow," the alien responds: what he does not follow, the "pass word" that he soon realizes is the key to American conversation, is the word "okay."[63] This perplexity is both conversational—is "okay" a crutch, or does it add meaning to the sentence?—and conceptual: what *does* it mean to say for oneself, "I do okay," especially amid the decadence and violence of Americans? This blurring of "okay" into a nebulous "liberty" (one not, in fact, embodied in the "carnage" of Americans' history or their more mundane routines) creates a covenant devoid of either blessing or curse—that is, of terms that govern it—and the worship not of the Unknowable Essence but of a "blonde miss teen age / america waving from a red white and blue flower / float as the goddess of liberty."[64]

"[American Journal]" gazes on the American people as "El-Hajj Malik El-Shabbaz" gazes on the person and names of Malcolm X and "John Brown" on Jacob Lawrence's series of paintings. There's another way to describe this shift in the object of attention: from an individual to an artwork to a public. "[American Journal]," that is, invites readers to do what Hayden himself felt his life and work had forced him to do: to step outside, at least momentarily, the broad-based American public in which they led their lives and consider it from the exterior. The failures that this perspective brings to our attention produce a critique—the alien's—whose searing nature I find difficult to understate and yet nearly impossible to accurately convey. Americans, put simply, have misunderstood what it means to be human.

This distancing, this objective and critical gaze on the American public, *alienates* readers from the broader American public. Put otherwise, the connection it forges between alienated reader and alien speaker produces what Michael Warner has described as a *counterpublic*: "[Counterpublics are] defined by their tension with a larger public. Their participants are marked off from persons or citizens in general. Discussion within such a public is understood to contravene the rules obtaining in the world at large, being structured by alternative dispositions or protocols, making different assumptions about what can be said or what goes without saying."[65] The "rules," "dispositions," and "protocols" at stake in "[American Journal]," the "different assumptions about what can be said or what goes without saying," are, indeed, the terms of covenant. Because the public has misapprehended them, those who do apprehend them—or who, at least, recognize the partiality of their apprehension—become, almost by definition, a counterpublic.

Apprehension requires, however, more than just the recognition of the general public's falling away from covenant. It also entails recognition of the covenantal counterpublic's obligations toward the general public. The alien, despite himself, is "curiously drawn" to Americans; though there is "much that repels," he says, "i am attracted / none the less." The alien is drawn to Americans precisely because of what they do not know, one segment of the "charming savages enlightened primitives brash / new comers lately sprung up in our galaxy."[66] He sees them much as Hayden sees Malcolm X: muddling through the process of learning to apprehend, of learning to know, of learning to learn the nature of their relationship to covenant and covenantal authority. In their shuffling uncertainty, he says, they express "their variousness their ingenuity / their elan vital and that some thing essence / quiddity i cannot penetrate or name."[67]

If Robert Hayden's poetry serves as a limit case of the covenantal poetics that this book has probed and explored, then "[American Journal]" tests the limits of those limits. But both poet and poem are "limit cases," in this regard, not simply because they stand at the border of lyric and covenantal or because of the seeming adequacy of "lyric" as a generic label. Rather, they accomplish what limit cases—as opposed to lim*inal* cases—in fact do: allow us to better see the shape and nature of the phenomenon at hand, a covenantal poetics enacted.

Coda

The House We Build Together

This scene shouldn't be too hard to imagine: a small Jewish boy, somewhere between the ages of five and eight, the tails of his long, black coat trailing behind him, cap barely holding to his head, runs with all the speed he can muster down New York City streets and turns, in a last effort, into a dead-end alley. The ten boys—his classmates, his neighbors—who have been chasing him, crying out that he's a dirty Jew, corner him against a wall. He climbs: up, into the windowsill. His cap falls off. His back is pressed to the glass as hands grab and swing at him. There's nowhere left to go.

It's 1945; the war in Europe has entered its endgame as the Pacific front crests.

Only once the group has cornered the Jewish boy does something remarkable happen. A man emerges from the doorway a few feet away, the black front and white collar of his thigh-length jacket making him look like some kind of priest or minister in cassock—even a Jew at prayer, the ends of a striped *tallit gadol* dangling over his shoulders. He places himself between the crowd and the boy and speaks to them of God's love, of an Americanness that knows nothing of national origins or religious difference, of blood that is literally shared among them all. The boy climbs down. "What is America to me?" the man asks—then begins to answer in rhyming quatrains. More than an idea or a symbol, it's the people—of "All races and religions," he insists, "that's America to me."[1] The song ends, and the ten boys turn to leave—joined by the eleventh whom they'd been pursuing. Their leader stoops to pick up the books that the Jewish child has dropped. He hands them to the boy and invites him to join the group. They leave together.

This is the plot of the 1945 RKO short film *The House I Live In*, which closely mirrors the story Louis Zukofsky told about his own youth—when, as a child, he recited a Yiddish translation of *Hiawatha* to ward off anti-Semitic bullies. More important than the two tales' shared conflict (too common, we can suppose), they both share a resolution: deploying verse to establish a covenantal public. Frank Sinatra, playing himself, appears in pseudoministerial garb as an ecumenical priest of an American civil religion grounded in religious pluralism and labor solidarity: two of the central themes of the title song, written by Lewis Allan, the activist nom de plume of Abel Meeropol, a public-school English teacher. This values-driven message, a pivot from wartime solidarity to solidarity on the postwar home front, earned the film a special 1946 Academy Award.

The House I Live In enacts many of the themes this book has engaged with and highlighted in the works of James Weldon Johnson, Charles Reznikoff, Lola Ridge, Louis Zukofsky, and Robert Hayden. It posits a moment in which verse is situated in time and space to establish a public and contribute to the democratic expansion of American civil religion—and thereby the American public itself. Yes, "The House I Live In" is a *song*, not a poem. But one of the key themes of *Situating Poetry* has been the reality that "written" verse also exists—sometimes even *primarily* exists—off the printed page. The situations in which poetry emerges and is deployed do not always match our expectations. We might be well suited to encounter, engage with, and learn from even seemingly page-bound avant-garde works (like Zukofsky's) by being willing, in this moment, to blur the line a little between "poem" and "popular song." The career of Abel Meeropol, like Johnson's, speaks to this blurring: he began as a poet, publishing his first volume, *The Dynasty of the Dust and Other Poems*, in 1929. After joining the Communist Party in the early 1930s, Meeropol increasingly turned to writing for situated publics: teachers' unions, the Communist Party USA, and Popular Front fund-raisers, revues, and group gatherings. In 1945, he left his job as a teacher at DeWitt Clinton High School in New York City and turned full-time to writing, working for Columbia, MGM, and NBC Television.[2]

"The House I Live In" itself seems to have begun on the page; it's the title of an undated antilynching poem (a theme to which Meeropol's writing turned again and again in the 1920s, '30s, and '40s—his most famous composition is the Billie Holiday standard "Strange Fruit").[3] By 1943, the song—now with more familiar lyrics and set to music by Earl Robinson—had been performed during a May Day rally in Union Square, and it debuted on-screen in the 1944 Universal Pictures USO revue *Follow the Boys*. In early 1945, a dinner party brought Frank Sinatra (at the height of both his early-career stardom and Popular Front activism) together with the screenwriter Albert Maltz and producer Frank Ross. As they sought a way to bring Sinatra's political activism to the screen and reach a broad, popular audience, Maltz's thoughts turned to Meeropol's song.[4]

As the ten-minute film opens, Sinatra stands in a recording studio, finishing a take of a hit love song, "If You Are But a Dream." They wrap, satisfied with what they have. The conductor tells Sinatra he needs five minutes to get ready for the next song, and Ol' Blue Eyes decides to step outside for a cigarette break. It's at this moment that the film cuts away to the chase scene; Sinatra steps into the alley just as the gang corners the Jewish boy against the studio window. The singer's first reaction is recognition: this is what boys do, his face says. He'll try to talk them out of it, but with good humor. So he asks a question with an obvious answer: Is there a fight brewing?

"We don't like him," one of the larger boys, blond-haired, who serves as their spokesman, explains. "We don't want him in our neighborhood or going to our school." Hearing this, the Jewish boy finally offers a retort: "I've been living here as long as you!" Maybe they're picking on the new kid; maybe they're picking a fight with someone they've just recently decided to loathe. When the singer asks why, a second boy from the crowd chimes in: "We don't like his religion!"

Now the singer can see this moment for what it is: these blond-haired boys in their striped short-sleeve collared shirts; this dark-haired cornered kid in a cap and black clothes. Even the shadows make the boy "look Jewish": as he stands in the window, they cast a thin black line down the side of his face where a curled forelock might fall.

These boys, Sinatra announces, must be "Nazi werewolves." They're taken aback. "I'm an American," he states by way of contrast and insists, a second time, that they're Nazis.

Now the protests start: their fathers are in the military. How could anyone compare Americans to Nazis? They're ready to fight *him* now, too.

It's at this point that Sinatra's sermon begins. They're all Americans, he explains, as long as they recognize that someone like Sinatra's father, who was born in Italy, can become as American as anyone born here. God created them all equally and loves them all equally. Jews and Christians work together on Navy bombers to defend the country. Jewish civilians donate blood that goes to help save the lives of Protestant soldiers: blood that, mixed in all their veins, upends the notions of descent-based nationalism. Americanness, Sinatra signals, emerges through the *mixing* of Jewish and Christian, native-born and immigrant, not autochthonous blood purity.

By the sermon's end—and it *is* a sermon—the gang of boys has decided to drop their pursuit of violence. Now they're more interested in getting Sinatra to prove that he's a singer. He opens the door to the studio, steps in, and changes his mind. He'll prove it. The orchestra swells. He begins to sing Meeropol's lyrics. America is "the dream that's been a-growing for 150 years," but "especially the people" of "all races and religions," "the grocer and the butcher," "the people that I meet." These words reinforce the sermon's message; as he concludes and steps inside, the orchestra shifts from Robinson's score to the notes of "America the Beautiful," a musical insistence that this song, too, belongs in the canonical liturgy of American civil religion. Publicity material from the film's release emphasizes this aspect. In the movie poster, for instance, Sinatra's depiction is quite clearly that of a clergyman tending to his flock, from his clothes to the lift of his arms to the boys' attentive faces.

But Sinatra's performance also acts as the means for creating and then transforming a public. For the bulk of the film, he's been talking to an audience composed exclusively of the gang of boys; he's placed himself as a physical barrier between them and the Jewish child, who lingers, hiding, in the window. Even as Sinatra begins to sing, this stays the same. But as Sinatra's voice rises, the Jewish boy slowly lowers himself down from the sill. He inches closer to the crowd, lingering at their rear. As the song ends and the film draws to a close, the boys turn to leave. The Jewish child, uncertain, stands still. But now something happens: one of the boys bends to pick up the books and hat that he's dropped and hands them to the Jewish child. The crowd of boys signal that they accept him as one of their own, and they leave together.

It's an easy and sentimental ending to a sentimental film. But that shouldn't lead us to overlook the song's role. Sinatra's sermon—his prose—merely persuades the boys to cease bullying. That's a win, certainly. But only with verse does he transform this audience into a public, and only through the shared experience of listening to the lyrics do they expand their public to include the Jewish child. Sinatra's rendition of "The House I Live In," situated in that studio alley, transforms the resolution from *ignoring* the outsider to acknowledging and accepting him as a member of a *shared public*.

And yet. When Abel Meeropol saw the film, he was furious. "Shit, they've ruined my song!" he shouted. He continued to make a scene, and, shortly, ushers removed him from the theater.[5] The film succeeded in creating a public—but failed to create the one the song envisioned. Its lyrics had been edited, excising references to America's founding history of revolution, the New Deal, and (most gallingly) more pointed lyrics about racial justice. The house that *Meeropol* lives in is "The same for black and white"; indeed, the closing stanza insists that it is, making specific reference to race, "A home where all are equal."[6] Meeropol's unedited lyrics accept the wartime patriotism of "My country right or wrong" but insist that this means that "if it's wrong, to set it right," a call to ongoing action for racial as well as economic and religion/immigrant-centered justice.

Meeropol did not let go of his song or his ideals or his anger at its presentation, rewriting "The House I Live In" for *Broadside*, the folk-revival publication whose contributors also included Bob Dylan, Pete Seeger, Julius Lester, Nina Simone, Janis Ian, and Arlo Guthrie. Published shortly before the 1964 presidential election, Meeropol's answer to his question, "What is America to me?" is bleak. "The house we live in," he notes, is no longer located amid the pluralism of race, religion, and occupation. Now Americans reside "On segregation street," neighbors to "racists," "bigots," and "jingoists."[7] By 1964, Meeropol swapped out "Democracy" for "hypocrisy" as the word that now defines America, whose leaders have "refined crude Nazi ways" while resisting integration and full civil rights. In place of the American Dream, Meeropol highlights "The freedom that's been shackled / For a hundred and eighty years." Turning to Sinatra's American/Nazi dichotomy, Meeropol's revision ends on a full-throated call to electoral action—but one from which concern with religious pluralism, labor rights, and immigration have been excised, replaced with a nearly single-minded focus on precisely that which was excluded from the song's most well-known performance.

The Maltz/Sinatra film is a testament to a postwar ideal of a religiously plural America—a turning point, perhaps, along with the 1947 feature *Gentleman's Agreement*, in the shifting, broadening concept of Americanness that Will Herberg identified and examined in *Protestant, Catholic, Jew* (1955). But precisely in this democratic, religiously plural, and immigrant-friendly expansion of an American public, *The House I Live In* highlights the omissions that Herberg himself observed of this triadic, religiously plural Americanness: even as it opened American identity and acceptance to Jews, Catholics, and eastern and southern European immigrants, this movement failed to include either African Americans or their churches and worship traditions, both of which continued to be seen as other.

These omissions also cast a harsh, unyielding spotlight on one of the central but mostly unspoken tensions that runs throughout *Situating Poetry*.

Attention to religious pluralism—as an ideal, an American reality, and a way of approaching poetry—allows us to move outside standard categories of poetic and literary classification and to recombine authors, groups, and works. In doing so, we can see the same potential that many writers and activists (whether believers, avowedly secular, or somewhere in the ambivalent middle) saw in religious pluralism to overcome racial divisions and anti-immigrant divides in the United States. But we know from history that this was not sufficient. So the crowd of white faces that assemble in the alley outside Sinatra's studio mandate that we confront, head-on, the reality that even deploying religious pluralism that succeeds in the establishment of a covenantal poetics may continue to exclude even in the same moment, even in the same *motion*, in which it expands the borders of inclusion. This might be true however noble its intentions. The risk (for which the film has been criticized by scholars as well as by Meeropol) is that precisely by bringing together Italian, Irish, English, and Jewish faces as equally American, it might reinforce the exclusion of African Americans.

The same critique might be made of the publics that Reznikoff, Ridge, and Zukofsky create. Each sympathized with the early civil rights movement—recall, for example, Ridge and Johnson's exchange about their belief in the power of literature ("especially the poetry," Johnson wrote) to help the cause.[8] So it's a matter of proximity and limits: not everyone can write (and write *well*) about everything. Ridge and Zukofsky focus on the experiences nearest them, into which they have the most insight and are best prepared to explore in verse. Ridge did write several race poems—and they're not among her strongest: the dialect of "Lullaby," for example, sits uneasily. For Zukofsky, it's a little more complicated. To fit the history of slavery and segregation into his complex, patterned historical vision places them among a swirl of historical injustices, while the primacy of personal experience relegates them largely to the background.

The case of Reznikoff's *Testimony* is more complex. In its final version, race serves as an important through line, one of the recurring section headings across time period and region, woven clearly into the fabric of his covenantal public. But the original version of *Testimony*, the 1934 "My Country 'Tis of Thee," foregrounds it. Instead of a focus on 1885–1915—the immigration era—he begins earlier. The first of the poem's three sections, "Southerners and Slaves," is a series of antebellum case histories. "Of Slaves" is the third of three subsections ("Of Murder" and "Two Letters" are the others), but it accounts for over half the text. In its final version, Reznikoff refounds the United States during the immigration era; in its original, during the reign of chattel slavery. As we've seen, an immigration-era focus proves instrumental to the ways *Testimony* creates a covenantal public. But it wasn't a change that came without a cost. Some people might see that as a sign of pluralism's (or covenant's) failure. Yet I'm not so sure: there's a line between difficult and uncertain, on the one hand, and impossible, on the other. These momentary publics, joined through poetry, prove the possibility of something more sustainable. Attention to religious pluralism is not a miracle cure but a way of better understanding those difficulties and addressing, sometimes even resolving, them.

We can see the ways understanding and resolution might play out, for example, in the afterlife of *God's Trombones*—perhaps precisely because it has been the least page-bound of the works examined here. And the life of "The House I Live In," from poem to song to film, gives us a further glimpse at how and why a work succeeds or fails in establishing a covenantal public. Both Paul Robeson and the African American folksinger Josh White recorded versions of "The House I Live In" in 1947, following a version of Meeropol's preferred lyrics. Indeed, White was regularly performing the song around New York City as Sinatra's film was in production—a version that Wendy Wall describes as a boldly "left-liberal, antifascist" iteration in contrast with film's emphasis on religious pluralism.[9] Both White's and Robeson's recordings outmatch the overarranged studio orchestration of Sinatra's and produce superior musical performances. As a Sinatra aficionado, I'll be blunt: his is pure schmaltz. (I actually prefer the version from 1994's widely panned *Duets II*, recorded with Neil Diamond, to the original: precisely because the deterioration of Sinatra's voice required changes to his phrasing, allowing Diamond—the king of schmaltz-as-sincerity—to take the lead. He can sell it; Sinatra can't.) Despite this, it's as a *Sinatra* song that "House" became a minor cultural touchstone. By the time of the Statue of Liberty's 1986 centennial celebration, at which Sinatra performed the song, it had been totally subsumed into Reagan-era civil religion, transformed from protest song to a paean to morning in America, just as Sinatra himself had moved from the Popular Front Left to the political Right over the course of the 1960s and '70s.

The reason, I would suggest, is that Sinatra managed to offer a broader invitation to public-formation in 1945 than either White or Robeson did in 1947. This is not to say that their performances did *not* establish covenantal publics; they certainly do appeal to and expand the discourse of American civil religion through theirs. Nor is it meant to totally decouple public-creation from aesthetic merit. But such merit alone cannot account, we've seen, for success or failure on these grounds; it is one element among many. Rather, it's a matter of *circulation*—the same question that bedeviled Zukofsky and Ridge, which has given lasting life to Johnson's *God's Trombones*, which Reznikoff reimagined as translation, and which has been overlooked in discussions of Hayden. Precisely by embedding the song within a narrative of public-creation, *The House I Live In* can invite its viewers to imagine themselves as part of this public in a way that recordings alone cannot. This holds for a Sinatra record as well as White's and Robeson's. Their live performances—at protests and rallies, in the small venues of the emerging folk scene—certainly could engage in public-creation just as effectively as (perhaps more than) Sinatra's film. In these contexts, as with the labor rallies in which Ridge's "Stone Face" was first circulated, the lyrics are situated. But as with "Stone Face" on the printed page, so with "The House I Live In" on an LP. *Circulating* this situatedness proves too difficult a task.

⁓

Links between popular song and modernist poetry have recurred throughout *Situating Poetry*, changing shape yet echoing and recalling earlier instances like a musical phrase. From Reznikoff's use of recitative to Johnson's blurring of score and prosody, pulpit speech and song, to Zukofsky's Yiddishized Bach, this has gone beyond the referentiality and engagement with recording technologies found, for instance, in Eliot's *Waste Land*. Rather, it has been crucial to their explorations of genre and of public-creation. So I should be careful to clarify, particularly in this coda focused on popular song, that I do not mean to conflate poetry with this closest of its "others"; I agree with Jahan Ramazani that "it's a misapprehension, . . . if not quite an insult, to confuse them."[10] Yet in this study, the dialogic relationship between these two modalities of creation and communication goes beyond the evocation of soundscape or efficacy of transmitting cultural memory. The dialogues I have explored have been probing tests of how publics might be created by a poem situated *as a poem* (on the page, at a protest, reading, or museum exhibit) and how genre might be deployed toward this end.

So why turn, in these closing pages, to popular culture and popular song? Beyond its usefulness in highlighting the ways that the interplay of circulation and genre force us to step outside familiar aesthetic and critical categories and in highlighting the limits of the attention to religious pluralism that I have been utilizing, it's a reminder that cultural revisions of American civil religion aren't just, to paraphrase Leonard Cohen, something I'm sitting up here on a stage thinking and writing about. They're real. They touch on and inform the careers of artists we might now think of as niche (Josh White) and who, like Sinatra, dominated American music and film (and Hollywood tabloids) for over half a century. Civil religious discourse permeated and continues to permeate American cultural production, drawing in writers and performers from Left and Right, religious and secular.

Yet juxtaposing poetry and song helps highlight what poetry—even *modernist* poetry—shares with song: the situatedness of composition and encounter; the ways poetry, like other modes of speech, strives toward the creation of publics. This is true of modernist poetry, too, despite its postures of alienation and isolation. Aren't these attitudes, at least as they're expressed in modernism, an insider's privileges—doesn't exile depend on having had, at some point, access? Zukofsky certainly thought so. In "Poem Beginning 'The,'" the send-up of *The Waste Land* that first drew him to Ezra Pound's attention and marked his debut as a modernist of note, he casts T. S. Eliot—but also Pound, Virginia Woolf, James Joyce, E. E. Cummings, and D. H. Lawrence—as "self-exiled men" whose despair at the twentieth century self-indulgently misses the point. Antisocial modernism, he sees, is just one posture among many, one way of building a public of similarly minded readers. It's also one that won't do for him, the Yiddish-speaking son of an immigrant mother "who never could sing Bach, never read Shakespeare," whose professors dismiss him as "a Jewish boy" who should go be his "Plato's Philo." "Assimilation is not hard, / and once the Faith's askew / I might as well look Shagetz just as much as Jew," he proclaims—but knows he *can't* look like a WASP, that his cultural citizenship will always be as temporary and contingent as Shylock's.[11]

The five writers examined at length in *Situating Poetry*—immigrants and their children; Jews, Catholics, Baha'is, Black Methodists; atheists and idiosyncratic believers; African Americans and ethnic whites—all strove, each in their own way, toward a prosocial modernism. Johnson, Ridge, Reznikoff, Zukofsky, and Hayden are notable not for *succeeding* in this quest—they do not always succeed—but for undertaking it and moving, along different vectors, toward a shared goal: the creation of a more democratic and pluralist American public through writing and reading poetry. Each moves toward this goal via engagement with the language, typology, and discourse of covenant. In doing so, they repurpose what's present in American cultural and political discourse, much as they repurpose Classical myth, literature in translation, biblical stories, historical documents, and popular culture.

By showing us this public-creating modernism situated in social spaces and specific modes of circulation, they offer us new ways to imagine the period, its poetry, and its genres. Applying pressure to limit cases, we see productive engagement with old genres that modernism supposedly discarded. All told, they suggest new ways of reading and imagining modernism and modern poetry, including and beyond the lyric. Their works are "democratic" not in the sense of being less difficult than those of a high modernist elite but in the ways they manipulate difficulty to insist on public *nomoi* of access and pluralism. While Eliot and Pound write paeans to the ruins of homes that they have moved away from, the writers studied here busy themselves with the blueprints of the house we might build together.

NOTES

Introduction

1. Yehoash, *Dos lied fun Hiavata* (New York: Ferlag Yehoash, 1910), 6.

2. Zukofsky mentions these incidents obliquely in *"A"-14* (New York: New Directions, 2011), 340; and more fully in a June 28, 1960, letter to Cid Corman (Folder 2, Box 18, Louis Zukofsky Collection, Harry Ransom Center, University of Texas at Austin). Mark Scroggins summarizes these accounts and others in *The Poem of a Life: A Biography of Louis Zukofsky* (Berkeley, CA: Shoemaker and Hoard, 2007), 3, 18.

3. James Weldon Johnson, *Along This Way*, in *Writings* (New York: Library of America, 2004), 315.

4. They throw pennies, yes, but at the son of a pants presser who is so poor that, on his death in 1950, his life savings came out to less than one dollar, willed to his synagogue. Zukofsky's verb, in his 1960 letter to Corman, was "toss."

5. Michael Warner, *Publics and Counterpublics* (Brooklyn, NY: Zone Books, 2002), 88.

6. Warner, 88.

7. Alan Jacobs, "Attending to Technology: Theses for Disputation," *New Atlantis*, Winter 2016, 17.

8. Warner, *Publics and Counterpublics*, 81.

9. Warner, 81.

10. Virginia Jackson, *Dickinson's Misery: A Theory of Lyric Reading* (Princeton, NJ: Princeton University Press, 2005); Virginia Jackson and Yopie Prins, eds., *The Lyric Theory Reader: A Critical Anthology* (Baltimore: Johns Hopkins University Press, 2013); Mark Jeffreys, "Ideologies of Lyric: A Problem of Genre in Contemporary Anglophone Poetics," *PMLA* 110, no. 2 (March 1995): 196–205. See also works that develop historically attuned practices of reading poetry, whether lyric or not (the following attend, in particular, to the theory and practice of prosody and rhythm), such as Meredith Martin, *The Rise and Fall of Meter: Poetry and English National Culture, 1860–1930* (Princeton, NJ: Princeton University Press, 2012); Sarah Ehlers, "Making It Old: The Victorian/Modern Divide in Twentieth-Century American Poetry," *MLQ* 73, no. 1 (March 2012): 37–67; and Michael Golston, *Rhythm and Race in Modernist Poetry and Science* (New York: Columbia University Press, 2008). Gillian White's *Lyric Shame: The "Lyric" Subject of Contemporary American Poetry* (Cambridge, MA: Harvard University Press,

2014) explores the debates in contemporary US poetics over what lyric is, means, and ought to be.

11. Jeffreys, "Ideologies of Lyric," 200; Virginia Jackson, "Who Reads Poetry?," *PMLA* 123, no. 1 (January 2008): 181–87.

12. Jackson, *Dickinson's Misery*, 10.

13. White, *Lyric Shame*, 2.

14. John Stuart Mill, "What Is Poetry?," in *The Broadview Anthology of Victorian Poetry and Poetic Theory*, ed. Thomas J. Collins and Vivienne J. Rundle (Peterborough, ON: Broadview, 1999), 1216.

15. William Butler Yeats, "Per Amica Silentia Lunae: Anima Hominis," in *Per Amica Silentia Lunae* (New York: Macmillan, 1918), 29.

16. Mill, "What Is Poetry?," 1216.

17. Virginia Jackson and Yopie Prins, introduction to section 8, "Avant-garde Anti-lyricism," in *Lyric Theory Reader*, 452. Gillian White also discusses avant-garde anti-lyricism and its connection to Mill and the history of lyric as genre and reading practice in the introduction to *Lyric Shame*, esp. 7–26.

18. Mike Chasar's *Everyday Reading: Poetry and Popular Culture in Modern America* (New York: Columbia University Press, 2012) is an excellent and provocative guide to the poetic contexts that these encounters overlook and erase.

19. Mill, "What Is Poetry?," 1213.

20. Jackson, "Who Reads Poetry?," 183.

21. T. S. Eliot, "The Social Function of Poetry," in *On Poetry and Poets* (New York: Farrar, Straus and Giroux, 1957), 5.

22. Barry McCrea, *Languages of the Night: Minor Languages and the Literary Imagination in Twentieth-Century Ireland and Europe* (New Haven, CT: Yale University Press, 2015).

23. Meredith Martin, *The Rise and Fall of Meter: Poetry and English National Culture, 1860–1930* (Princeton, NJ: Princeton University Press, 2012), 204.

24. Dorothy Wang, *Thinking Its Presence: Form, Race, and Subjectivity in Contemporary Asian American Poetry* (Stanford, CA: Stanford University Press, 2014), 20.

25. Wang, xx.

26. Wang, xxii.

27. Cary Nelson, *Repression and Recovery: Modern American Poetry and the Politics of Cultural Memory, 1910–1945* (Madison: University of Wisconsin Press, 1992), 4.

28. Philip Gorski, *American Covenant: A History of American Civil Religion from the Puritans to the Present* (Princeton, NJ: Princeton University Press, 2017), 110.

29. The major figure in this field of study is still Sacvan Bercovitch, particularly his *Puritan Origins of the American Self* (New Haven, CT: Yale University Press, 1975), *The American Jeremiad* (Madison: University of Wisconsin Press, 1978), and *The Rites of Assent: Transformations in the Symbolic Construction of America* (New York: Routledge, 1993). Nan Goodman's and Michael P. Kramer's edited volume, *The Turn around Religion in America: Literature, Culture, and the Work of Sacvan Bercovitch* (Burlington, VT: Ashgate, 2011), and a 2014 roundtable, "Short Reflections on Sacvan Bercovitch's *The American Jeremiad*," *Common-Place* 14, no. 4, offer both a retrospective view of Bercovitch's influence and forays into how his work can continue to converse with contemporary scholarship. More recently, Michael Hoberman has explored the

interactions between Puritan thinking about Jews and Colonial-era encounters with them (*New England / New Israel: Jews and Puritans in Early America* [Amherst: University of Massachusetts Press, 2011]), while Shalom Goldman has studied what he terms "Puritan Hebraism" (*Hebrew and the Bible in America: The First Two Centuries*, ed. Goldman [Lebanon, NH: Brandeis University Press, 1994]; *God's Sacred Tongue: Hebrew and the American Imagination* [Chapel Hill: University of North Carolina Press, 2004]). Meanwhile, scholars such as Tracy Fessenden (*Culture and Redemption: Religion, the Secular, and American Literature* [Princeton, NJ: Princeton University Press, 2006]) have taken the study of American biblical typology in early American literature and rhetoric in new directions.

30. Arthur Hertzberg, "The New England Puritans and the Jews," in Goldman, *Hebrew and the Bible in America*, 105.

31. Warner, *Publics and Counterpublics*, 56.

32. Martin P. Kramer offers a cogent description in his reflection on the fortieth anniversary of Bercovitch's *American Jeremiad*: "In America, he suggested, consensus did not necessarily mean ideological uniformity or behavioral conformism but 'symbolic cohesion,' not uncritical allegiance but a shared rhetoric that could sustain a complex constellation of competing values and even encourage dissent—as long as it was dissent in the name of America, as long as consent and dissent were made to correspond." Kramer, "The Jews and the Jeremiad," *Common-Place* 14, no. 4 (Summer 2014), http://commonplace.online/article/the-jews-and-the-jeremiad/.

33. Gorski, *American Covenant*, 96.

34. Michael Walzer, *Exodus and Revolution* (New York: Basic Books, 1986), 7.

35. James Darsey, *The Prophetic Tradition and Radical Rhetoric in America* (New York: New York University Press, 1999); Melanie J. Wright, *Moses in America: The Cultural Uses of Biblical Narrative* (New York: Oxford University Press, 2002). Particular emphasis has been placed on the African American encounter with American biblical discourse. This is the focus of Rhondda Robinson Thomas's *Claiming Exodus: A History of Afro-American Identity, 1775–1903* (Baylor, TX: Baylor University Press, 2013), as well as Philip Gorski's discussions of Frederick Douglass and W. E. B. DuBois in *American Covenant* and Wright's reading of Zora Neale Hurston's *Moses, Man of the Mountain* in *Moses in America* (2002). Joanna Brooks's *American Lazarus: Religion and the Rise of African-American and Native American Literatures* (New York: Oxford University Press, 2003) is an indispensable study in this regard.

36. This, more or less, is what Charles Taylor means when he defines a "secular age" as one in which "there are no more naïve theists, just as there are no naïve atheists"—that is, "we have moved from a naïve acceptance of [God's, spiritual creatures'] reality, to a sense that either to affirm or deny them is to enter a disputed terrain." Taylor, *A Secular Age* (Cambridge, MA: Belknap Press of Harvard University Press, 2007), 30.

37. Warner, *Publics and Counterpublics*, 56. By distinguishing my approach from studies of modernism *and* religion, I mean to make a contrast between the goals of this study and those of important recent works on modernism and religion, such as Pericles Lewis's *Religious Experience and the Modernist Novel* (Cambridge: Cambridge University Press, 2010), Anthony Domestico's *Poetry and Theology in the Modernist Period* (Baltimore: Johns Hopkins University Press, 2017), Alan Jacobs's *The Year of*

Our Lord 1943: Christian Humanism in an Age of Crisis (New York: Oxford University Press, 2018), and Tracy Fessenden's *Culture and Redemption: Religion, the Secular, and American Literature* (Princeton, NJ: Princeton University Press, 2007).

38. Wang, *Thinking Its Presence*; Anthony Reed, *Freedom Time: The Poetics and Politics of Black Experimental Writing* (Baltimore: Johns Hopkins University Press, 2016).

39. Steven S. Lee, *The Ethnic Avant-Garde: Minority Cultures and World Revolution* (New York: Columbia University Press, 2017).

40. The approach I outline in this paragraph builds on the multi- and postethnic approaches to Jewish literary and cultural studies offered by Jonathan Freedman, *Klezmer America: Jewishness, Ethnicity, Modernity* (New York: Columbia University Press, 2008); Dean Franco, *Race, Rights, and Recognition: Jewish American Literature since 1969* (Ithaca, NY: Cornell University Press, 2012); and Benjamin Schreier, *The Impossible Jew: Identity and the Reconstruction of Jewish American Literary History* (New York: New York University Press, 2015).

41. Will Herberg, *Protestant, Catholic, Jew: An Essay in American Religious Sociology* (Garden City, NY: Doubleday, 1955).

42. See, for instance, the essays on Zukofsky, Reznikoff, and George Oppen in *Radical Poetics and Secular Jewish Culture*, ed. Stephen Miller and Daniel Morris (Tuscaloosa: University of Alabama Press, 2010); and *The Objectivist Nexus*, ed. Rachel Blau DuPlessis and Peter Quartermain (Tuscaloosa: University of Alabama Press, 1999).

43. For example, Henry Louis Gates Jr., *The Signifying Monkey* (New York: Oxford University Press, 1988); Houston Baker Jr., *Blues, Ideology, and Afro-American Literature: A Vernacular Theory* (Chicago: University of Chicago Press, 1984); Baker, *Afro-American Poetics: Revisions of Harlem and the Black Aesthetic* (Madison: University of Wisconsin Press, 1988); and Eric Sundquist, *The Hammers of Creation: Folk Culture in Modern African-American Fiction* (Athens: University of Georgia Press, 1997).

44. Major works in this vein include Cary Nelson, *Revolutionary Memory* (New York: Routledge, 2001); Nancy Berke, *Women Poets on the Left* (Gainesville: University Press of Florida, 2001); Caroline Maun, *Mosaic of Fire* (Columbia: University of South Carolina Press, 2012); John Timberman Newcomb, *How Did Poetry Survive?* (Urbana: University of Illinois Press, 2012); Terese Svoboda, *Anything That Burns You: A Portrait of Lola Ridge, Radical Poet* (Tucson, AZ: Schaffner, 2016); and Belinda Wheeler, "Lola Ridge's Pivotal Editorial Role at *Broom*," *PMLA* 127, no. 2 (March 2012): 283–91.

45. James Weldon Johnson to Lola Ridge, March 16, 1925; and Countee Cullen to Lola Ridge, n.d.; both courtesy of Elaine Sproat.

46. "The Spring Books of Viking Press, 1927," Folder 222, Box 61, James Weldon and Grace Nail Johnson Collection, Beinecke Rare Book and Manuscript Library, Yale University, New Haven, CT.

47. Search for *God's Trombones* or the title of any individual poem in the collection on YouTube. You'll find dozens of videos of their *contemporary* performances in African American churches.

48. Robert Hayden, "A Certain Vision," in *Collected Prose*, ed. Frederick Glaysher (Ann Arbor: University of Michigan Press, 1984), 94. Hayden would also write the preface to the 1968 Atheneum edition of *The New Negro*.

49. This is the address listed on the copyright page of the self-printed *Nine Plays* (New York, 1927).

50. Some scholarship has also attempted to link Zukofsky to the American Yiddish avant-garde. The most persuasive cases are Ariel Resnikoff's "Louis Zukofsky and Mikhl Likht, 'A Test of Jewish American Modernist Poetics,'" *jacket-2*, September 2013; and Sarah Ponichtera's PhD dissertation, "Yiddish and the Avant-Garde in American Jewish Poetry" (Columbia University, 2012), which she generously shared with me.

51. Hillel Rogoff, "Di 'Gheto' an englishe poema fun der ist sayd," *Forverts*, December 22, 1918.

52. Louis Zukofsky to Harriet Monroe, September 1, 1920, Folder 3, Box 43, *Poetry: A Magazine of Verse* Records 1895–1961, Special Collections Research Center, University of Chicago Library, Chicago, IL.

53. Svoboda, *Anything That Burns You*, 130.

1 • *A Congregation of Readers*

1. Johnson insists as much in his autobiography, *Along This Way*, in *Writings* (New York: Library of America, 2004). Imani Perry's *May We Forever Stand: A History of the Black National Anthem* (Chapel Hill: University of North Carolina Press, 2018) traces this at length.

2. Johnson, *Along This Way*, 301–2.

3. Johnson, 301–2.

4. Johnson, 187.

5. He knew it, and the inconsistencies of American racial dynamics, well enough to pass for a Black Cuban (rather than a Black Floridian) while traveling between Jacksonville and Atlanta—and so avoided being moved to the Jim Crow car at the Georgia border (Johnson, 205).

6. Michael Warner, *Publics and Counterpublics* (Brooklyn, NY: Zone Books, 2002), 81.

7. Warner, 81.

8. Bonnie Costello, *The Plural of Us: Poetry and Community in Auden and Others* (Princeton, NJ: Princeton University Press, 2017), 5, 13.

9. Brander Matthews, "Introduction to *Fifty Years and Other Poems*," in *Complete Poems*, by James Weldon Johnson (New York: Penguin, 2000), 115–16.

10. Imani Perry, *May We Forever Stand: A History of the Black National Anthem* (Chapel Hill: University of North Carolina Press, 2018), 12.

11. In this, I'm drawing on the legal theorist Robert Cover's analysis of the development of a plurality of interpretive communities. For Cover, constitutional and legal meaning emerge from the narratives and *nomoi* of communities; I'm arguing that something similar occurs on the level of civil religious discourse. See Cover, "The Supreme Court, 1982 Term—Foreword: *Nomos* and Narrative," *Harvard Law Review* 97, no. 4 (1983–84): 26–33.

12. James Weldon Johnson, "Lift Ev'ry Voice and Sing," in *Writings*, 875.

13. Cover, "*Nomos* and Narrative," 34. In *American Covenant: A History of American Civil Religion from the Puritans to the Present* (Princeton, NJ: Princeton University Press, 2017), Philip Gorski observes something similar about the revisionary civil religious project contained in the writing and politics of Abraham Lincoln and, especially, Frederick Douglass (see, e.g., 107–8).

14. Johnson, "Lift Ev'ry Voice," 875.

15. James Weldon Johnson, "Race Prejudice and the Negro Artist," in *Writings*, 755, 763–64.

16. Kwame Anthony Appiah eloquently depicts art and cultural projection as being subject to claims from both the local and the global:

> We can respond to art that is not ours; indeed, we can fully respond to "our" art only if we move beyond thinking of it as ours and start to respond to it as art. But equally important is the human connection. My people–human beings–made the Great Wall of China, the Chrysler Building, the Sistine Chapel: these things were made by creatures like me, through the exercise of skill and imagination. I do not have those skills, and my imagination spins different dreams. Nevertheless, that potential is also in me. The connection through a local identity is as imaginary as the connection through humanity. The Nigerian's link to the Benin bronze, like mine, is a connection made in the imagination; but to say this isn't to pronounce either of them unreal. They are among the realest connections that we have.

Appiah, *Cosmopolitanism: Ethics in a World of Strangers* (New York: Norton, 2006), 135.

17. Johnson, "Race Prejudice and the Negro Artist," 764, 765.

18. To offer a handful of examples from among many, Johnson declared in a May 1922 *New York Age* editorial, "I wish my readers to think of the production of poets by a race as a vital thing. It is vital not only as an indication of the development of the race but it is vital as to the place and recognition which that race is given by the world at large." James Weldon Johnson, "A Real Poet," in *Writings*, 646. In an April 10, 1924, address at Howard University titled "American Negro Poets and Poetry," he impressed on his audience that "the matter of Aframerican poets and their poetry does have a distinct bearing on the Race Question." Box 76, Folder 466, James Weldon and Grace Nail Johnson Papers, Beinecke Rare Book and Manuscript Library, Yale University, New Haven, CT. Notes for a talk titled "Contributions of the Negro to American Culture" express a similar sentiment. Box 76, Folder 487, James Weldon and Grace Nail Johnson Papers. In "Convention—and the Negro in American Fiction," a May 7, 1931, lecture at Fisk University, he called on young writers to alter the conventions that make for poor depictions of African Americans in US fiction. Box 76, Folder 490, Johnson Papers.

19. James Weldon Johnson, "The Dilemma of the Negro Artist," in *Writings*, 751.

20. William Stanley Braithwaite to James Weldon Johnson, March 29, 1913, Box 3, Folder 55, Johnson Papers. Johnson kept abreast of developments in the modernist avant-garde, reading Pound, Eliot, Joyce, and Stein—and sending the latter a copy of *God's Trombones*. This gift is noted in an undated letter from Stein (Box 20, Folder 459, Johnson Papers) and in a January 20, 1935, letter from Johnson to Carl Van Vechten (Box 21, Folder 502, Johnson Papers). Immediately after the US embargo on Joyce's *Ulysses* was lifted, Johnson ordered a copy of it (Box 4, Folder 58, Johnson Papers).

21. John Timberman Newcomb, *Would Poetry Disappear? American Verse and the Crisis of Modernity* (Columbus: Ohio State University Press, 2004), xv–xvi.

22. James Weldon Johnson, "Preface to *God's Trombones*," in *Writings*, 837.

23. Other early contributors to this journal included William Carlos Williams and Witter Bynner, as well as Leonora Speyer, winner of the 1927 Pulitzer Prize. George Hutchinson reads *The Freeman* against *The Dial* as the two competing progeny of *The Seven Arts*. While *The Dial* placed more emphasis on—and became far more influential in—promoting *The Seven Arts*' literary/cultural agenda, it also "became unabashedly highbrow and emphasized that American writers worked 'in the same *milieu* and in the same tradition of letters as the Europeans,' that 'we are all in the Western-civilized-Christian-American tradition.'" Hutchinson, *The Harlem Renaissance in Black and White* (Cambridge, MA: Harvard University Press, 1996), 117. *The Freeman*, with its name purchased from an African American paper in Indianapolis, was *The Dial*'s socialist/progressive, anti-imperialist alternative, in possession of a worldview in much closer alignment with that of the publications of the New Negro movement.

24. Johnson, "Preface to *God's Trombones*," 839.

25. Marcellus Blount, "The Preacherly Text: African American Poetry and Vernacular Performance," *PMLA* 107, no. 3 (1992): 589. In the thirty years since Blount's article appeared, scholarship's engagement with his reading has been conspicuously absent.

26. Johnson, "Convention—and the Negro in American Fiction." In Johnson's introductory remarks to an October 1929 reading of *God's Trombones* at the Institute of Pacific Relations, he further notes that he deliberately chose "not to paint the oldtime [sic] preacher in his external comic aspects." Box 77, Folder 513, Johnson Papers.

27. Johnson, "Preface to *God's Trombones*," 836, 834.

28. When Johnson returned from the consular service in 1914, he found that Jacksonville had become a boomtown for the nascent motion-picture business. Excited, perhaps, by the possibilities of this new form, he "thought to make a try at this new art field" (*Along This Way*, 461). Johnson sold three scenarios: *Aunt Mandy's Chicken Dinner* (June 25, 1914), *Do You Believe in Ghosts?* (July 9, 1914), and either *The Black Billionaire* or the frankly repellant *Why Don't You Get a Lady of Your Own?*, which, in presenting the African American male as at once violently sexual and sexually violent, incorporates every stereotype Johnson's criticism would later rail against. Johnson's first biographer, Eugene Levy, glosses over this period in his career, as did Johnson himself, writing in his autobiography only, "We saw the exhibition of the first picture and were so disappointed in it that we were actually ashamed to see the others" (*Along This Way*, 461). Nonetheless, this little-remarked low point survives in the lacunae, a negative against which he pushed in his career as poet, mentor to and promoter of younger New Negro writers, newspaper editorialist, and secretary of the NAACP.

29. TS synopsis, Box 74, Folder 436, Johnson Papers.

30. "Memo—J.W.J.–W.E.B. DuB.," Box 60, Folder 217, Johnson Papers.

31. Lines from this poem are taken, unless otherwise noted, from the final, clean TS, ca. 1927–28, Box 60, Folder 217, Johnson Papers.

32. An earlier draft of the poem reads, "You wondered whether he were seer or clown," pointing toward a slightly more nuanced view of this poem's function: to plant doubts about stereotypes in the reader's mind, which would then be completely dissolved once they had "heard" him preach for themselves. Original TS with author revisions, Box 60, Folder 217, Johnson Papers.

33. Caroline Goeser, *Picturing the New Negro: Harlem Renaissance Print Culture and Modern Black Identity* (Lawrence: University Press of Kansas, 2007), 141–42.

34. "Program: The New World Dancers," Box 62, Folder 236, Johnson Papers.

35. syracuse.com, "The Paul Robeson Performing Arts Company: *God's Trombones*," YouTube, February 25, 2015, http://youtu.be/7az47nDJ6aQ.

36. *The Ed Sullivan Show*, episode 29, season 19, "Easter Show," aired March 26, 1967, on CBS.

37. Blount, "Preacherly Text," 589.

38. Johnson, "Preface to *God's Trombones*," 839.

39. Ben Glaser, "Folk Iambics: Prosody, Vestiges, and Sterling Brown's *Outline for the Study of the Poetry of American Negroes*," *PMLA* 129, no. 3 (2014): 418. See also Michael Golston's *Rhythm and Race in Modernist Poetry and Science* (New York: Columbia University Press, 2008) on modernist "theories of rhythm as blood- and race-based, as stimulated by environmental factors, as integral to a 'primitive' layer of the world that Modernism seeks to make available, and as 'a subconscious possession'" (58).

40. Johnson, "Preface to *God's Trombones*," 840.

41. James Weldon Johnson, "Reading at Columbia University, December 24, 1935," *PennSound*, accessed April 19, 2019, http://writing.upenn.edu/pennsound/x/Johnson-JW.php. The 1938 record comes from James Weldon Johnson, "The Creation," *Voices of Black America: Historical Readings of Speeches, Poetry, Humor, and Drama* (Naxos Audiobooks, 2002).

42. For example, three of five lines in the third stanza: "And the light," "And the darkness," "And the light." And so on throughout the poem.

43. Something similar occurs as the preacher is transformed and dignified in "Jasper Jones": steadily iambic lines begin to end on phrases—e.g., "of his spell," "at his will"—that can be read as anapests.

44. Yopie Prins, "What Is Historical Poetics?," *Modern Language Quarterly* 77, no. 1 (March 2016): 14.

45. As Adelaide Morris notes in her entry on documentary poetics in the *Princeton Encyclopedia of Poetry and Poetics* (Princeton, NJ: Princeton University Press, 2012), the category "is less a systematic theory or doctrine of a kind of poetry than an array of strategies and techniques" (372). *God's Trombones* represents one of these techniques, the origins of which precede the publication of the first readily recognized documentary poems.

46. Paula Marie Seniors, *Beyond Lift Every Voice and Sing: The Culture of Uplift, Identity, and Politics in Black Musical Theater* (Columbus: Ohio State University Press, 2009), 33.

47. The third major anthology of this period—*The Book of American Negro Poetry* (1922)—was likewise an endeavor in documenting African American literary and cultural productions by collecting, editing, and arranging texts.

48. Unlike the contemporaneous development of documentary poetics within the avant-garde, Johnson's documentary poetics are not fragmentary, insofar as his "original poetic voice" appears "almost totally subsumed by the sources from which he worked": that is, the remembered documents of traditional sermons from his youth, the prosody (such as it is) of the King James Bible, and the phrases of the idiomatic vernacular he does include. The quoted phrases come from David Ten Eyck's discus-

sion of Ezra Pound's documentary practices and refer to the change in Pound's documentary method during the 1930s, in *Ezra Pound's Adams Cantos* (London: Bloomsbury, 2012), 35. Rather than historical documents framed by lyric and narrative verse, in the Adams Cantos, the documentary source serves as the poem to the exclusion of other modes or voices. This reapplication of Ten Eyck's words is intended to highlight Johnson's similarity and his dissimilarity from these practices: at the same time that he prefigures the techniques of Pound and Reznikoff, his production of a documentary poetics also utilizes nineteenth-century modes they rejected.

49. For which many scholars have criticized him. See, e.g., Henry Louis Gates Jr.'s *The Signifying Monkey* (New York: Oxford University Press, 1988) and Eric Sundquist's *The Hammers of Creation: Folk Culture in Modern African-American Fiction* (Athens: University of Georgia Press, 1997).

50. Ten Eyck, *Ezra Pound's Adams Cantos*, 38.

51. Edward Keyes Whitley, *American Bards: Walt Whitman and Other Unlikely Candidates for National Poet* (Chapel Hill: University of North Carolina Press, 2010), 16.

52. Gorski, *American Covenant*, 128.

53. James Weldon Johnson, "Listen Lord: A Prayer," in *Writings*, 841.

54. Charles Reznikoff, "Israel," in *The Poems of Charles Reznikoff: 1918–1975*, ed. Seamus Cooney (Boston: Black Sparrow, 2005), 73.

55. Noelle Morrissette, *James Weldon Johnson's Modern Soundscapes* (Iowa City: University of Iowa Press, 2013), 119, 124.

56. James Weldon Johnson, "The Prodigal Son," in *Writings*, 846.

57. Johnson, 847.

58. Johnson, 846.

59. James Weldon Johnson, *The Autobiography of an Ex-Colored Man*, in *Writings*, 60.

60. Johnson, 70.

61. Johnson, "Prodigal Son," 847 (emphasis added).

62. Johnson, *Autobiography of an Ex-Colored Man*, 127.

63. Johnson, "Prodigal Son," 848.

64. Johnson, *Autobiography of an Ex-Colored Man*, 82.

65. Johnson, "Prodigal Son," 846.

66. Johnson, *Autobiography of an Ex-Colored Man*, 81–82.

67. Johnson, 6.

68. Johnson, "Prodigal Son," 848.

69. Johnson, "Race Prejudice and the Negro Artist," 746.

70. Johnson, "Prodigal Son," 845.

71. These artists were not alone: the crucifixion was used as a trope for Jewish suffering among Yiddish writers and artists, most notably Marc Chagall; and for labor martyrdom, including, as we will see in chapter 3, Lola Ridge's poetry. See Goeser, *Picturing the New Negro*, 228–43; on Douglas and Johnson, 216–18. See also Gorski's discussion of Du Bois's crucifixion tales (*American Covenant*, 120–23).

72. The development of this poem reveals Johnson's interest in the psychology of violence. In early drafts ("The Rapist" and "The Eternal Savage"), his primary concern is sexual rather than racial violence, attempting to debunk justifications of lynching by presenting the reality of sexual violence—that its potential exists in men of *all* races and that African American men cannot be uniquely blamed for it. These early versions of

"Brothers" are among drafts of poems included for consideration in *Fifty Years*, which he compiled in or around 1917. Box 59, Folder 195, Johnson Papers.

73. A clean, apparently final typescript of this poem can be found in Box 74, Folder 409, Johnson Papers.

74. Johnson, *Autobiography of an Ex-Colored Man*, 112.

75. Johnson, 113.

76. Johnson, *Along This Way*, 315.

77. Johnson, *Along This Way*, 315.

78. James Weldon Johnson, "The Crucifixion," in *Writings*, 856, 857.

79. Johnson, 857.

80. Johnson quotes this testimony in his autobiography, *Along This Way* (543–44). His essay "Lynching—America's National Disgrace" (1924) likewise describes the history of lynching as a particular, racially driven subset of mob violence; it is, therefore, a question of "the maintenance of order, good government and civilized society" to stamp it out (in *Writings*, 729).

81. Johnson, *Along This Way*, 534.

82. Johnson, "Crucifixion," 857.

83. Johnson, "Prodigal Son," 846–47.

84. Johnson, 848.

85. In Johnson's "Noah Built the Ark," God destroys the sinful crowd of humanity but promises, in an echo of the spirituals, "No more will I judge the world by flood—/ Next time I'll rain down fire" (in *Writings*, 855). (Here, the document interpolated is "O Mary Don't You Weep," which contains the couplet "God gave Noah the rainbow sign / no more water, but fire next time." This is the same couplet James Baldwin cites in the title of *The Fire Next Time*.) "Let My People Go" turns directly to "All you sons of Pharaoh" to ask, "Who do you think can hold God's people / When the Lord God himself has said, / Let my people go?" (864). (Here, the source is "Go Down, Moses.")

86. Johnson, "Prodigal Son," 848.

87. Whitley, *American Bards*, 16.

88. James Weldon Johnson, "The Judgment Day," in *Writings*, 865.

89. Johnson, 866.

90. Johnson, 866.

91. Johnson, 867. In both "Brothers" and "A Texas Carnival," the victims are killed not by rope but by fire, their cries and the sight, sound, smell, and result of burning flesh described graphically. Fire, there and elsewhere, is one of the central aspects of Johnson's discussions of lynching.

92. And of the lynch mob in "A Texas Carnival."

93. Johnson, "Judgment Day," 867.

94. Johnson, 867.

95. Johnson, *Along This Way*, 315.

2 • Renewing the Covenant

1. This was the magazine's second iteration, resuscitated for three issues by William Carlos Williams. The first series, which ran a decade earlier, originated during a conversation between Williams and Robert McAlmon in 1920—during a party hosted

in Lola Ridge's apartment. William Carlos Williams, *The Autobiography of William Carlos Williams* (New York: New Directions, 1967), 171–72.

2. Founded by Mary Mowbray-Clarke and Madge Jennison in 1916, Sunwise Turn also resembles the bookstore founded by the protagonist of Reznikoff's 1930 novel *By the Waters of Manhattan*. Alfred Kreymborg, Alfred Stieglitz, Amy Lowell, Thorstein Veblen, Lytton Strachey, and Robert Frost all passed through its doors. The enterprise was partially funded by the modernist publisher Harold Loeb and Mowbray-Clarke's husband, John Frederick Mowbray-Clarke, had helped to organize the 1913 Armory Show exhibition that introduced Americans to the experiments of European visual art. See Terese Svoboda, *Anything That Burns You: A Portrait of Lola Ridge, Radical Poet* (Tucson, AZ: Schaffner, 2016), 170–71; and Lawrence Rainey, *Institutions of Modernism: Literary Elites and Public Culture* (New Haven, CT: Yale University Press, 1999), 65; and Madge Jenison, *The Sunwise Turn: A Human Comedy of Bookselling* (New York: E. P. Dutton, 1923), 8.

3. For a more detailed discussion of the connection between Reznikoff's poetry and his parents' craftsmanship, see Joshua Logan Wall, "Family Business: Charles Reznikoff in Text and Textile," *Studies in American Jewish Literature* 37, no. 1 (Spring 2018): 37–55.

4. Philip Gorski, for instance, draws a distinction between a conquest narrative based in blood sacrifice and blood descent, undergirding nativist and religious-nationalist discourses of Americanness, and that of a wide, mainstream middle of American civil religious discourse. (The distinction might be put, in Colonial terms, as that between, respectively, Increase and Cotton Mather, on the one hand, and John Winthrop, on the other.) See, e.g., Gorski, *American Covenant: A History of American Civil Religion from the Puritans to the Present* (Princeton, NJ: Princeton University Press, 2017), 20–21, 29, 55, 99, 107.

5. Henry Roth, *Call It Sleep* (New York: Noonday, 1991), 61.

6. Rita Barnard, "Modern American Fiction," in *The Cambridge Companion to American Modernism*, ed. Walter Kalaidjian (Cambridge: Cambridge University Press, 2005), 50; Joshua L. Miller, *Accented America: The Cultural Politics of Multilingual Modernism* (New York: Oxford University Press, 2011), 4–6; Hana Wirth-Nesher, *Call It English: The Languages of Jewish American Literature* (Princeton, NJ: Princeton University Press, 2005), 83–84.

7. Leonard Bernstein, "What Is a Recitative / Leonard Bernstein: Omnibus: 'American Musical Comedy,'" YouTube, October 7, 2015, http://youtube.com/watch?v=IDq4KqP7Pxs. Originally aired on *American Television Presents: "American Musical Comedy,"* ABC Television Network, October 7, 1956.

8. Michael Davidson, *Ghostlier Demarcations: Modern Poetry and the Material World* (Berkeley: University of California Press, 1997), 156.

9. Joan Shelley Rubin, *Songs of Ourselves: The Uses of Poetry in America* (Cambridge, MA: Harvard University Press, 2010), 118, 136–59, and esp. 207–26.

10. Activist social documentary, detailed by Paula Rabinowitz in *They Must Be Represented: The Politics of Documentary* (London: Verso, 1994), was an aesthetic phenomenon with origins distinct from those of high modernist documentary poetics (though, in practice, the two are often intertwined). Whereas the latter derives poetry from prior documents, the former is overwhelmingly visual, defined by the aesthetics

of photography and film, even in literary works, and, as William Stott puts it in his seminal work, *Documentary Expression and Thirties America* (Chicago: University of Chicago Press, 1973), has "an axe to grind" (21). Social documentary, both Rabinowitz and Stott acknowledge, often resembles (or even *is*) propaganda. The aesthetic "is instrumental, and its people tend, like the innocent victims in most propaganda, to be simplified and ennobled—sentimentalized, in a word" (Stott, 57). By the "inward turn" of modernist epic, I mean the way in which even while modernist epics (and antiepics) seek to "contain history," they engage that history through the voice of the poet talking or thinking to themselves: *"A"* follows the tracks of Zukofsky's mind, the reader perched on his shoulder as he writes; Pound's *Cantos* likewise allows the reader to overhear the poet's experience of reading, e.g., Andreas Divus's 1537 translation of Homer into Latin (as in Canto I) or the letters of Sigismondo Malatesta (in the later Malatesta Cantos).

11. Eliot Weinberger, introduction to *Testimony: The United States (1885–1915): Recitative*, by Charles Reznikoff (Boston: Black Sparrow, 2015), xiii, xii.

12. L. S. Dembo, "Charles Reznikoff," *Contemporary Literature* 10, no. 2 (1969): 194–95.

13. Todd Carmody discusses Reznikoff's *Holocaust* in this vein, comparing it with Holocaust accounts and writings that seek to elicit sympathy rather than apprehension, in "The Banality of the Document: Charles Reznikoff's *Holocaust* and Ineloquent Empathy," *Journal of Modern Literature* 32, no. 1 (2008): 86–110.

14. Charles Bernstein, "Reznikoff's Nearness," in *The Objectivist Nexus: Essays in Cultural Poetics*, ed. Rachel Blau DuPlessis and Peter Quartermain (Tuscaloosa: University of Alabama Press, 1999), 225.

15. Ranen Omer-Sherman, *Diaspora and Zionism in Jewish American Literature: Lazarus, Syrkin, Reznikoff, and Roth* (Lebanon, NH: University Press of New England, 2002), 103. See also Maeera Shreiber, "'None Are Like You, Shulamite': Linguistic Longings in Jewish American Verse," *Prooftexts* 30, no. 1 (2010): 35–60, esp. 49.

16. On "avant-garde anti-lyricism," see the discussion in Virginia Jackson and Yopie Prins, introduction to section 8, "Avant-Garde Anti-lyricism," in *The Lyric Theory Reader: A Critical Anthology* (Baltimore: Johns Hopkins University Press, 2013), 451–59. In *Muriel Rukeyser's "The Book of the Dead"* (Columbia: University of Missouri Press, 1997), Tim Dayton likewise casts Muriel Rukeyser's book-length sequence (and, by extension, the Left modernist documentary poetics it exemplifies) as "attempts to break with the self-enclosed quality of the modern lyrical subject" (1) and says that "reportage" emerged from "the limitations of lyric poetry" (62).

17. Stephen Fredman, *A Menorah for Athena: Charles Reznikoff and the Jewish Dilemmas of Objectivist Poetry* (Chicago: University of Chicago Press, 2001), 163; Correspondence, Charles Reznikoff to Albert Lewin, September 17, 1933, in *Selected Letters of Charles Reznikoff, 1917–1976*, ed. Milton Hindus (Boston: Black Sparrow, 1997), 200–201.

18. "Early History of a Seamstress" was then reprinted, now as memoir again, in *Family Chronicle* (New York: Charles Reznikoff, 1963).

19. Charles Reznikoff, "Israel," in *The Poems of Charles Reznikoff: 1918–1975*, ed. Seamus Cooney (Boston: Black Sparrow, 2005), 63.

20. Reznikoff, 63.

21. Reznikoff, 65. This section of "Israel" is a redacted version of Genesis 37:19–28. Reznikoff varies from both the KJV and 1917 Jewish Publication Society (JPS) translations throughout this passage, however. In some places ("ba'al ha-kholomot" as "the master of dreams" rather than "this dreamer"), he follows the Hebrew; in others (retaining the KJV's "spicery, balm, and myrrh" as the goods carried by the Ishmaelite caravan to which they sell Joseph), he veers from it. I make this point to highlight the fact that Reznikoff's translations are more than simply redacted versions of already-existing English translations. While he clearly looked to them, their voices are by no means definitive—just as the Hebrew text itself is not.

22. Reznikoff, 66, 67.

23. The passage from which these lines are drawn, Genesis 46:18–20, is not, in the Hebrew, spoken by Joseph. Reznikoff takes Pharaoh's instructions to Joseph, that he offer these goods to his family on behalf of the state, and places them into Joseph's mouth. This new, unprompted context makes the emphasis on material wealth intrinsic both to Joseph and to his brothers—who actually take part in this scene in Reznikoff's version.

24. Reznikoff, *Poems*, 70. Although the Hebrew slaves' taking of wealth also occurs in the biblical account, the departure of Israel from Egypt on the night of the Passover takes thirteen verses in Hebrew (Exodus 12:19–42; in the JPS translation, four paragraphs of English) and the packing of gold, silver, and jewels is contained in a single *pasuk*. In Reznikoff's version, the departure occurs rapidly, in only seven short lines, two of which describe the material wealth taken out. In other words, a very generously calculated 7.7 percent of the Hebrew account (12:35 is significantly shorter than most of the verses in the passage) against 28.6 percent of Reznikoff's account is devoted to describing the luxury goods that go with the Hebrew slaves out of Egypt.

25. Even the seemingly secular rhetoric of Wilsonian progressivism (which Gorski is too quick to set outside the discourse of American civil religion) and progressivism after Wilson falls within the tradition of—and on a continuum with—the language of biblical exceptionalism. If a "war to end all wars" is not a messianic dream fit for Isaiah or John the Revelator, then nothing is.

26. For instance, the source texts for section 4 of "King David" (Reznikoff, *Poems*, 81–83) are, in order, 1 Samuel 20:1–3, 1 Samuel 22:1–5, 1 Samuel 23:23, 1 Samuel 23:14, 1 Samuel 24:1–3, 1 Samuel 27:1–12, 1 Samuel 22:7–8, 1 Samuel 21:2–10, 1 Samuel 22:9–19, and 1 Samuel 25:44.

27. Much of this "psalm" is drawn from 2 Samuel 22:2–51, which appears again in altered form as Psalm 18, though the introductory lines, which frame David's words within the context of his rise from sheepherder to king of Israel, draw on 2 Samuel 7:8–9, 18–19, and 1 Chronicles 17:7 and 17:16. The lines from 2 Samuel 7:8–9 were initially spoken by *God* (!) to the prophet Nathan in the context of building the Temple.

28. In section 3 of the poem, subtitled "Michal," she interrupts the proceedings to predict this will be her fate even in the event of domestic harmony: "The grave men who will write / the history of the kings of Israel and the wars of God, / will not trouble to write of our happiness" (Reznikoff, *Poems*, 81).

29. The Talmud Bavli (Sandhedrin 19b) calls 2 Samuel 21:8 a "confused passage." The difficulty stems from the fact that a marriage of Michal and Adriel would not have been permissible according to Jewish law; the Talmud concludes that another of Saul's daughters, Meirab, gave birth to the children but Michal raised them.

30. The 1917 JPS translation refers to "the five sons of Michal . . . whom she bore," but the revised 2000 JPS translation reads, "Merab" (it retains the *Hebrew* reading of "Michal," however). Its note on this verse observes that Hebrew and (Greek) Septuagint editions are divided on this point as well, with the Hebrew tending (but not exclusively) toward "Michal" and the Septuagint likewise toward "Merab." The Hebrew verb is from the root *yod-lamed-dalet*, "to give birth."

31. Reznikoff, *Poems*, 88–90.

32. Jahan Ramazani, *Poetry and Its Others: News, Prayer, Song, and the Dialogue of Genres* (Chicago: University of Chicago Press, 2014), 5. His discussion of a dialogic poetics extends across 1–16.

33. Michael Davidson gestures toward the intersection of translation and testimony/*Testimony* but sees it as a metaphor for the lengthy, revisionary composition of Reznikoff's long poem: "The continuity linking the several editions of *Testimony* is the act of translation, whether from witness to judge, from court transcript to case report in the reporter volumes, from first-person testimony to third-person narration, from prose to verse" (*Ghostlier Demarcations*, 153).

34. Charles Reznikoff and Reinhold Schiffer, "The Poet in His Milieu," in *Charles Reznikoff: Man and Poet*, ed. Milton Hindus (Orono, ME: National Poetry Foundation, 1984), 123–24. Stephen Fredman, following the recollections of the "Objectivist" poet George Oppen, believes that Reznikoff was probably more fluent in Yiddish than he acknowledged in interviews. Stephen Fredman, *A Menorah for Athena: Charles Reznikoff and the Jewish Dilemmas of Objectivist Poetry* (Chicago: The University of Chicago Press, 2001), 24.

35. Reznikoff and Schiffer, 124.

36. Charles Reznikoff, *By the Waters of Manhattan* (Boston: Black Sparrow, 2009), 52; Fredman, *Menorah for Athena*, 41. This scene, with slight differences, appears in *By the Waters of Manhattan*, *Family Chronicle*, and "Early History of a Writer." It refers to Reznikoff's maternal grandfather, for whom Hebrew was at once the sacred language of liturgy and Torah study and the language of a nascent Jewish literary culture. After his death, his widow, who could not read Hebrew, destroyed the manuscript of his poetry for fear it could be deemed "anarchist"—or that the neighbors and authorities might conclude that all foreign manuscripts were inherently anarchist.

37. Charles Reznikoff, *By the Well of Living and Seeing*, in *Poems*, 249.

38. Critics have read Reznikoff's relationship with Hebrew through a matrix of loss. Fredman, Finkelstein (*Not One of Them in Place*, 2001), and Shreiber (*Singing in a Strange Land*, 2007) all read Reznikoff's lack of formal Hebrew study as synecdoche for his dispossession from Jewish cultural patrimony. For a longer discussion of Reznikoff as a poet of successful inheritance, rather than disinheritance, see Joshua Logan Wall, "Family Business: Charles Reznikoff in Text and Textile," *SAJL* 37, no. 1 (Spring 2018), 37–55.

39. Reznikoff and Schiffer, "The Poet in His Milieu," 121. In a 1923 letter, he mentions "working very hard at" Hebrew (Reznikoff to Albert Lewin, March 1923, in *Selected Letters*, 37).

40. In the oft-discussed poems 14–16 (as numbered in *Poems: 1918–1975*), he laments the "difficult[y]" of Hebrew, a "Zion" from which he has been "exiled" (Reznikoff, *Poems*, 58). The first poem of *Jerusalem the Golden* finds the poetic speaker likewise lamenting, "I have married and married the speech of strangers" (Reznikoff, 93). See

Fredman, *Menorah for Athena*, 23–26; and Shreiber, "None Are Like You," 43–49, for lengthier discussions of these poems.

41. Barry McCrea, *Languages of the Night: Minor Languages and the Literary Imagination in Twentieth-Century Ireland and Europe* (New Haven, CT: Yale University Press, 2015), 30.

42. McCrea, xii.

43. McCrea, 32, 45.

44. Virginia Woolf, "On Not Knowing Greek," in *The Common Reader* (New York: Harvest Books, 1984), 23–38. Whatever degree of fluency Reznikoff attained was, by all accounts, nonconversational: a pure literacy, the inverse of his childhood's multilingualism.

45. Charles Reznikoff, "14," in *Poems*, 58.

46. Reznikoff's father, hearing him pronounce the words, was dumbfounded, exclaiming, "That's Arabic!" (Reznikoff and Schiffer, "The Poet in His Milieu," 121). In some ways, his relationship to Hebrew mimics the multilingual practices of T. S. Eliot, Ezra Pound, and H. D.: classical content (the Bible, Yehuda Halevi) filtered through a modernist aurality (the modernist/Zionist reconstruction of Hebrew).

47. Charles Reznikoff, "Joshua at Shechem," in *Poems*, 113. Shreiber, "None Are Like You, Shulamite," 45–46, reads this as a resistance to an exclusively (and territorially) Zionist claim on the language.

48. I mean this in distinction from Walter Benjamin's belief that "all translation is only a somewhat provisional way of coming to terms with the foreignness of languages," a coming to terms that, in its ultimate, messianic aspiration, would eliminate foreignness (or at least transform it into something rather foreign from itself) through the achievement of an ideal language—the "final, conclusive, decisive stage of all linguistic creation," the "higher and purer linguistic air" of the translated text over the original. Benjamin, "The Task of the Translator," trans. Harry Zohn, in *The Translation Studies Reader*, ed. Lawrence Venuti (New York: Routledge, 2002), 19. For Reznikoff, by contrast, linguistic foreignness prompts an encounter between the individual and the language that simulates the encounter between the individual as subject and a second individual as other. The foreignness of Hebrew, this is to say, is not dissimilar from the foreignness of the beggars Reznikoff notices on New York's streets.

49. In this way, Reznikoff's translations attempt to avoid the tension between translation as a means to construct original poetic authorship and translation as a means, through fealty to the original, to "foreignize" the language. The dynamics of his translation, therefore, differ more markedly from those of his contemporaries (like Pound or Zukofsky) who saw themselves as translators than from those, like Woolf, who did not.

50. While all three utilize translation as a means to reinvigorate English, Reznikoff's translational practices thus differ from those of his contemporaries and colleagues Ezra Pound and Louis Zukofsky. All three treat translation as a project of recovery, but Pound and Zukofsky only recover what has been or most likely will/would be suppressed by other translations into English: the spirited, chatty, and eroticized anti-imperialism of Pound's Sextus Propertius, for example, or Zukofsky's attention to the *sound* of the original, which ultimately culminated in his theory of homophonic translation. Reznikoff, on the other hand, seeks to recover that which has been suppressed *by the very text he sets out to translate*.

51. Walt Whitman, "Song of Myself," *Leaves of Grass (The First [1855] Edition)*, (New York: Penguin Books, 1959), 85.

52. Injunctions to care for people in these categories appear, among other places, in Exodus 22:20–22, Deuteronomy 14:29, Jeremiah 7:6, and Isaiah 58:7. The passage in Isaiah has been emphasized in Judaism by its traditional reading as the Haftarah portion in the Yom Kippur liturgy.

53. Charles Reznikoff, "Testimony," in *Poems*, 207–10.

54. Robert Alter, *The Art of Biblical Poetry* (New York: Basic Books, 1985), 27.

55. Classicists, translators, and other scholars have also observed this quality. The opening chapter of Eric Auerbach's *Mimesis*, "Odysseus' Scar," may be the best known of these discussions. The objects, details, and events of Homeric verse, he writes, "[take] place . . . in a local and temporal present which is absolute." Auerbach, *Mimesis: The Representation of Reality in Western Literature*, trans. Willard R. Trask (Princeton, NJ: Princeton University Press, 2003), 7.

56. Historicist readings of biblical poetic form at times suggest "that the ancient Hebrew writers generally avoided verse narrative precisely because of its associations with pagan mythology" (Alter, *Art of Biblical Poetry*, 28); one might perhaps seek an affinity between this interpretation and Reznikoff's unwriting of American foundation myths.

57. Alter, 39.

58. Fredman, *Menorah for Athena*, 30–31. See also chapter 6 of Alter's *Art of Biblical Narrative*, "Characterization and the Art of Reticence" (114–30).

59. Reznikoff, "Testimony," 207.

60. C. Bernstein, "Reznikoff's Nearness," 210–27.

61. Reznikoff, *Testimony*, 580.

62. Reznikoff, 5.

63. Richard Weisberg, *Poethics and Other Strategies of Law and Literature* (New York: Columbia University Press, 1992), 5, 8.

64. Robert Cover, "The Supreme Court, 1982 Term—Foreword: *Nomos* and Narrative," *Harvard Law Review* 97, no. 4 (1983–84): 9.

65. Gorski, *American Covenant*, 128 (emphasis in original).

66. Gorski, 55. He finds this divergence, in the United States, beginning during the Colonial period, when Increase Mather's notion of election set a covenant of blood descent against a more inclusive covenant of divine law. Secularized, we can easily see these terms translated to a blood- or descent-based nationalism/nativism and a more flexible, fluid concept founded in legal precedent and democratic norms.

67. Reznikoff, "Israel," 73.

68. Ramazani, *Poetry and Its Others*, 47, 60. His discussion of poetry and law extends from pages 46 through 62.

69. Christianity, with consistency among communions and denominations, holds that the full verse, including "Thou shalt have no other gods before me," constitutes the first commandment; Catholicism and some Protestant denominations read the first commandment as including the prohibition on graven images (that is, through Exodus 20:6). For Judaism, the prohibitions against worshipping other gods and against graven images together constitute the second commandment.

70. Reznikoff, "Israel," 70.

71. 1 Samuel 8:19–20 and Ezekiel 20:32.
72. Reznikoff, "Israel," 70.
73. Reznikoff, 71.
74. Deuteronomy 6:4–5.
75. Reznikoff, "Israel," 73.
76. See, for example, Exodus 31:18, 32:15, or 34:29.

3 • Immigrant Publics

1. In *Anything That Burns You: A Portrait of Lola Ridge, Radical Poet* (Tucson: Schaffner, 2016), Terese Svoboda discusses Ridge's time at Yaddo on pages 247–55. Ridge's drug use was not abusive but prescribed for various medical ailments—though the side effects of the very drugs she was instructed to take correspond to many of the symptoms she described. Ridge was very likely addicted to both Gynergen and Corax (librium) during her time at Yaddo, each of which could cause sleeplessness and hallucinations—the former during use and the latter during withdrawal (250–51).

2. Svoboda, 256.

3. Percy Hutchison, "Religious Fervor and Beauty in Miss Ridge's Poem," *New York Times*, December 8, 1929.

4. Ridge figures in the accounts of this period offered by Cary Nelson in *Repression and Recovery: Modern American Poetry and the Politics of Cultural Memory, 1910–1945* (Madison: University of Wisconsin Press, 1992) and *Revolutionary Memory* (New York: Routledge, 2001). Al Filreis's *Counter-Revolution of the Word: The Conservative Attack on Modern Poetry, 1945–1960* (Chapel Hill: University of North Carolina Press, 2008) offers a detailed history of the postwar politics of poetic canonization. Nancy Berke's *Women Poets on the Left: Lola Ridge, Genevieve Taggart, and Margaret Walker* (Gainesville: University Press of Florida, 2001), Caroline Maun's *Mosaic of Fire: The Work of Lola Ridge, Evelyn Scott, Charlotte Wilder, and Kay Boyle* (Columbia: University of South Carolina Press, 2012), and Svoboda's *Anything That Burns You* offer feminist accounts of Ridge's failed recoveries.

5. Mike Chasar, *Everyday Reading: Poetry and Popular Culture in Modern America* (New York: Columbia University Press, 2012), 6.

6. Chasar, 8.

7. Lola Ridge, "Morning Ride," in *Red Flag* (New York: Viking, 1927), 67. This is to distinguish, following David Ten Eyck's *Ezra Pound's Adams Cantos* (London: Bloomsbury, 2012), between the early documentary form of the Malatesta Cantos, in which the document is framed within lyric and narrative modes (44–51), and the "late" documentary of the Adams Cantos, in which lyric and narrative are suppressed (54).

8. Ridge, "Morning Ride," 67.

9. Ridge, 67.

10. Marilynne Robinson, cover blurb to *Tinkers*, by Paul Harding (New York: Bellevue Literary Press, 2009).

11. Ridge, "Morning Ride," 67.

12. Michelle Leggot's article "Verses and Beyond: The Antipodean Poetry of Lola Ridge," *Ka Mate Ka Ora: A New Zealand Journal of Poetry and Poetics* 12 (March 2013), and part 1 of Terese Svoboda's *Anything That Burns You* survey this early, formally

traditional poetry. They reveal an early interest in questions of national self-definition, geography, and the experience of encountering a specific place.

13. For the biographical details in this paragraph and the next, I draw on the details in Terese Svoboda's *Anything That Burns You*. Ridge's deliberate obscuring—at times, outright fabrication—of her biography makes this work a central resource for my own contextualization of her career, as well as for readers of Ridge in the twenty-first century.

14. She would reunite with him in New Orleans in 1914, as she and her second husband, David Lawson, traveled the country. They would remain together for most of the next three years, until Ridge and Lawson left Keith in Detroit on their return to New York City.

15. Michael North, *The Dialect of Modernism: Race, Language, and Twentieth-Century Literature* (New York: Oxford University Press, 2012), 162.

16. Lola Ridge, "The Ghetto," in *The Ghetto and Other Poems* (New York: B. W. Huebsch, 1918), 26.

17. Michael Warner, *Publics and Counterpublics* (Brooklyn, NY: Zone Books, 2002), 80.

18. Ridge's literary executor, Elaine Sproat, also maintains that she did not live on the Lower East Side.

19. Svoboda, *Anything That Burns You*, 59, 101, 152, 373.

20. Lola Ridge, "The Ghetto," *New Republic*, April 13, 1918, 326. The version published in *The Ghetto and Other Poems* reads, "Cool, inaccessible air / Is floating in velvety blackness shot with steel-blue lights" (3).

21. Ridge, "Ghetto," 326.

22. Ridge, 327–28.

23. Ridge, 327–28.

24. Thorstein Veblen, "A Policy of Reconstruction," *New Republic*, April 13, 1918, 320.

25. "Contributors to This Issue," *New Republic*, April 13, 1918, 335.

26. Ridge, "Ghetto," 328.

27. Ridge, *Ghetto*, 4.

28. Ridge, 24–25.

29. Lola Ridge, "To the American People," in *Ghetto and Other Poems*, v.

30. Lola Ridge, "Three Men Die," in *Dance of Fire* (New York: Harrison Smith and Robert Haas, 1935), 61.

31. Ridge, *Ghetto*, 9.

32. Ridge, 11.

33. Ridge, 15.

34. Ridge, 13.

35. Ridge, 19, 21.

36. Ridge, "Ghetto," 328; Ridge, *Ghetto*, 22–23.

37. Ridge, *Ghetto*, 24–26.

38. Life, of course, is also that promised by the Mosaic covenant. "Therefore choose life," the dying Moses enjoins his people, "that you and your children may live" (Deuteronomy 30:19).

39. Cf. Sacvan Bercovitch, *The Puritan Origins of the American Self* (New Haven, CT: Yale University Press, 1975).

40. Luke 22:19–20.

41. Harold Loeb, *The Way It Was* (New York: Criterion, 1959), 103. See also, Belinda Wheeler, "Lola Ridge's Pivotal Editorial Role at *Broom*," *PMLA* 127, no. 2 (March 2012): 285, note 2.

42. Svoboda, *Anything That Burns You*, 177; Belinda Wheeler, "Lola Ridge's Pivotal Editorial Role at *Broom*," *PMLA* 127, no. 2 (March 2012): 284.

43. Lola Ridge to Harold Loeb, March 25, 1922, in Wheeler, "Ridge's Pivotal Editorial Role," 287.

44. Lola Ridge to Harold Loeb, February 1, 1922, in Wheeler, "Ridge's Pivotal Editorial Role," 287.

45. Lola Ridge to Harold Loeb, January 2, 1923, in Wheeler, "Ridge's Pivotal Editorial Role," 289.

46. Lola Ridge to Harold Loeb, September 26, 1922, in Wheeler, "Ridge's Pivotal Editorial Role," 288.

47. Lola Ridge to Harold Loeb, n.d., in Wheeler, "Ridge's Pivotal Editorial Role," 288.

48. Ridge to Loeb, February 1, 1922, 287.

49. See North's *Dialect of Modernism*, esp. chap. 6, "Race, the American Language, and the Americanist Avant-Garde" (127–46).

50. Ridge to Loeb, February 1, 1922, 289–90.

51. Ridge to Loeb, n.d., 288.

52. North, *Dialect of Modernism*, 147, 128, 129.

53. "Prize Contest," *Broom* 4, no. 1 (December 1922), 74.

54. William Carlos Williams, *In the American Grain* (New York: New Directions, 2009), 231.

55. Williams, 143, 27, 28.

56. Harris Feinsod, *The Poetry of the Americas: From Good Neighbors to Countercultures* (New York: Oxford University Press, 2018), 138; see, generally, chap. 3, "The Ruins of Inter-Americanism" (137–89).

57. Ridge to Loeb, February 1, 1922, 290.

58. Svoboda, *Anything That Burns You*, 3–4, 292, 313–15.

59. For example, poet laureate Tracy K. Smith's 2018 essay in the *New York Times*, "Politics and Poetry," notes particularly the work of Danez Smith, Justin Philip Reed, CA Conrad, and Evie Shockley. And Smith herself is among the most accomplished contemporary producers of such work. *New York Times Sunday Book Review*, December 16, 2018, 1.

60. Daniel Tobin, introduction to *Light in Hand: Selected Early Poems of Lola Ridge*, ed. Daniel Tobin (Niantic, CT: Quale, 2007), xxxiii, xxxvi. Tobin's assessment reflects the attitude that other scholars of Ridge's work—and partisans on her behalf—have expressed to me in conversation.

61. Tobin, xxxi. His critique entails a long list of attributes found within *Firehead* and *Dance of Fire* that might indeed seem without merit for the sake of expressing the quarrel of self with self—but need not be dismissed as mere rhetoric with a different understanding of her poetics: the poetry is "a staged oracle for the poet's visionary proclivities" (xxxvi); her "tone is strident, bombastic, full of self-regard" (xxx) and employs "an antiquated mode of address" (xxxvi), "grandiose diction, . . . syntactical inversions, . . . hyperbolic imagery" (xxx), "a series of stylized gestures" (xxxiv), and "archaism and bathos" (xxxv).

62. "Anything that burns you must come out whether it be propaganda or not," Ridge once declared in an interview—a statement of poetics that Svoboda deems central enough to serve as the title of her biography (Svoboda, *Anything That Burns You*, 104).

63. As opposed, in the second half of the twentieth century, to "pop," "pulp," and the ironically titled "genre" genres—but also, in the nineteenth century, to other, more clearly gendered and/or ethnically marked genres: "poetess" verse, for example.

64. Nelson, *Revolutionary Memory*, 51; Svoboda, *Anything That Burns You*, 313.

65. "Labor Martyr Immortalized in Poem, 'Stone Face,' by Lola Ridge, with Photo of Tom Mooney," poster, in *Radical Responses to the Great Depression*, University of Michigan Special Collections Library and University of Michigan Library Digital Collections, Ann Arbor, MI, accessed April 24, 2017, http://quod.lib.umich.edu/s/sclradic/x-sce00669/sce00669.tif.

66. Virginia Jackson, *Dickinson's Misery: A Theory of Lyric Reading* (Princeton, NJ: Princeton University Press, 2005), 7.

67. See Nelson, *Revolutionary Memory*, 51–53.

68. Lola Ridge, "Stone Face," in *Dance of Fire*, 57–58.

69. Berke, *Women Poets on the Left*, 63.

70. Warner, *Publics and Counterpublics*, 87.

71. Warner, 90.

72. Lola Ridge, "Via Ignis," in *Dance of Fire*, 35, 18.

4 • Louis Zukofsky and the Poetics of Exodus

1. Hugh Kenner, "'A'," *New York Times Sunday Book Review*, March 14, 1976, 2.

2. Don't confuse this group with Ayn Rand's Objecti*vism*—for one thing, they were almost all of the political Left. For another, not only were they poets rather than novelists, in whatever genre you choose, but they were simply better *writers* than Rand and her acolytes.

3. Alan Golding, "Louis Zukofsky and the Avant-Garde Textbook," *Chicago Review* 55, nos. 3–4 (Autumn 2010): 30.

4. Louis Zukofsky, *A Test of Poetry* (New York: C.Z., 1980), 52, 67, 99.

5. Louis Zukofsky, "'Mantis,' An Interpretation," in *ANEW: Complete Shorter Poetry* (New York: New Directions, 2011), 67.

6. Louis Zukofsky, *"A"* (New York: New Directions, 2011), 22–23.

7. Hugh Seidman, "Louis Zukofsky at the Polytechnic Institute of Brooklyn (1958–61)," *Paideuma* 7, no. 3 (Winter 1978): 553–55.

8. Mark Scroggins, *The Poem of a Life: A Biography of Louis Zukofsky* (New York: Shoemaker and Hoard, 2007), 174, 188–89.

9. The claim itself, frequently cited, originated with Eric Homberger's 1986 book *American Writers and Radical Politics, 1900–1939: Equivocal Commitments* (New York: Palgrave Macmillan). In its final chapter, "Communism and Objectivism," he concludes that, as Zukofsky's aesthetics began to clash with the politicized aesthetics of leftist editors and magazines, "Zukofsky . . . wrote for the desk drawer" (182). The claim has been frequently cited since and was reprinted, along with a revised version of the chapter, in the 1999 edited collection *The Objectivist Nexus: Essays in Cultural Poetics* (ed. Rachel Blau DuPlessis and Peter Quartermain [Tuscaloosa: University of Alabama

Press, 1999]), a key scholarly starting point for people interested in Zukofsky, Charles Reznikoff, George Oppen, or others within the loose "Objectivist" group.

10. Cary Nelson, *Repression and Recovery: Modern American Poetry and the Politics of Cultural Memory, 1910–1945* (Madison: University of Wisconsin Press, 1992), 4.

11. "Easter and Passover," *New York Times*, April 16, 1927, 14.

12. Barry Ahearn, introduction to Zukofsky, *"A"*, xiii.

13. Zukofsky, *"A"*, 38.

14. Louis Zukofsky, "Poetry / For My Son When He Can Read," in *Prepositions: The Collected Critical Essays of Louis Zukofsky* (New York: Horizon, 1967), 11.

15. The notes and outline can be found in Box 4, Folder 13, of the Louis Zukofsky Collection, Harry Ransom Humanities Research Center, University of Texas–Austin. Scroggins notes that it was carried in Zukofsky's wallet (*Poem of a Life*, 87), while both he and Ahearn date the origin of the outline to 1927–28, with notes added through 1934–35. Barry Ahearn, *"A": An Introduction* (Berkeley: University of California Press, 1983), 38.

16. Zukofsky, *"A"*, 3.

17. Regina Schwartz, *Sacramental Poetics at the Dawn of Secularism: When God Left the World* (Stanford, CA: Stanford University Press, 2008), 13.

18. Schwartz, 8.

19. Schwartz, 42.

20. Zukofsky, *"A"*, 83.

21. Zukofsky, 3.

22. Zukofsky, 2.

23. Zukofsky, 2.

24. Ahearn's *"A": An Introduction* confirms that this image adorned the cover in 1928 (42). As we'll see shortly, the cover also helps bind *"A"* and its Exodus to the Yiddish newspaper *Der Tog*.

25. Zukofsky, *"A"*, 3, 2.

26. Zukofsky, 5, 28, 30, 88, 95, 98, 54, 70, 75. Magnus also recalls the wealthy Roman general Gnaeus Pompeius Magnus—Pompey the Great—who was a member of Caesar's first triumvirate and is linked, either by pun or etymology, to the word "pompous."

27. Zukofsky, 63.

28. Zukofsky, 32.

29. Zukofsky, 25, 26, 30.

30. Exodus 4:10. This occurs in "A"-6 and "A"-8 at 24, 29, 30, and 34, reappearing at 63.

31. Zukofsky, *"A"*, 32–33.

32. Zukofsky, 35–36.

33. On Zukofsky's correspondence, see Scroggins, *Poem of a Life*, 12.

34. In this, Zukofsky's depiction of political time finds an analogue not in Marxist dialectics but in the writings and rhetoric of Abraham Lincoln, Frederick Douglass, and American civil religious discourse in their wake. As Philip Gorski observes, in *American Covenant: A History of Civil Religion from the Puritans to the Present* (Princeton, NJ: Princeton University Press, 2017), "Lincoln and Douglass *transformed the revival cycle into a progressive spiral*: the point was not to return to the eternal social order of a bygone golden age, nor even to recover the original meaning of the founding principles; rather, it was to more fully realize the moral meaning of those principles, even when that meant abandoning established interpretations" (96; emphasis in original).

35. Zukofsky, "A", 74, 36.

36. Zukofsky, 70.

37. Zukofsky, 43, 104–5. Light appears as an explicit subject or event throughout "A"-8, for instance, on 44, 49–52, 58, 76, 92, 96, 97, 99, and 104–5.

38. Zukofsky, 55.

39. Some readers might recall that the Bible promises a *four*-hundred-year exile from Canaan, but Judaism, traditionally, calculates this to include time spent outside the land in freedom as well as the slavery that constituted three-quarters of the period.

40. Zukofsky, "A", 83.

41. Zukofsky, 54. See also 47, 50, 75, and 90.

42. Zukofsky, 83–86.

43. Zukofsky, 86.

44. Zukofsky, 112.

45. See Deborah Dash Moore, *G.I. Jews: How World War II Changed a Generation* (Cambridge, MA: Harvard University Press, 2004), esp. 22–48. Saul Bellow's early novels also testify to this experience: impatient to join up, Augie March (like Bellow himself) joins the Merchant Marine in a sudden, somewhat jarring plot turn (*The Adventures of Augie March* [New York: Viking, 1953]). In his first novel, *Dangling Man* (New York: Vanguard Press, 1944), the narrator "dangles" between civilian and military life as he waits for his draft notice to arrive.

46. Zukofsky, "A", 121.

47. James Frazer, *The Golden Bough: A Study in Magic and Religion*, abridged ed. (New York: Macmillan, 1922), 233.

48. Zukofsky, "A", 112.

49. Jewish liturgy appears elsewhere in "A"-10, twined together with the Catholic Mass, and is also affected by the Nazi/Vichy inversion. Consider for example, "The Giver of life makes the dying come" (Zukofsky, 120), an allusion to, inversion of, and compression of the "Mkhayei Meitim" section of the daily Amidah prayers: "You give life to the dead and have great power to save. He sustains the living with loving-kindness, and with great compassion revives the dead. He supports the fallen, heals the sick, sets captives free, and keeps faith with those who sleep in the dust. Who is like you and to whom can you be compared, O King who brings death and gives life?" Here, the promised resurrection of the dead is transformed into simple murder—not because God does not exist, or because of the violent reality of religious warfare, but because of the Nazi Black Mass.

50. Zukofsky, 112.

51. Zukofsky, 119.

52. Zukofsky, 123.

53. Zukofsky, 118, 115, 120.

54. Zukofsky, 113–14, 119.

55. Zukofsky, 114, 117.

56. Zukofsky, 116.

57. Zukofsky, 86.

58. Alan Jacobs, *The Year of Our Lord 1943: Christian Humanism in an Age of Crisis* (New York: Oxford University Press, 2018).

59. Zukofsky, "A", 1.

60. "2,500 Jews Mourn Sholem Aleichem," *New York Times*, June 18, 1916, 5. The correct name of the prayer mentioned is "El Malei Rachamim," with an *R*.

61. "Yiddish Poet Hears Praise of His Work," *New York Times*, December 21, 1913, 2.

62. The precise year of the first performance of the *St. Matthew Passion* is uncertain, and Zukofsky probably believed that it was in 1729—the consensus among music historians prior to 1975.

63. Michael Warner, *Publics and Counter Publics* (Brooklyn, NY: Zone Books, 2002), 16.

64. Warner, 16.

65. Zukofsky, *"A"*, 12, 14.

66. At the turn of the twentieth century, a contentious debate developed over whether there was a "national language" of the Jewish people—and, if so, whether this language was Yiddish or Hebrew. The beginning of a full-blown "language war" between the two camps is typically dated to the 1908 Tzhernovits (Czernowitz) Conference, at which European Jewish intellectuals and writers debated precisely the question of such a national language.

67. Zukofsky, *"A"*, 13.

68. See Karen Leick, "Popular Modernism: Little Magazines and the American Daily Press," *PMLA* 123, no. 1 (2008): 125–39.

69. "'A'-4," in "Notes to 'A'," *Z-site: A Companion to the Works of Louis Zukofsky*, accessed October 8, 2019, http://www.z-site.net/textual-notes/#A4.

70. Zukofsky, *"A"*, 12.

71. Louis Zukofsky to Hugh Kenner, January 30, 1974, in *The Selected Letters of Louis Zukofsky*, ed. Barry Ahearn (2013), 326, accessed January 30, 2022, https://z-site.net/selected-letters-of-louis-zukofsky/. Beyond what Zukofsky listed in his letter, Yehoash's works also drew on the conceits of English Romanticism, Tamburlaine, the Buddha, and others.

72. At the time of Yehoash's death in January 1927, he was an editor at *Der Tog*. The last installment it published ran on May 6, 1927—the books of Zechariah and Malachi. His Yiddish Tanakh was also published as a book in 1926 (and again in 1938 and 1941).

73. Louis Zukofsky to Harriet Monroe, September 1, 1920, Box 43, Folder 3, *Poetry: A Magazine of Verse* Records 1895–1961, Special Collections Research Center, University of Chicago Library, Chicago, IL.

74. Rather than destroying or discarding these works, Zukofsky prepared them as a self-deprecating typescript, sending a copy to Lorine Niedecker, his correspondent and fellow "Objectivist" poet. Holograph and typescript are in Box 15, Folder 2, Louis Zukofsky Collection.

75. He says so explicitly and claims the newspaper printing as his working source in a letter to Hugh Kenner. Louis Zukofsky to Hugh Kenner, October 20, 1976, Box 50, Folder 4, Hugh Kenner Collection, Harry Ransom Humanities Research Center, University of Texas–Austin.

76. This is the same Nahum Syrkin whose daughter, Marie, married Charles Reznikoff.

77. For example, Norman Finkelstein's *Not One of Them in Place: Modern Poetry and Jewish American Identity* (Albany: SUNY Press, 2001), 46–53; Ariel Resnikoff, "Louis Zukofsky and Mikhl Likht, 'A Test of Jewish American Modernist Poetics,'" *jacket-2*, September 2013, https://jacket2.org/commentary/ariel-resnikoff-louis-zukofsky-and

-mikhl-likht-test-jewish-american-modernist-poetics-p-0; and Sarah Ponichetera, "Yiddish and the Avant-Garde in American Jewish Poetry" (PhD diss., Columbia University, 2012).

78. In Zukofsky's index, "light" receives roughly one hundred entries.

79. Studies of the poetry of Emma Lazarus suggest that her works associate the image of the lamp or torch with both Jewish consciousness and "America's historical advantage over the 'ancient lands' . . . attained through its use of the Hebrew's immortalizing lamp of truth as a basis for its own political and social vision." Daniel Marom, "Who Is the 'Mother of Exiles'? An Inquiry into Jewish Aspects of Emma Lazarus's 'The New Colossus,'" *Prooftexts* 20, no. 3 (Fall 2000): 248. See also Max Cavitch, "Emma Lazarus and the Golem of Liberty," *American Literary History* 18, no. 1 (Spring 2006): 1–28; and Shira Wolosky, "An American Jewish Typology: Emma Lazarus and the Figure of Christ," *Prooftexts* 16, no. 2 (May 1996): 113–25. This re-Judaized/Hebraicized lamp of truth enters American thought especially, they argue, through "The New Colossus." There is circumstantial evidence, this is, that in the United States, a torch or lamp carried connotations beyond a generalized "truth" or "knowledge" even without considering *Der Tog*'s masthead.

80. Zukofsky, *"A"*, 17.

81. Compare this image, for instance, with the New York skyline of George Grosz's 1934 painting *Lower Manhattan*.

82. See Zukofsky, *"A"*, 8, 19, and (esp.) 21.

83. Zukofsky, 199.

84. Scroggins, *Poem of a Life*, 335–37.

85. Hugh Kenner, "More Than Pretty Music," *National Review*, November 19, 1960, 318–20.

86. Scroggins, *Poem of a Life*, 154.

87. Louis Zukofsky, "Mantis," in *ANEW*, 65.

88. Zukofsky, "'Mantis,' An Interpretation," 70.

89. Zukofsky, "Mantis," 66.

90. Zukofsky, "'Mantis,' An Interpretation," 71.

91. *Z-site: A Companion to the Works of Louis Zukofsky*, accessed October 8, 2019, http://www.z-site.net.

92. The University of Alabama Press has published three important collections: *Upper Limit Music: The Writing of Louis Zukofsky* (ed. Mark Scroggins, 1997); *The Objectivist Nexus: Essays in Cultural Poetics* (ed. Rachel Blau DuPlessis and Peter Quartermain, 1999); and *Radical Poetics and Secular Jewish Culture* (ed. Stephen Miller and Daniel Morris, 2010).

5 • *A Covenantal Limit Case*

1. Jacob Lawrence, *The Legend of John Brown* (Detroit: Detroit Institute of Arts, 1978), 6.

2. Laurence Goldstein and Robert Chrisman, introduction to *Robert Hayden: Essays on the Poetry*, ed. Laurence Goldstein and Robert Chrisman (Ann Arbor: University of Michigan Press, 2001), 1.

3. Derek Smith, *Robert Hayden in Verse: New Histories of African American Poetry and the Black Arts Era* (Ann Arbor: University of Michigan Press, 2018), 5–6, 202–3.

4. Michael Warner, *Publics and Counterpublics* (Brooklyn, NY: Zone Books, 2002), 81.

5. Warner, 55.

6. Robert Hayden, "A Certain Vision," in *Collected Prose*, ed. Frederick Glaysher (Ann Arbor: University of Michigan Press, 1984), 94.

7. Robert Hayden, "These Are My People," in *Heart-Shape in the Dust* (Detroit: Falcon, 1940), 63.

8. Robert Hayden, "Speech," in *Heart-Shape in the Dust*, 27.

9. Warner, *Publics and Counterpublics*, 56.

10. It plays this role in the earliest of the three monographs devoted to Hayden, John Hatcher's *From the Auroral Darkness: The Life and Poetry of Robert Hayden* (Oxford, UK: George Ronald, 1984) and Pontheolla T. Williams's *Robert Hayden: A Critical Analysis of His Poetry* (Urbana: University of Illinois Press, 1987) and serves a key framing function in more recent articles, including Brian Conniff's "Answering the *Waste Land*: Robert Hayden and the Rise of the African American Poetic Sequence," *African American Review* 33, no. 3 (Autumn 1999): 487–506; and Tim DeJong's "'Nothing Human Is Foreign': Polyphony and Recognition in the Poetry of Robert Hayden," *College Literature* 43, no. 3 (Summer 2016): 481–508. Even Smith's *Robert Hayden in Verse*, which rejects traditional readings of the incident's centrality to Hayden's career and reception, devotes significant time to rereading the event.

11. Hatcher, *Auroral Darkness*, 37.

12. Quoted in Smith, *Hayden in Verse*, 26.

13. Dudley Randall to Robert Hayden, April 29, 1966, quoted in Melba Joyce Boyd, *Wrestling with the Muse: Dudley Randall and the Broadside Press* (New York: Columbia University Press, 2003), 129–30.

14. See Smith, *Hayden in Verse*, 18–40.

15. To offer two later examples of this transformation of commemorative verse to a genre associated with anthologies, consider *Starting Today: 100 Poems for Obama's First 100 Days* (Iowa City: University of Iowa Press, 2010), which expands on the explicitly commemorative, occasional nature of Elizabeth Alexander's inaugural poem by adding others written during—and in order to mark—the first months of Obama's presidency. Carolyn Forche's 1993 anthology *Against Forgetting: Twentieth Century Poetry of Witness* (New York: W. W. Norton) is widely credited with *creating* (or at least codifying and popularizing) our ability to recognize a genre: the poetry of witness. Yet the act of witness, as I've argued in chapters on Charles Reznikoff and Lola Ridge, is itself a form of commemoration. Forche's anthology, this is to say, establishes a genre that participates in and radically transforms the older genre of commemorative verse.

16. Ossie Davis, "Why I Eulogized Malcolm X," in *For Malcolm: Poems on the Life and Death of Malcolm X*, ed. Dudley Randall (Detroit: Broadside, 1967), xxiii (emphasis in original), xxiv.

17. Robert Hayden, "El-Hajj Malik El-Shabbaz," in Randall, *For Malcolm*, 14. All citations refer to this edition, unless otherwise indicated.

18. Hayden, 14.

19. Hayden, 14.

20. Hayden, 14.

21. Hayden, 14. As revised for 1970's *Words in the Mourning Time* and all subsequent collections, the first line quoted here reads, "false dawn of vision." Robert Hayden,

"El-Hajj Malik El-Shabbaz," in *Words in the Mourning Time* (New York: October House, 1970), 38; Hayden, "El-Hajj Malik El-Shabbaz, in *Collected Poems* (New York: Liveright, 2013), 87.

22. Hayden, "El-Hajj Malik El-Shabbaz," 15.

23. Hayden, 16.

24. Hayden, 14–16.

25. Hayden, 16.

26. See Peter Sacks's *The English Elegy: Studies in the Genre from Spenser to Yeats* (Baltimore: Johns Hopkins University Press, 1985) for a study of the modern elegy as (intuitively) a poetry of mourning. Jahan Ramazani's *The Poetry of Mourning: The Modern Elegy from Hardy to Heaney* (Chicago: University of Chicago Press, 1994) explores the ways in which modern elegy establishes itself as elegy by questioning and even rejecting the traditional norms of the genre.

27. Robert Hayden, "The Poet and His Art: A Conversation," in *How I Write/1* (New York: Harcourt, Brace, Jovanovich, 1972), 135.

28. Robert Hayden, "Foreword to 'A Portfolio of Recent American Poetry,'" in *Collected Prose*, 66.

29. Robert Hayden, "A Certain Vision," in *Collected Prose*, 111.

30. Hayden, "Foreword," 66.

31. This wandering among names also mirrors and echoes the instability of *Hayden's* name. Born Asa Bundy Sheffey, he was rechristened (but not legally renamed) Robert Hayden by his foster parents. Throughout his adult life, the slippage between these two names would pose problems for Hayden as he (among other things) attempted to finalize employment and procure a US passport and is the explicit subject of his poem "Names."

32. We know this because it's Hayden's description of himself at this time, however much his activity on the region's political Left might suggest otherwise: "I was a Baptist when I went to Ann Arbor," he recalled in 1977 (Hayden, "Certain Vision," 110).

33. Hayden, 111.

34. The textual contradictions to this description prove the point: there is also a covenant at Sinai and reams of rabbinic commentaries that attempt to prove that Abraham in fact fulfilled all its terms in his own life; the New Testament by its very nature supersedes an older covenant; and Christian anti-Semitism might, on some level, be understood as the reaction against the de facto challenge to the singularity of Christian covenant that the continuing existence of Jews presents.

35. Richard Chenevix Trench, *On the Study of Words: Lectures Addressed (Originally) to the Pupils at the Diocesan Training School, Winchester* (London: Macmillan, 1876), 272.

36. Hayden, "Certain Vision," 110.

37. Robert Hayden, "A Conversation during the Bicentennial," in *Collected Prose*, 84.

38. Hayden, 84.

39. Frederick J. Cummings, preface to *The Legend of John Brown*, by Jacob Lawrence (Detroit: Detroit Institute of Arts, 1976), 6.

40. See Warner, *Publics and Counterpublics*, 87–88; and Lauren Berlant, *The Female Complaint: The Unfinished Business of Sentimentality in American Culture* (Durham, NC: Duke University Press, 2008), 4.

41. Robert Hayden, "John Brown," in Lawrence, *Legend of John Brown*, 43.

42. Ellen Sharp, "Introduction," 10–14, in Lawrence, *Legend of John Brown*, 13.
43. Lawrence, 36.
44. Hayden, "John Brown," 41.
45. Hayden, 41.
46. Hayden, 43.
47. Hayden, 43.
48. This range is on display in the poems that accompany "John Brown" in the 1982 edition of *American Journal*: the title poem contains no punctuation marks at all; "The Rag Man" punctuates for standard syntax; and "A Letter from Phillis Wheatley" punctuates according to the syntax of the eighteenth-century voice that Hayden captures.
49. Hayden, "John Brown," 41.
50. Hayden, 43.
51. Hayden, 43.
52. Lawrence, *Legend of John Brown*, 31–32.
53. Hayden, "John Brown," 43.
54. Hayden, 43.
55. Hayden, 43.
56. Hayden, 43.
57. Hayden, 43.
58. Robert Hayden, "[American Journal]," in *American Journal* (New York: Liveright, 1982), 57, 60.
59. Laurence Goldstein, Hayden's colleague for many years at the University of Michigan, recalls that Hayden was fascinated by major events in the space program but deeply worried that it drew attention toward other worlds (the moon) that would be more rightly applied to *this* world (the Earth, its people). He also tried to direct writing students toward exploring the space program in verse. Goldstein, conversation with the author, April 20, 2019.
60. Hayden, "[American Journal]," 57, 60.
61. Hayden, 57, 59.
62. Hayden, 58.
63. Hayden, 58.
64. Hayden, 59.
65. Warner, *Publics and Counterpublics*, 56.
66. Hayden, "[American Journal]," 60, 57.
67. Hayden, 60.

Coda

1. Albert Maltz, writer, *The House I Live In* (RKO Radio Pictures, 1945), film.
2. See Nancy Kovaleff Baker, "Abel Meeropol (a.k.a. Lewis Allan): Political Commentator and Social Conscience," *American Music* 20, no. 1 (Spring 2002): 25–79, esp. 23–36.
3. Baker, 54–55.
4. Art Simon, "The House I Live In: Albert Maltz and the Fight Against Anti-Semitism," in *Un-American Hollywood: Politics and Film in the Blacklist Era*, ed. Frank Krutnick (New Brunswick, NJ: Rutgers University Press, 2007), 173–74.
5. Simon, 181; Wendy Wall, *Inventing the American Way: The Politics of Consensus from the New Deal to the Civil Rights Movement* (New York: Oxford University Press, 2008), 157.

6. Baker, "Abel Meeropol," 55–56.

7. Baker, 67–68.

8. James Weldon Johnson to Lola Ridge, March 16, 1925 (letter courtesy of Elaine Sproat).

9. Wall, *Inventing the American Way*, 155–59.

10. Jahan Ramazani, *Poetry and Its Others: News, Song, and the Dialogue of Genres* (Chicago: University of Chicago Press, 2014), 237.

11. Louis Zukofsky, "Poem Beginning 'The,'" in *ANEW: Complete Shorter Poems* (New York: New Directions, 2011), 15–18.

INDEX

"A". *See under* Zukofsky, Louis (works)
advertisements, 96–99, 114–16, 151–56; for Wrigley's chewing gum, 154, 155–56. *See also* cigarettes
Aleichem, Sholem, 146–47
Allan, Lewis. *See* Meeropol, Abel (Lewis Allan)
American Dream, 167, 172–73, 188–90
"[American Journal]." *See under* Hayden, Robert (works)
American Law Book Company. See *Corpus Juris* (legal encyclopedia)
anthologies, 7–8, 94, 126, 127–29, 170–72, 225n15
anti-Semitism, 1–2, 156, 191–94
apprehension, 126, 172–75, 176, 179, 186, 190. *See also* misapprehension
attention, 3–5, 9, 12, 19, 80, 96, 124–26, 178–80, 189. *See also* distraction
Auden, W. H., 145, 169, 175
audiences, 9–10, 26–27, 45–46, 129, 144–45, 146, 161–62, 168–69, 194; at performance of Bach's *St. Matthew Passion*, 133–35; and translation, 131

Bach, Johann Sebastian: *Mass in B-Minor*, 141–42; *St. Matthew Passion*, 129–31, 132–35, 139, 146–48, 156
Baha'i faith, 172
Baha'u'llah, 172–73, 175, 186
Bible: crucifixion narrative, 52–56, 93, 132, 133; Deuteronomy, 46, 87–88, 139; Exodus, 86–87, 136; Genesis, 41–43, 69–72; Gospel of Matthew, 156; Hebrew Bible, 11, 69–73, 78, 79–84, 84–89, 134, 139; Judges, 88; King James Bible, 33–34, 41–44, 47–48, 73, 78, 161; Leviticus, 87; Luther's German translation, 73; Proverbs, 88; 2 Samuel, 72–73
Black Arts Movement, 169, 170
Broom, 112–18; advertisement for, 114–16, 122–23; 1922 "American" issue, 113–17, 122–23
Brown, John (historical figure), 165–67; "John Brown" (poem) (*see under* Hayden, Robert [works])

Cardozo, Benjamin, 82–83
Carter's Little Liver Pills, 96, 97
Christian humanism, 145
Christianity. *See* Bible; Christian humanism; communion; congregations; covenant: Eucharistic; Easter; Mass (Catholic); passion play; prayer; preacherly text; preachers; Protestant Reformation; sacramental poetics; typology: Christological
cigarettes: in "A", 135, 137–38, 143; billboard advertisements, 152; Camel (brand), 137, 152, 153; Helmar (brand), 152, 154, 155; in *House I Live In, The* (film), 193; newspaper advertisements, 152–55
circulation, 4–5, 19, 133–34, 147–49, 157, 198–200; across time, 5, 118, 124–25, 133, 148, 178; between languages, 133–34, 147–57; of people, 96–98, 101, 103–4, 107–12, 115–18, 124–25, 130–31, 133–39, 140–45, 147–48, 156–57, 158–61; of texts, 12, 94–102, 104–6, 111–12, 115–18, 118–26, 127–31, 147–48, 157–62, 170–71, 198

citizenship, 5, 13, 34, 59, 64–65, 68–69, 193–94, 199; and covenant, 10, 61–63, 68–69, 84–87, 101, 129–30, 193–94; and immigration, 84–85, 103–4, 123, 193–94; and race, 29, 40, 46
civil religion, 10–14, 38–40, 65, 67–69, 83–84, 104–5, 129–31, 176–77, 192, 197–200; and African American experience, 27–29; and Baha'i faith, 176–77; Fourth of July, 109–10; Manifest Destiny, 110; and modernism, 33, 199–200; and publics, 30–31, 38, 45–46, 130
classrooms, 7, 15, 95, 127–29, 157, 161
Cohen, Leonard, 198–99
Cole and Johnson, 24, 26, 48
commemorative verse, 30–31, 45, 57, 65, 166–67, 170–71, 174, 178–80, 183–85, 225n15
communion, 109, 111–12, 133, 141, 144
concrete poetry, 181
congregations, 31–32, 35–36, 38–39, 45–46, 55–59, 142, 174
Contact, 60
conversions, 13, 172–74, 175, 176–77
Corpus Juris (legal encyclopedia), 60, 67–68, 82–83
cosmopolitanism, 2, 24, 29, 67, 112, 206n16, 206n17
counterpublics, 11, 13, 40, 168, 189–90
courtrooms, 61–62, 64–66, 72, 74, 79, 84, 174
covenant, 31, 45–46, 46–48, 55–59, 129–34, 159, 172–75, 182–90; in Baha'i faith, 172, 176–77; Biblical, 62–63, 69, 71–73, 172; broken covenants, 48–52, 55–59, 131, 141–45, 167; circumcision, 172; civic, 173; covenantal poetics, 84–89, 109, 133–34, 139, 161, 167–68, 174–75, 179, 186, 190, 196; covenantal time, 184; Eucharistic, 112, 132–33, 144; and immigration, 101–2, 124, 141–45; in law, 46; misapprehended, 172–73; and name-changes, 172–74; reparation of, 145–48, 156–57
covenantal authority, 58–59, 145, 158–59, 172–74, 178, 188, 190; law as, 31–32, 46–47, 55–56, 59, 62, 84–86, 88; poetry as, 133–34, 145
Crane, Hart, 113, 114, 117, 125
"Creation, The." *See under* Johnson, James Weldon (works)
"Crucifixion, The." *See under* Johnson, James Weldon (works)

Davenport, Guy, 157, 161
David (biblical king), 72–73
Davis, Ossie, 171
Detroit, 18–19, 103, 165–66, 168, 169, 175, 177–78
Detroit Institute of Arts, 165–67, 178, 180
dialect verse, 30–31, 40, 52–53, 196
disenchantment, 84, 132–33
distraction, 96–98, 101, 160. *See also* attention
documentary poetics, 30–31, 40–41, 43–45, 47–48, 50, 65–66, 95–99, 208n48, 211n10
Douglas, Aaron, 48, 169
dramatic monologue, 187
Dunbar, Paul Laurence, 34–35, 40–41

Easter, 39, 129–30, 132–33, 146
Ed Sullivan Show, The, 39
ekphrastic poetry, 5, 166–67, 178–86, 187
elegy, 5, 171, 174–75
"El-Hajj Malik El-Shabbazz." *See under* Hayden, Robert (works)
Eliot, T. S., 7–8, 48, 141, 145, 199–200
epic, 5, 62, 65–66, 68, 71, 79; and anti-epic, 62, 68, 79
eulogy, 171, 174–75, 178
Exodus (biblical event), 71, 130–31, 133–39, 146

failure, 71–2, 82–4, 94–6, 119–20, 134, 180–81, 188–89, 198–99
Fisk University, 34, 48, 169, 170
Five (1951 film), 38
Ford, Henry, 121, 136, 139, 143
For Malcolm: Poems on the Life and Death of Malcolm X, 169, 170–72, 178
France en Liberté, La, 140–45, 171
Frank, Leo, 95–96, 98
Freeman, The, 33, 207n23
free verse, 32–33, 52–53
fugue, 130–31, 133, 136, 137
funerals, 45, 146–47, 171–72

genre, 3–5, 5–10, 61–63, 63–67, 118, 120, 166–68, 170–72, 178–79, 187, 198–200
genteel poetry, 26, 32, 33
Gershwin, George and Ira, 63–64
"Ghetto, The." *See under* Ridge, Lola (works)
God's Trombones (album by Fred Waring and His Pennsylvanians), 38–39, 59

God's Trombones (jazz album by Chris Crenshaw), 36
God's Trombones (poetry collection). *See under* Johnson, James Weldon (works)
God's Trombones (setting by Gordon Myers), 36
Goldman, Emma, 100, 112, 118

Hayden, Erma, 175–76
Hayden, Robert, 15, 165–90, 198, 199; and the American Dream, 167; Baha'i faith, 172, 175–77, 186; and civil religious discourse, 11; conversion, 175, 176–77; and covenant, 166–67, 172–75, 176–77, 179, 182–90; documentary poetry, 179; First World Festival of Negro Arts Grand Prix de la Poesie, 169; Fisk University Writers' Conference, 169, 170; influence of Lola Ridge and James Weldon Johnson on, 16, 167–68; involvement with labor movement, 168; name, 175, 226n31; as "People's Poet" of Detroit, 168–69; on poetry and religion, 175–77; political views, 168; relationship with Black Arts Movement, 166, 169, 170; religious beliefs, 13, 172, 175–77; use of punctuation, 182–83, 185–86; views on American history, 167, 189
Hayden, Robert (works): *American Journal* (book), 179, 186–87; "[American Journal]" (poem), 167, 186–90; *Collected Poems*, 179, 186; early poetry ("'Prentice Pieces"), 167–69; "El-Hajj Malik El-Shabbaz," 167, 169, 170–75, 178–79, 181–82, 186–89; *Heart-Shape in the Dust*, 167–69; "John Brown," 166–67, 169, 170, 178–86, 187–89; "Middle Passage," 179; "Mourning Poem for the Queen of Sunday," 174; *Selected Poems*, 169; "Speech," 168; "These Are My People," 168; "Those Winter Sundays," 175; "Words in the Mourning Time," 174
Hebrew, 62, 69, 74–84, 87, 89
Herberg, Will, 14, 130, 195
historical poetics, 6, 43, 120
House I Live In, The (film), 191–98
"House I Live In, The" (song), 191–95, 197–98
Huebsch, B. W., 111–12

immigration, 84–85, 102–5, 112, 123, 133–34, 193–94, 196–97; forced migration, 143–44; internal migration, 136–37; Johnson-Reed Act, 105; and poetics, 101, 115–18, 148–49; refugees, 142–43
indigeneity, 101, 115–18, 123–24
intensification (biblical poetic device), 79–81, 87
Inzikhism (Yiddish literary movement), 151
Islam, 171–74. *See also* Nation of Islam
"Israel" (poem). *See under* Reznikoff, Charles (works)

Jacksonville, 23–26, 53, 59, 207n28
Jacob (biblical patriarch), 70–71
jargon, 148–49, 155–56
Jasper, John, 34–35, 40–41
Jeffers, Robinson, 93
Jewish history, 14, 68–73, 84, 109–10, 140–41, 143, 148–49, 159
Jewish immigration to United States, 14, 60, 64–65, 107–12, 137–38, 149–50
Jewish Studies, 14
"John Brown" (poem). *See under* Hayden, Robert (works)
Johnson, James Weldon, 15–19, 23–59, 168–69, 174–75, 185, 196–98, 199; and anti-lynching legislation, 24–25, 33, 51–52, 54; and civil religious discourse, 11; and cosmopolitanism, 24, 29–30, 206n18; correspondence with Lola Ridge, 16, 196; on dialect and vernacular, 26, 30–31, 40–42; drafts and composition of *God's Trombones*, 40–46; and film, 34–35, 207n28; and genteel verse, 26, 32; and interpolation, 47–52; and law, 32; multilingualism, 24; near-lynching, 2, 24, 53; performances of *God's Trombones*, 36–40; religion, 13, 46, 175; Senate testimony, 54–55; and sheet music, 41, 43–44; songwriting, 23–29, 32, 48
Johnson, James Weldon (works); *Along This Way*, 23–24; *Aunt Mandy's Kitchen Dinner*, 34–35, 207n28; *Autobiography of an Ex-Colored Man*, 47–52, 53; *Book of American Negro Poetry*, 33, 47; *Book of American Negro Spirituals*, 43–44, 47; "Brothers—American Drama," 52–53, 209n72; "Creation," 31–32, 32–33, 38–46; "Crucifixion," 52–56; "Dilemma of the Negro Artist," 30, 51; *Fifty Years and Other Poems*, 26; "Glory of the Day Was in Her Face," 26, 28; "Go Down, Death," 36, 38; *God's Trombones*, 5, 15–16, 30–32, 32–59, 78, 122, 168, 174, 197–98; "Judgment Day," 57–59, 185; "Let My People

Johnson, James Weldon (works) (*continued*) Go," 44; "Lift Every Voice and Sing," 23–32, 38, 65; "My Lady's Lips Am Like de Honey," 26–27; "Noah Built That Ark," 44; preface to *God's Trombones*, 34–35, 40–42; "Prodigal Son," 36, 37, 48–52, 55–56; "Race Prejudice and the Negro Artist," 29–30, 51; "Reverend Jasper Jones," 35–36, 45; *Saint Peter Relates an Incident*, 26; "Texas Carnival," 52–53
Johnson, J. Rosamond, 23–24, 44
Judaism, 14, 86–89, 129–31, 142–44, 172
"Judgment Day, The." *See under* Johnson, James Weldon (works)

Kenner, Hugh, 127, 150, 157, 162
"King David" (poem). *See under* Reznikoff, Charles (works)

labor movement, 5, 95, 120–26, 138, 144, 149; abuse by management, 65, 78–79, 135–36; rallies, 5, 12, 15, 120–21, 124, 168, 198; strikes, 155
Language poetry, 7, 9
law, 5, 32, 46–47, 52–56, 79, 82–89; biblical, 69, 86–89; Reznikoff on, 66. *See also* courtrooms
Lawrence, Jacob, 165–67; *Frederick Douglass*, 165, 178; *Harriet Tubman*, 165, 178; *Legend of John Brown, The*, 165–67, 178–86, 189
Lawson, David, 103
Legend of John Brown, The (exhibition portfolio), 177–80, 181, 184
Legend of John Brown, The (series of paintings). *See under* Lawrence, Jacob
leitmotif, 80–81, 82
Leyeles, Aron Glantz, 151
Loeb, Harold, 112–14
Longfellow, Henry Wadsworth. See *Song of Hiawatha, The*
lynching, 2, 24–25, 50, 52–55, 58, 105, 168, 192–93, 209n72. *See also* Frank, Leo
lyric poetry, 4–5, 5–10, 25–26, 93–94, 120, 166–67, 187–88, 190; anti-lyric, 5, 7, 8, 61–62, 68, 79; lyric reading, 7, 45, 79, 94–95, 122, 161, 166; lyric speech, 32, 36, 40, 102

"Mantis." *See under* Zukofsky, Louis (works)
Mass (Catholic), 133, 141–45, 157, 222n49; Black, 141–42; Easter, 133. *See also* Bach, Johann Sebastian: *Mass in B-Minor*

Mayan art, 115–18, 123–24
Meeropol, Abel (Lewis Allan), 192, 194–95
memory, 86, 94, 110, 139, 170, 198
Menorah Journal, 69, 149
Michal (biblical queen), 72–73, 74, 214n30
Mill, John Stuart, 6–7, 9
misapprehension, 167, 172–73, 176, 188, 190, 198. *See also* apprehension
mobs, 46–48, 52–56, 58–59, 191, 193–94
modernism, 5, 8, 10–14, 30–32, 32–33, 95–96, 149–51, 156, 198–200; Americanist avant-garde, 100–102, 114, 115, 117; in vernacular languages, 75–77; Yiddish modernism, 150–51
Mooney, Tom, 120–26
"Morning Ride." *See under* Ridge, Lola (works)
Moses, 70, 82, 89, 136–37, 139, 176
motley, 110, 131, 146, 148, 156
multilingualism, 1–2, 14–15, 19, 24, 74–75, 147–48. *See also* Hebrew; translation; Yiddish
museums, 5, 7, 113, 165–67, 179–80, 184–85. *See also* Detroit Institute of Arts
music, 132–33, 144, 157, 188, 192–200; and Charles Reznikoff, 62–64, 66; and James Weldon Johnson, 23–24, 26–27, 31, 38–39, 43–44, 48, 57; and Louis Zukofsky, 128, 137; and Yehoash, 147. *See also* Bach, Johann Sebastian; Cole and Johnson; fugue; Gershwin, George and Ira; recitative; songwriting; syncopation
"My Country 'Tis of Thee" (poem). *See under* Reznikoff, Charles (works)
"My Country 'Tis of Thee" (song), 29, 31, 60–61, 63–64, 77, 188

NAACP, 24–25, 27, 33, 51
Nation, The, 120–21
National Review, 157
Nation of Islam, 171
Nazi Germany, 131, 140–45, 157, 159, 193
New Criticism, 6, 9
New Masses, 98–99, 101, 136, 158
New Negro, The, 16, 33, 167–68
New Republic, The, 102, 103–7
newspapers, 61, 95–98, 102, 148, 150–56, 159–61

New York City, 1–2, 16, 24, 48–49, 100, 132–39, 140, 191; Carnegie Hall, 132–34, 138–39, 146–47, 149; Ellis Island, 102–3; Lower East Side, 101, 103, 107–12, 132, 146–47; skyline, 96, 152
Niger, Shmuel, 151

"Objectivist" poetry, 65–67, 69, 127, 141, 149, 161, 220n2
Objectivist Press, The, 82, 128
"Objectivists" Anthology, An, 149
Of Thee I Sing (Gershwin musical), 63–64
Oppen, George, 82, 127–28, 157

parallelism, 79–81, 87
parataxis, 42, 81–82
Paris, 131, 140–41
passion play, 132
Passover, 129–31, 137–39, 142–44; Haggadah, 132; Seder, 130, 132–33, 139, 144; Ten Plagues, 134–35
Paul Robeson Performing Arts Theater, 38
Pétain, Phillipe, 140, 143
pluralism, 3, 5, 12, 78, 104, 191–93, 195–200; economic pluralism, 134; racial pluralism, 13–14, 123, 168, 175, 195–98; religious pluralism, 13–14, 129–31, 138, 176–77, 192–95
Poetry: A Magazine of Verse, 18, 32, 103, 118, 127, 149–50, 158, 161
political cartoons, 152–53, 155
postsecularism, 176
Pound, Ezra, 45, 76, 100, 127, 199–200; *ABC of Reading*, 128; *Cantos*, 44, 68, 95–96, 182
prayer, 39, 45, 87–88, 174–76, 191, 222n49. *See also* Mass (Catholic); preachers; *sh'ma* (Jewish prayer)
preacherly text, 34–35, 40–41, 47–48
preachers, 30–32, 33–36, 40–46
"Prodigal Son, The." *See under* Johnson, James Weldon (works)
propaganda, 119–20, 211–12n10
prosody, 30, 33–34, 40–46, 78, 82, 198
Protestant Reformation, 132–33
publics, 2–5, 7, 95, 101–2, 122, 178–86, 195–200; American public, 10, 11, 129–31, 187–90, 192, 195, 197–200; commemorative, 170–72, 174–75, 177–80, 184; covenantal, 39–40, 45–47, 58–59, 61–63, 78, 105, 111–12, 130–31, 132–34, 139, 145, 156–57, 167, 174–75, 178–80, 185–86, 187, 189–90, 197; creation of, 25–26, 33, 35–36, 38–40, 45–46, 57, 124–25, 128–29, 132–34, 139, 142–43, 145, 147–48, 151, 156, 161, 166–69, 170–71, 178, 185–86, 197–200; ephemeral, 125–26, 197; and genre, 10, 78, 102, 166; Michael Warner on, 3–4, 11, 25, 102, 124, 147–48, 166, 189–90; multiracial, 38–39, 40–41, 58–59, 168; and museum exhibitions, 166–67, 177–79, 184–86; and musical performance, 25–28, 142–43, 147–48, 156, 194–97; and translation, 156–57

Randall, Dudley, 169, 170
Rankine, Claudia, 7
reading, 60, 62–63, 94–99, 144, 157–62, 176–77, 181. *See under* lyric poetry
Rebecca (biblical matriarch), 70–71
recitative, 63–67, 67–72, 76–77, 78, 84, 88–89, 101, 198
redemptive constitutionalism, 29–32, 84
Reznikoff, Charles, 16–19, 60–89, 94, 109, 128, 149, 157, 174–75, 185, 196–97, 199; and civil religious discourse, 11, 60, 67–69; documentary poetry, 65–66, 67–68, 69–73; and genre, 15; and Hebrew, 62, 69, 74–84, 84–89, 214n36; and law, 60, 66, 79, 82–84, 85–89; as legal editor, 60, 67–68, 82; on "Objectivist" poetry, 65–67; recitative, 64–67, 69, 76–77; religion, 13, 175; self-publishing, 60–61; translation, 13, 62, 69–73, 74–84, 84–89, 213n21, 213n23, 213n24, 215nn48–50; and Yiddish, 74–75; and Zionism, 67
Reznikoff, Charles (works): *By the Waters of Manhattan: An Annual*, 67, 69; *By the Waters of Manhattan* (novel), 69; *Holocaust*, 68; "Israel," 47, 67–71, 75, 78, 82–83, 84–89, 213n21, 213n23, 213n24; "Joshua at Shechem," 76–77; "King David," 67–69, 72–73, 74–75, 78, 82–83, 84–89; "My Country 'Tis of Thee: Oratorical and Poetical Gestures," 60, 67, 82, 196–97; shorter poems, 74–75, 76; *Testimony* (1934 prose poem), 80–81; "Testimony" (1941 poem), 78–80; *Testimony* (multi-decade poetic project), 60, 62, 68, 72, 77–84, 85, 174, 196–97; *Testimony: The United States (1885–1915): Recitative* (1978), 64, 79, 81–82; verse dramas, 68

Ridge, Lola, 15–19, 93–126, 128, 129, 167–68, 171, 196, 198, 199, 217n1; Catholicism, 13, 176; and civil religious discourse, 11; correspondence with Harold Loeb, 113–14; correspondence with James Weldon Johnson, 16, 196; criticism of later poetry, 119, 219n61; and documentary poetics, 95–99; early life, 100–101; editor of *Broom*, 112–18; on Gertrude Stein, 114; immigration to United States, 100–101, 102–4; influence on Robert Hayden, 167–68; labor activism, 118–26; and misogyny, 94, 112; and modernism, 112, 122–26; name, 100; political radicalism, 105–8, 110–11, 118–26; and propaganda, 119–20; relationship with son, 100–101; reviews in Yiddish press, 18; views on modernism, 99–100

Ridge, Lola (works): *Dance of Fire*, 119–21, 124–26, 167; *Firehead*, 93, 119, 124, 126, 167; "Ghetto," 101, 103–12, 114, 124, 126; *Ghetto and Other Poems*, 103, 107–12, 167; "Lullaby," 196; "Morning Ride," 95–99, 158–60; *Red Flag*, 15–16, 95, 122; "Stone Face," 5, 120–26, 198; "Three Men Die," 109; "To the American People," 108–9; "Via Ignis," 125

Robeson, Paul, 197–98
Roth, Henry, 63
ruins, 117–18, 124, 142, 200

Sacco and Vanzetti, 94, 100, 107, 118
Sacks, Jonathan, 191–200
sacramental poetics, 132–33, 144
secularization, 13, 132, 175–76, 203n36
sestina, 157–61
Sharp, Ellen, 178–80, 183
sh'ma (Jewish prayer), 87–88
Sinai, 84–89, 137, 142
Sinatra, Frank, 192–95, 197–98
slavery, 33–34, 71, 86–87, 135–39, 143–44, 157, 180, 196–97
solidarity, 14, 95–96, 98–99, 101–2, 120, 122, 192
Song of Hiawatha, The, 2, 9, 127, 147
songwriting, 23–29, 32, 41, 43–44, 48, 63–64, 192, 194–95
sonnet, 18, 118, 125, 128–29, 134
Spinoza, Baruch, 128–29, 133, 145, 149
Stein, Gertrude, 100, 112, 114, 118
"Stone Face." *See under* Ridge, Lola (works)
subways, 158–61

Sunwise Turn, The (bookstore), 16–17, 61, 211n2
syncopation, 41–42
Syrkin, Marie, 67, 75
Syrkin, Nahum, 67, 150

Taupin, René, 140
Testimony (poem). *See under* Reznikoff, Charles (works)
textbooks, 7, 120, 126
Tog, Der (Yiddish newspaper), 150–56
Tolson, Melvin, 169
translation, 13, 77–84, 84–89, 131, 148–57, 198, 215nn48–50; and circulation, 149–57; from Hebrew, 68–73, 74–75, 85–88; as public speech act, 2–3, 9–10, 156–57; from Yiddish, 149–52; into Yiddish, 2–3, 147, 150
Twitchell-Waas, Jeffrey, 161
typology (biblical), 10–11, 30–31, 67–69, 71–73, 83–84, 133–39, 199–200, 203n29; Babylon, 48–49; birthright, 50; chosen people, 55, 71; Christological, 101, 109–12, 123–24, 130–31, 142, 144, 181, 185, 209n71; covenant, 11–12, 45–46, 71, 78, 146, 199; Egypt, 134–39, 144, 152–55; Israelites, 10–11, 88–89; Promised Land, 11, 46, 55, 69, 108–9, 134; prophets, 11–12, 45–46, 77, 78–79, 159, 180–84; Zion, 67

Veblen, Thorstein, 105–6

White, Josh, 197–98
Williams, William Carlos, 18, 101, 114, 115–18, 127, 141, 158
Wilson, Woodrow, 16, 24, 30, 105, 120
witnessing, 62, 66, 69–72, 74, 78, 88–89, 109, 142–43
Woolf, Virginia, 74, 76
World War II, 131, 136, 140–45, 149, 191, 193–94; fall of Paris, 140–41; invasion of France, 140–45

X, Malcolm, 170–75, 176, 179, 182, 186

Yeats, W. B., 6–7, 9, 119–20
Yehoash (Solomon Bloomgarden), 1–2, 18, 147–48, 150–52, 223n72; "Af di khurves," 152; at Carnegie Hall, 147; *Dos lid fun Hayavata*, 1–2, 59, 127, 147, 150, 191; "Shimone-san,"

150–51; in *Tog*, 150–52; translations into Yiddish, 150; "Tsu der zun," 150–51; Zukofsky on, 18, 150
Yiddish, 1–2, 60, 74–75, 105, 109–10, 145–57
Yiddish newspapers, 131, 148, 150–57

Zukofsky, Louis, 16–19, 82, 127–62, 171, 174–75, 196, 198, 199; and Bach, 129–31, 132–35, 199; and civil religious discourse, 11, 129–31, 138; correspondence with Harriet Monroe, 150; correspondence with Hugh Kenner, 150; early notes for *"A"*, 131–32, 156; encounter with anti-Semitic bullies, 1–2, 9–10, 59, 127, 150, 156, 191–92; *France en Liberté, La*, 140–45, 171; and genre, 15; and immigration, 132, 133–34, 137–38, 199; and Judaism, 129–30, 132, 145, 175; and Lola Ridge Memorial Prize, 94; as "Objectivist" poet, 127, 141, 149, 161; reaction to World War II, 140–41; and Spinoza, 128–29, 133, 145, 160–61; theories of history, 137–39; and translation, 18, 131, 133–34, 149–57; use of Christian typology, 144; use of Exodus, 130–31, 132–39, 142–44, 146, 148–52, 156–57; on Yehoash, 18, 150; Yiddish language, 1–3, 18, 132, 149–53; Yiddish newspapers, 18, 150–57; and Yiddish poetry, 1–3, 18, 127, 150–52; *Z-Site*, 161–62

Zukofsky, Louis (works): *55 Poems*, 127, 161; *"A"*, 125, 127, 129, 131–32, 145; "A"-1, 130–31, 132, 134–35, 138–39, 146–47, 149, 152–56; "A"-3, 147; "A"-4, 147–51, 155–57; "A"-5, 152; "A"-6, 130–31, 136–37, 143, 149; "A"-8, 131, 137–38, 143, 144, 149, 153; "A"-10, 131, 140–45, 157, 171, 174, 222n49; "A"-12, 157; *"A" 1–12*, 157; *ALL: Collected Short Poems*, 161; *ANEW*, 127; *First Half of "A"-9*, 129; "Mantis," 157–62; "'Mantis,' An Interpretation," 128–29, 157–62; "Paris" (see "A"-10); "Poem Beginning 'The'," 152, 199; "Poetry / For My Son When He Can Read," 131–32; *Selected Letters* (online), 161; *Selected Poems*, 161; "Sincerity and Objectification, With Special Reference to the Work of Charles Reznikoff," 149; *Test of Poetry*, 127–29, 161
Zukofsky, Paul, 131, 144–45, 157, 161
Zukofsky, Pinchos, 18, 138, 150

www.ingramcontent.com/pod-product-compliance
Lightning Source LLC
Chambersburg PA
CBHW020649230426
43665CB00008B/361